# The Mindful Schools Curriculum for Adolescents

## Advance Praise

"*The Mindful Schools Curriculum for Adolescents* by Oren Jay Sofer and Matthew Brensilver is a timely and valuable contribution to the field of Mindfulness in Education. The curriculum does a wonderful job creating connection and making mindfulness relevant to the adolescent context. This resource is a must-have for anyone sharing mindfulness with teens!"

—**Meena Srinivasan, author of *SEL Every Day: Integrating Social and Emotional Learning with Instruction in Secondary Classrooms* and *Teach, Breathe, Learn: Mindfulness In and Out of the Classroom***

"An absolute must-read for every person teaching mindfulness to teens and young adults. Oren Jay Sofer and Matthew Brensilver have combined their many years of experience teaching mindfulness for adolescents and developing curriculum for Mindful Schools with their decades of personal mindfulness meditation practice to create a clear, engaging, very down-to-earth and step-by-step classroom approach. And as an extra bonus, each chapter offers the science background with citations for the reader who wants to know more."

—**Christiane Wolf, M.D., Ph.D., coauthor of *A Clinician's Guide to Teaching Mindfulness***

"This comprehensive and beautifully designed curriculum is sure to become a classic in the field. It offers carefully crafted lessons with helpful examples, study and practice questions, and scientific evidence to back it up. I would recommend this to anyone who wishes to teach mindfulness to adolescents, although I have no doubt it would be relevant to teaching adults as well!"

—**Diana Winston, director of Mindfulness Education at UCLA's Mindful Awareness Research Center, and author of *The Little Book of Being***

"Teaching mindfulness is an art; teaching mindfulness to adolescents is a rare art. In this thorough, well-researched, and creative curriculum, the authors offer innovative and timely tools for sharing the powerful practice of mindfulness with teens and adolescents. This book will serve well anyone who is seeking guidance on how to teach mindfulness to adolescents."

—**Bonnie Duran, Ph.D., Professor, University of Washington School of Social work, Public Health, and Indigenous Wellness Research Institute**

NORTON BOOKS IN EDUCATION

# The Mindful Schools Curriculum for Adolescents

TOOLS FOR DEVELOPING AWARENESS

Oren Jay Sofer and Matthew Brensilver

W. W. NORTON & COMPANY
*Independent Publishers Since 1923*

**Note to Readers:** Models and/or techniques described in this volume are illustrative or are included for general informational purposes only; neither the publisher nor the author(s) can guarantee the efficacy or appropriateness of any particular recommendation in every circumstance.

Copyright © 2019 by Mindful Schools

For information about permission to reproduce selections from this book, write to
Permissions, W. W. Norton & Company, Inc., 500 Fifth Avenue, New York, NY 10110

For information about special discounts for bulk purchases, please contact
W. W. Norton Special Sales at specialsales@wwnorton.com or 800-233-4830
Manufacturing by Sheridan Books
Book design by Vicki Fischman
Production manager: Katelyn MacKenzie

Library of Congress Cataloging-in-Publication Data

ISBN: 978-0-393-71391-6 (pbk.)

W. W. Norton & Company, Inc., 500 Fifth Avenue, New York, N.Y. 10110

www.wwnorton.com
W. W. Norton & Company Ltd., 15 Carlisle Street, London W1D 3BS

1  2  3  4  5  6  7  8  9  0.

For the classroom teachers who do the essential work of opening the hearts and minds of youth and children, and for the youth they serve. May we see that another world is possible, and make that a reality.    —*Oren Jay Sofer*


For Jacob & Gabriel                    —*Matthew Brensilver*

# CONTENTS

# Acknowledgments

This version of the curriculum was co-created by Matthew Brensilver and Oren Jay Sofer. It stands on the shoulders of the former program directors, Megan Cowan and Chris McKenna. Many others have generously contributed to previous iterations of the curricula over the years, including Vinny Ferraro, Laurie Grossman, Richard Shankman, Kate Munding, Daniel Rechtschaffen, Martina Schneider, Kevin Griffin, Gary Buck, Marvin Belzer, and Diana Winston. We have benefited substantially from the students who have received these lessons and the educators who have provided feedback. We thank Mindful Schools for supporting this project. We also wish to acknowledge Randy Fernando, who was instrumental in the evolution of Mindful Schools. Lastly, we are deeply grateful for the wisdom and kindness of our own teachers, without whom this book would not exist.

# The Mindful Schools Curriculum for Adolescents

# Welcome to the Mindful Schools
# Adolescent Curriculum

We are very happy that you are reading this and are grateful for your commitment to practice and share mindfulness. We sincerely hope that this curriculum supports your efforts to foster self-awareness, empathy, and wisdom in yourself and in the young people in your care.

We view this curriculum not as a manual to be rigidly followed, but as a vehicle for you to share your own kindness, skill, and wisdom. *The scripts are not intended to be read verbatim.* In our years teaching adolescents, we have been impressed by the way that curricula serve as living documents. The lessons that are taught are the convergence of our minds and your minds. We are delighted to imagine all the ways you might innovate and build upon this curriculum.

In this brief introduction, we wish to highlight several underlying principles of this curriculum.

**Developmentally appropriate with potential for depth.** This curriculum is designed for young people ages 13 to 20. We have tailored the lessons to the particular developmental needs of adolescents, tying the practices to their most pressing concerns. At the same time, we've attempted to preserve the radical potentials of mindfulness. The practices unfolded in these lessons can be explored at different depths and may catalyze important understandings and prosocial orientations in the young people you teach.

**Founded on behavioral science.** Mindfulness is about mitigating stress and promoting flourishing. These aims are supported and energized by numerous lines of scientific research: behavioral change, psychotherapy research, clinical neuroscience, evolutionary psychology, and emotion regulation research. The

curriculum draws—explicitly and implicitly—from these bodies of knowledge. Sometimes, a scientific finding underscores a particular concept or practice and is explored explicitly in the lessons. Many of the lessons also include a "Science Supplement" that highlights relevant research to provide you with a fuller understanding of the scientific context. The curriculum also draws on a prominent model of the mechanisms of mindfulness from Tang, Hölzel, & Posner (2015). The key beneficial mechanisms of mindfulness include enhanced emotion regulation, attention stability, and self-awareness.

We regard our role of disseminating mindfulness research seriously. We take care to ensure that the personal confidence we have in mindfulness does not distort our estimation of its scientific basis. We aspire to offer training and resources that present mindfulness in a compelling and digestible manner, while honoring the complexity of scientific findings. The benefits of mindfulness are well-documented in adults, and neuroscientific studies offer plausible evidence regarding the mechanisms of these changes. Those data provide reason for optimism regarding the emerging science on mindfulness in students. We are actively engaged in understanding the emerging research and are committed to being responsive to new scientific findings. With this perspective in mind, we also wish to express our deep enthusiasm for integrating mindfulness into schools and the lives of young people.

**Structured and adaptable.** We attempt to provide a framework to guide your teaching, with flexibility to add or drop lesson components depending on the context. The transcripts present one possible version of the lesson, rather than lines to be read verbatim.

The curriculum is a vehicle through which you can share your own skills and insights. It depends on your own embodiment of mindfulness, the familiarity you have developed with your mind, as well as the teaching skills you have acquired outside the context of mindfulness.

**Secularity.** Mindful Schools is unequivocally committed to a thoroughly secular approach to mindfulness practice. We are steadfastly committed to integrating mindfulness in education in a way that neither advances nor inhibits the religious beliefs (or lack of beliefs) of educators or students. This enduring commitment reflects our fundamental value of inclusivity. Only a thoroughly secular articulation of mindfulness avoids excluding people who might otherwise be interested in the practice. To fully honor the autonomy of students and our community members, the secularity of mindfulness is of paramount concern. (See our Guidelines for Secular Teaching of Mindfulness for specific recommendations.)

**Integration of Social-Emotional Learning (SEL) components.** The boundaries between mindfulness-based and SEL curricula are understandably fuzzy. The key skills of mindfulness (emotion regulation, attention stability, and self-awareness) have substantial overlap with the key skills of SEL (self-awareness, self-management, social awareness, relationships skills, and responsible decision making). We have attempted to integrate some components of SEL and blend them with mindfulness practice in the belief that this integration is synergistic.

**Three versions of foundational lesson.** There are many different ways to describe mindfulness and explain its relevance. Accordingly, we have created three different foundational lessons. We hope you will feel free to choose or adapt them to suit the needs of your particular context.

## Structure of the Curriculum

We believe that teaching mindfulness lessons at regular intervals with a clear, repeated structure enhances their effectiveness. We highly recommend drawing a clear distinction between the mindfulness lesson and any previous activities. We have standardized the lesson structure and included repetition of key curriculum components to support learning.

The lessons are intended to be completed in 20 to 30 minutes. That said, in a cohesive and expressive class environment, exploration and conversation may extend the lesson time beyond 30 minutes. In general, we've erred on the side of giving you more information and options rather than fewer in the lessons. *You can expand or condense them according to your needs, your students and the overall context.*

The main goals of the curriculum are fourfold:

1. To articulate the relevance of mindfulness for adolescents.
2. To provide the basic instructions and support needed to develop their capacity for self-awareness and self-regulation.
3. To provide time for formal mindfulness practice.
4. To create emotional safety sufficient to share and explore their inner experience.

In an important sense, everything else is extra. If you only have 2 minutes, then do 2 minutes of mindful breathing. If you have 10 minutes, do some practice and then ask a few questions to seed a short discussion.

We have structured the curriculum to include a brief exercise to transition to the mindfulness lesson. This can be important in establishing a tone conducive to inner exploration and development. We outline several options for this transitional activity in the beginning of the curriculum, though you may choose to integrate your own movement-based practices.

Next, each lesson introduces a rationale for mindfulness practice. Establishing and reinforcing a sense of the material's relevance is an essential part of teaching adolescents. The curriculum attempts to do so using contemporary examples and frameworks that link mindfulness to on-the-ground realities of adolescent lives.

The conceptual framework provides a way to discuss the particular practice skills being developed. Next, there is a period of guided practice. During this time, the students remain quiet and practice (often seated) while the teacher provides suggestions for how to direct their attention. Each practice period begins with the same initial set of instructions for establishing mindfulness of the body. Regardless of the particular practice being explored, establishing mindfulness of the body supports the necessary foundations of presence, focus, and ease for further practice. Then, a new set of practice instructions is introduced and practiced within a container of silence and stillness.

Following the practice period, the curriculum includes several questions you can use to prompt dialogue about their experience and normalize the most predictable, common challenges: struggles with concentration, the power of distractions, restlessness, grogginess, liking, and disliking. The aim of the discussion is to get the students talking about their practice, to pique their interest, to clarify any questions they might have about the techniques or their experience, and to build a sense of safety and trust among the group. Depending on the level of class-wide trust, you might probe with questions that ask for a show of hands, yes-or-no questions, or open-ended questions that require a higher level of disclosure. To the extent that some students are willing to risk sharing openly, they set a high bar for honesty and emotional intelligence. You can then support the whole class to embrace these values.

We also outline some suggested journal-writing activities. Students can do these seated at their desks, perhaps in a notebook specifically dedicated to mindfulness. For each lesson, we've offered possible take-home practices. These activities are not required, and may not be appropriate in some contexts. Please use your judgment to determine the appropriateness of journaling and take-home practices.

All the core lessons are accompanied by a "Science Supplement" highlighting relevant scientific findings for the day's lesson. You might choose to find developmentally appropriate ways to incorporate these studies into the lesson. They are primarily intended to provide a scientific background for you and to create more confidence in the scientific underpinnings of mindfulness practice.

Each of the core 18 lessons includes a one-page handout outlining its key aspects; these can be distributed to the students. Feel free to edit these to suit your needs and style. Some lessons also contain "Alternate Activities," "Teacher Notes," and/or references for further reading. These are all meant to supplement your understanding of the lesson and provide more flexibility for how you offer it in your classroom.

We hope this curriculum serves you well. We are *sincerely grateful* for all the work you do, and trust that your efforts will bring benefits to many.

# Guidelines for Secular Teaching of Mindfulness

Mindful Schools arose from a simple experience: a few mindfulness practitioners sharing their love of the practice with students in several Oakland, California schools. The founders sought to articulate the practices in the most inclusive way possible. We continue to wish that everyone feels equally welcome in our community, regardless of religious orientation.

Our enduring commitment to secularity reflects the fundamental value of inclusivity. Only a thoroughly secular articulation of mindfulness avoids excluding people who might otherwise be interested in the practice. To fully honor the autonomy of students and our community members, the secularity of mindfulness is of paramount concern.

In sharing mindfulness, it is first important to clarify and affirm our intentions. When we share mindfulness, we are not attempting to impose a comprehensive belief system. Nor are we attempting to advance or inhibit any religious commitments that students or educators may hold. Our objective is simple: to support the well-being of students and educators by sharing simple practices and psychoeducation, and to develop an attitude of inquiry around how the mind works.

In this spirit, we wanted to offer some recommendations to support secular teaching:

1. Mindfulness practices should be articulated in the primary instructional language or languages (in the case of bilingual education).
2. No classroom can be conducted in a completely value-neutral manner, and it is reasonable to affirm humanistic values such as kindness, cooperation, empathy, or concentration. However, mindfulness is not an attempt to teach a comprehensive ethical system.
3. Teach the practices in a direct, experiential manner whereby practitioners can examine the validity of the claims within their own subjective experience (e.g., when doing seated mindfulness practice, students can directly perceive the attention wandering away from the mindfulness anchor). The spirit is one of encouraging curiosity, as if conducting an experiment with one's own mind and body.
4. Do not assert or intimate claims about metaphysics (e.g., "The nature of the universe is love"). If such questions or comments arise from students, support their curiosity while clarifying the scope of mindfulness practice and redirect the conversation to the subjective or empirical realm.
5. Frame mindfulness as a practice about subjective experiences rather than about overarching truths of the universe.
6. Do not include symbols or artifacts closely linked to a particular religious tradition (e.g., making particular gestures with one's hands, bowing, using religious props, and so on).
7. Do not substantiate the practices on the basis of religious figures or texts. At the same time, take care not to denigrate religious practices or texts.
8. Teach in a manner consistent with current scientific understandings of human biology and behavior.

We hope these guidelines support you in your teaching.

## What is Mindfulness?

As mindfulness gains cultural momentum, there is a risk that its definition becomes more muddled. If we are to practice effectively and teach these practices to our students and communities, conceptual clarity is important. Of course, no single person or group has the authority to provide the one and only definition of mindfulness. This is an open and evolving conversation among practitioners, scientists, and scholars. We do not claim to offer the definitive version of mindfulness, but instead share a definition that has been productive in our practice and teaching, and is supported by the scientific research on mindfulness. We hope it will be helpful for you in teaching this curriculum.

Mindfulness can be considered a *state*, a *trait*, or a *practice*. We can have a moment of mindfulness (*state*) and also have a habitual tendency of mindfulness (*trait*). We can do the intentional formal *practice* of mindfulness using different postures and activities: seated mindfulness, mindful walking, or mindful eating, for example. The formal practice of mindfulness leads to more moments of mindfulness and ultimately improved trait-level mindfulness. Higher trait-level mindfulness means that we're more mindful even when we're not consciously *trying* to be mindful. This is critically important: We're learning to create a healthy *habit* of mindfulness.

Below is a diagram that highlights two components of mindfulness: present-time awareness and equanimity.

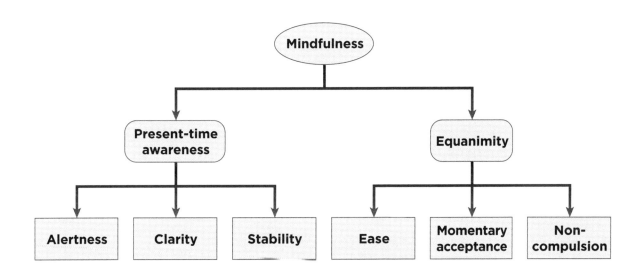

A CONCEPTUAL MODEL OF MINDFULNESS
*Source: Brensilver*

## Present-Time Awareness

The first component, present-time awareness, is perhaps the most familiar aspect of mindfulness. It refers to a stable, clear, and alert awareness of momentary experience. In present-time awareness, we are awake and alive to the moment. We know sensory experience—sights, sounds, sensations, thoughts—and we *know* that we're *knowing*. When we're on "automatic pilot" we're still *having* experience, but there's virtually no mindfulness present. We are still knowing something (sights, sounds, sensations, thoughts) but we *don't know that we're knowing*. Present-time awareness is thus a kind of *meta-awareness*, where we have rich contact with sensory experience *and* we know it's sensory experience arising in the field of awareness.

Present-time awareness is depicted as a combination of *stability*, *clarity*, and *alertness*. Imagine looking through a telescope at the moon. If the telescope were shaking, it would be difficult to fully take in the sight of the moon. Similarly, *stability* of our attention is important for present-time awareness. The moon would also be obscured if the lens were out of focus. In mindfulness practice, our "vision" becomes *clearer*. We're able to detect more and more subtle features of our experience. Lastly, we must be *alert* to the present moment. If we looked through a steady and focused telescope but were sleepy, lapsing in and out of awareness, we would miss the grandeur of the moon. Mindfulness steadies the attention, focuses the attention, and remains alert to the object of our attention.

## Equanimity

While present-time awareness has important benefits on its own, the second component of mindfulness—equanimity, depicted on the previous page—is critically important. Equanimity can be defined as a sense of cognitive-emotional balance where there is no compulsion to act out our preferences. It has a number of connotations: ease, non-reactivity, non-manipulation of experience, and the toleration of the arising, intensification, weakening, and disappearance of subjective experiences. Equanimity is the balance point between suppression of experience on the one hand, and entanglement with experience on the other. There is now evidence that present-time awareness without equanimity fails to deliver the same psychological benefits obtained from the combination of present-time awareness and equanimity.

Equanimity is often confused with indifference or passive acceptance of suffering in the world. This is a misunderstanding. In the diagram, we include "momentary acceptance" to denote that equanimity marks our relation to present-time experience, not objective conditions in the world. We can be equanimous with our present-time experience, but be deeply committed to changing and improving the conditions in the world.

In sum, we define mindfulness as attending to present-moment experience with openness and curiosity (equanimity). Our definition is similar to other common definitions of mindfulness. For example, Jon Kabat-Zinn, a leading figure in the mindfulness movement and member of the Mindful Schools Advisory Board, defined mindfulness as "the awareness that emerges through paying attention on purpose, in the present moment, and non-judgmentally to the unfolding of experience moment by moment." In this definition, "non-judgmentally" relates to the momentary acceptance component of equanimity.

Future research will seek to better understand the components of mindfulness, how they work together, and how they confer benefits in our personal and professional lives. Of course, you and your students can do research in the laboratory of your own minds! As you practice, you might examine how present-time awareness and equanimity function together. This exploration will support greater clarity and nuance as we think about, practice, and teach mindfulness.

# Working with Adolescents

Teaching mindfulness to different ages requires more than targeted curricula. Young people of different ages have unique needs, and teaching requires particular skills from the instructor.

Adolescents are in a developmental process of individuation. They are forming a sense of self and all that entails, including comparative and evaluative thought (comparing self to other; feelings of inferiority and superiority, and so on) and a heightened awareness of meaning. For mindfulness programs to be successful with teens, they must take this shift into account. Success in this realm is tied to developing three related skill sets.

1. **Creating Relevance:** Using explicit content to answer adolescents' underlying questions: *Why should I do this? Why is it interesting? How will it benefit me?*
2. **Creating Connection:** Using interpersonal skills to create safety, connection, and an easy flow of engagement with young people.
3. **Working with Resistance:** Creatively addressing adolescent behavior in a way that provides structure while still respecting their autonomy.

## I. CREATING RELEVANCE

One of the main tasks for a mindfulness instructor is to keep students interested and engaged by making their teaching relevant to students' lives. Relying on this curriculum exclusively will be insufficient for doing this. We encourage you to develop a variety of different, personalized material to engage kids—idiosyncratic lessons, rhetorical devices, stories, or examples. You must attune to the true concerns of the adolescents, and speak directly to those concerns. This is the true art of teaching adolescents.

Here are a few examples of ways you can build upon the curriculum material:

– **Use Metaphor, Myth, and Story:** Learn how to tell a good story and use language symbolically. Having a key image or metaphor (sometimes called a "hook") can be a useful way of drawing students in. The three versions of the first lesson in this curriculum each use different hooks.

– **Integrate other Disciplines:** Mindfulness teachers often draw on different fields to make their teaching relevant to students. The Science Supplements in this curriculum provide additional information to weave into lessons.

– **Use Current Events and Multimedia:** Try tying your lessons to examples the kids recognize. Without being gimmicky, use lyrics, scenes from TV, movies, commercials, or other media to illustrate a point or initiate a discussion in your lessons.

## II. CREATING CONNECTION

Developmentally, teens are undergoing major shifts in their sense of self and their relationships. As a mindfulness instructor, one of your key tasks is to create an experience in which young people feel safe, seen, and able to explore their identities. This happens *implicitly* through your relationship as well as *explicitly* through your words.

As facilitators, we are continually honing our ability to bring a stable, grounded presence to others, to read subtle cues, and to use the relationship itself as a vehicle for our teaching. Below is an overview of some of these areas that will be essential in your use of this curriculum.

**Create a Safe Container.** Do everything you can to create an environment in which young people are most likely to feel safe sharing with each other.

– Make the physical space comfortable and supportive; experiment with seating arrangements and lighting.

- Use a set routine for beginning and ending mindfulness that helps students recognize the shift and settle (see our suggestions, or create your own).

- Create a culture of respect with "community agreements" or guidelines for how students engage with one another. Try doing some team-building exercises.

- Consciously greet your students, being sure to make eye contact and/or physical gestures, depending on the context.

**Prioritize Attunement and Relationship.** One of the things young people need most is empathic attunement. When teaching adolescents, the *quality of our attention and presence* is as important as the *explicit content we are delivering.* Attune to your kids, sensing where they're at and what they need. This won't work if it's a technique or intervention. It must be a genuine expression of your own deep interest in knowing who they are. Watch out for any mindset of "fixing" students or getting overly attached to a particular outcome. Instead, aim to meet them with a spirit of openness and care, which will build trust.

**Attend to Your Internal State.** Adolescents are still learning to self-regulate by orienting to the nervous systems of adults. Many are desperately seeking a grounded and stable presence to help them relax and settle. In this regard, our own nervous system is our primary intervention when teaching adolescents. Pay attention to how you are feeling when you teach; develop your capacity for offering a solid, responsive presence in the room.

**Use Your Voice Skillfully.** Our internal state is transmitted in many ways: through body language, posture, facial expression, and to a large degree *through our voice.* Our state of mind is reflected as much in the pitch, tone, rhythm, and pace of our speech as by the words we speak. A calm and confident speaker can transmit a sense of ease and spaciousness, creating a safe and clear space for learning. Speak with awareness, taking pauses and allowing for natural silences. This creates a "relaxed power" and gentle authority in your teaching that students sense intuitively.

**Use Language Skillfully.** Give students *invitations* to practice rather than *commands.* "Let your eyes close" versus "Close your eyes," conveys a sense of autonomy and choice. Stay alert to any tendency or habit to use your authority in the classroom to attempt to dictate, control, or manipulate students' behavior rather than to invite their genuine engagement.

**Track Nonverbal Information.** Just as our own internal state is reflected through our bodies and our voices, so too are the internal experiences of young people reflected through their body language. Develop your ability to pick up on subtle, nonverbal information in the room. Use your intuition and the sensations in your own body to help "read the room" and determine what's needed to best support the group in any given moment.

**Be Authentic and Use Self-Disclosure.** Young people have an incredibly sensitive internal meter for authenticity. If you're putting on a front, trying to get their approval, or allowing your own unresolved adolescent issues to take over, they'll pick up on it. Bring your own authentic self to the dialogue. Develop your own language for teaching mindfulness that reflects your experience and is appropriate to the context within which you teach. When appropriate, be willing to "self-disclose," to share openly about your personal experience as a way of creating connection and modeling strength through vulnerability.

**Develop Group Facilitation Skills.** One way that humans experience interpersonal safety is through a lively "back-and-forth" exchange of information between members of a group. This flowing exchange produces a state of safety, ease, and interest—an ideal "learning readiness." Engage students by turning didactic content into discussions. We have integrated questions and invitations to our discussion throughout the lessons. You may build on this by honing your ability to ask compelling questions, to draw out the group by varying open-ended and closed (yes/no) questions, to ask clarifying questions, and to synthesize their responses in order to tie the discussion back to the lesson.

## III. WORKING WITH RESISTANCE

It's natural for adolescents to assert their autonomy. Encountering "resistance" and behavioral issues is one of the most common challenges for educators. Here are some suggestions:

**Learn to See "Resistance" as Information.** One of the greatest challenges to working effectively with resistance is our very interpretation of behavior as "resistance"! Our view of a student's actions as "resistance" can inhibit our ability to connect with them. Instead, we can learn to understand such behavior as valuable information about a teen's needs. We can see it as an attempt to communicate their inner experience, to self-regulate, or to exercise autonomy. This shift in our own thinking helps us stay connected to intentions of curiosity and care, creating new possibilities for engaging.

**Handle Your Internal State.** It can be very frustrating when one or more students seem to do everything they can to undermine our intentions or inhibit learning in the classroom. Our ability to respond effectively to such behavior issues is proportional to our capacity to manage our internal reactivity. Here are a few tips for handling reactivity.

– **Monitor your responses:** Mindfully track your inner experience and find balance in the moment. Take time outside of class as needed to investigate emotions. Imagine a worst-case scenario to face your fears. What's the worst that can happen? Once we acknowledge that, it has less power. The more you work through your feelings outside of class, the easier it will be to stay clear, grounded, and calm in class.

– **Check your assumptions:** Watch out for thoughts that assume we know what is happening for the student, or that attribute malicious intentions to their behavior. They may actually be recieving our care, whether they show it or not.

– **Don't take it personally:** The more we take a situation personally, feeling threatened, judging ourselves, or seeking approval, the less likely we are to respond in an appropriate, creative, or skillful way. Remember that there are many factors in a student's life that have nothing to do with you.

– **Redefine success:** Watch out for the belief that you are solely responsible for rescuing anyone. Shift your definition of success from a particular outcome to the integrity of your intention and the quality of the relationship you build with the kids.

**Engage the Resistance.** To "engage the resistance" means to work directly with the young people who are acting out. Try to find a way to redirect their energy, to meet the needs they are trying to meet by acting out, and/or to win them over. The level of conversation and strategy will vary depending on the age of the students. Here are a few best practices:

– **Prioritize connection:** Strengthen your ability to connect empathically and prioritize the quality of the relationship. Ultimately, we can't make anyone do anything, but how we engage often communicates more than what we say.

– **Seek to understand their needs:** Stretch to imagine the students' concerns. Ask questions and really listen to what they say. Inquire, directly or indirectly, what matters for them. "What do you need right now?" can be a powerful question.

- **Problem-solve together:** As you identify what's going on, have a conversation and brainstorm ways students can meet their needs that also honor you and the other students in the room. Communicate clearly your need to balance your care for them with your duty to protect everyone's right to learn.

- **Set clear limits and boundaries:** Creating a simple structure or agreement for behavior etiquette helps students to know what we expect of them and why. Following through on the limits you set sends a clear message that you will respect everyone's right to learn. Be sure to make your requests clear, specific, and doable, and to share the reasons behind what you are asking them to do. This inherently acknowledges their autonomy and helps create buy-in.

- **Walk or sit near the student:** Depending on the context, physical contact can be settling, providing comfort or attention in an unobtrusive way.

- **Elevate them:** Give the student a special role to help them feel like they belong.

- **Use it to teach:** Name what's happening in the room and include it in the lesson.

**Refine the Container.** Sometimes, it can be helpful to go back and redefine the ground rules. Consider doing a "reset" with your class: discuss everyone's needs; create group agreements and norms; and work to reestablish a culture of respect.

**Get Support.** While you may be the only person standing up in front of the classroom, you're not alone. Turn to friends and colleagues for support. Seek consultation from peers or mentors. Try obtaining one-on-one support for the student, which can be very effective in addressing behavior issues. You can also be creative and enlist the support of other students. Use the behavior issue as a teachable moment, and involve the whole class in an honest conversation about learning and collaboration. What do the other students need to be able to learn? Do they have ideas about how to work together to address the situation? Encourage them to speak up or help set behavior norms.

# Transitional Activities

Making a clear line between mindfulness lessons and other school activities can help students switch gears and participate more fully. With this in mind, we want to provide some short, simple mindful movement practices to shift gears and help students to settle.

We recommend doing one short activity at the beginning of each mindfulness session to help create circumstances most conducive for mindfulness practice. Most of them focus on shifting the body to a state of rest and relaxation by coordinating simple movements with breathing. You can also use these activities at other times during your school day, to make transitions smoother, before a test, or before any significant activity.

Some of these movements will be novel and unusual for students. Use your judgment to determine the appropriateness of the particular activity. In some groups, it will be necessary to have a sufficiently strong basis developed beforehand in order for students to perform some of these movements without evoking too much self-consciousness.

## Lesson Introduction

Just like stretching before playing a sport or warming up your voice before singing, it's helpful to do something to shift gears and get your body and mind ready for mindfulness. We can be mindful anytime, but these periods of dedicated practice are like training, so we want to put ourselves in the best possible state when we train.

### ACTIVITY 1: COORDINATED BREATHING

This activity can be done while sitting in a chair, and coordinates breathing with simple hand movements. Begin with hands resting on the thighs, palms up. Leaving elbows bent, breathe in while raising the hands slowly, palms up, as if you were lifting a tray. Say out loud to the students, "Breathing in" as they mimic you. Turn the palms down and lower the hands back to the thighs, as you breathe out, saying "Breathing out." Repeat four or five times. In order to keep the position of the arms comfortable, the range of motion for this activity is small. The hands should not rise above the shoulders at any point.

### ACTIVITY 2: SINKING DOWN* (STANDING)

Establish a stable standing posture, with the feet hip width apart and parallel. Knees are soft, not locked. Breathing in, raise hands and arms up and out to the sides of the body (as if you were beginning to make a snow angel). At the apex, allow the hands to come together above the head, with palms facing down. Breathing out, lower the hands in front of the body, palms facing down, as if they were sinking through honey. Bend the knees slightly so the weight of the body settles as the hands float down. Repeat three or four times, breathing in as the hands and arms rise out to the sides, breathing out as they sink down in front of the body.

### ACTIVITY 3: STRING PUPPET (STANDING)

This activity is similar to "Sinking Down," but in reverse. Gently lift the arms from the wrists, as if you were a marionette with strings attached at each wrist, and a puppeteer were pulling them from above. Breathe in as you raise the arms all the way up until the fingers point at the sky. As you breathe out, lower the arms slowly out to the sides as if you were smoothing out a sheet. Feel the hands growing heavy as the arms sink lower. If you like, you can allow the knees to bend and the body to sink slightly as the arms float downward. Repeat four or five times.

### ACTIVITY 4: RUB HANDS, MASSAGE FACE

This activity can be done while sitting or standing. Have the students breathe in as they turn their palms up as if carrying a tray. As they breathe out, slowly turn the palms over and then bring them together forcefully in one clapping motion. Rub the hands together steadily and vigorously to generate heat. Repeat three or four times. After the last time, have students use the bases of the palms to massage the eyes and eye sockets. Massage the cheeks and cheekbones, rubbing down the face gently but firmly. Finally, massage the neck and occipital region at the base of the skull.

**ACTIVITY 5: VISUAL ORIENTING**

This activity is done while sitting. Invite the students to look slowly around the room, orienting to their surroundings. You can use the prompt, "Let your eyes go where they want to go." Demonstrate this, looking around the room slowly and naturally, allowing your eyes, head, and neck to move in an easy, coordinated fashion. You can call this a mindfulness of seeing practice, and explain that orienting to our surroundings in this way engages our nervous system in a way that helps us to feel safe, relaxed, and settled.

For variation, invite the students to notice, for example, something they have never seen before in the class; the different colors, lines, and shapes of the visual field; or something they enjoy looking at.

**REFERENCES & FURTHER READING**

Bishop, S. R., Lau, M., Shapiro, S., Carlson, L., Anderson, N. D., Carmody, J., . . . & Devins, G. (2004). Mindfulness: A proposed operational definition. *Clinical Psychology: Science and Practice, 11*, 230–241.

Brown, K. W., Ryan, R. M., & Creswell, J. D. (2007). Mindfulness: Theoretical foundations and evidence for its salutary effects. *Psychological Inquiry, 18*, 211–237.

Desbordes, G., Gard, T., Hoge, E. A., Hölzel, B. K., Kerr, C., Lazar, S. W., . . . & Vago, D. R. (2014). Moving beyond mindfulness: Defining equanimity as an outcome measure in meditation and contemplative research. *Mindfulness, 6*, 356–372.

Lindsay, E. K., Young, S., Smyth, J. M., Brown, K. W., & Creswell, J. D. (2018). Acceptance lowers stress reactivity: Dismantling mindfulness training in a randomized controlled trial. *Psychoneuroendocrinology, 87*, 63–73.

Pearson, M. R., Lawless, A. K., Brown, D. B., & Bravo, A. J. (2015). Mindfulness and emotional outcomes: Identifying subgroups of college students using latent profile analysis. *Personality and Individual Differences, 76*, 33–38.

Tang, Y. Y., Hölzel, B. K., & Posner, M. I. (2015). The neuroscience of mindfulness meditation. *Nature Reviews Neuroscience, 16*(4), 213–225.

Wang, C., Collet, J. P., & Lau, J. (2004). The effect of tai chi on health outcomes in patients with chronic conditions: A systematic review. *Archives of Internal Medicine, 164*, 493–550.

Young, S. (2013). *What is mindfulness? A comprehensive overview.* Shinzen.org.

* Many of these practices, specifically "sinking down" and "string puppet" come directly out of tai chi chuan and related systems of qigong.

# INTRO TO MINDFULNESS: MIND POWER

## The Basics

This lesson is one of our three possible introductory lessons. It takes a distinctive approach to describing mindfulness as a method for taking back our power over the habits of mind that boss us around. While the practice described here is very similar to each of the other introductory lessons, the framing is different and may be more or less appropriate for your group of adolescents.

---

### LEARNING OBJECTIVES

1.  To define mindfulness.
2.  To demonstrate the sitting posture for mindfulness practice.
3.  To practice mindfulness of the body by relaxing and feeling gravity.

---

### LESSON 1.1 IN BRIEF: A SYNOPSIS

## Intro to Mindfulness: Mind Power

**1. Our minds can be aware, or on autopilot.**
Discuss the difference between being on "autopilot" and being mindful. Use an example, e.g., the story of Tesla's self-driving car.

**2. Make a case for mindfulness.**
**Mindfulness** is the process of paying attention to what's happening right now in our own experience in a curious and open way. It takes us off autopilot; helps us quiet our mind and pay attention; supports better choices and more happiness.

Engage the students with a series of questions. Have you ever . . .

- Said something you wish you could take back? Did something that you later regretted?

- Noticed your mind thinking about something over and over, and it wouldn't stop?

- Not been able to sleep because your mind kept spinning, or your body felt restless?

- Had trouble focusing in class, or spaced out when your teacher called on you?

- Noticed that some days certain things bug you, but other days you're totally fine?

- Is your mind always trustworthy? Should we always obey what our mind tells us to do?

Our minds boss us around; so do our reactions to others' behaviors.

**3. Explain the role of mindfulness.**

Mindfulness gives us back our power, to know when to listen to our mind and when to ignore it. We can develop habits of mind that lead to more happiness and emotional freedom. Mindfulness helps us to observe the mind and begin to understand how it works. Invite students to join you in an experiment to observe and train their own minds.

## Mindfulness of Body: Practice Instructions

Do about one minute of practice to begin.

+ Sit in a posture that is comfortable yet upright, feet on the floor and hands in your lap.

+ Let your eyes close, or gaze down at the ground in front of you.

+ Ring the bell, putting all of your attention into hearing.

+ Begin to let your body relax by feeling the weight of gravity. Notice its heaviness and where it touches the ground. If you like, say "relax, relax" silently inside.

+ Take a few deep breaths, noticing any ease or relaxation on the exhalation.

+ As your body settles, become aware of your whole body sitting. Feel the sensations of sitting.

+ Sit like this for a few minutes, noticing whatever happens in your body.

+ Ring the bell, listening to the entire sound.

+ When you're ready, let your eyes open and look around the room.

Discuss what the students noticed. Time permitting, practice again for another two to three minutes.

 **Discussion Questions**

+ What did you notice? How did that feel? How many people noticed that you felt more relaxed? Did anyone have the opposite reaction where you actually got more anxious?

+ Do we make our best decisions when we're really agitated? Do you think being relaxed might help us listen to our own wisdom and make good choices?

+ How else might this practice be useful in your life? (*Offer some suggestions*)

 **Take-Home Practice**

1. As a reflection, study your mind to see when you feel like it's bossing you around and when you feel like you're making your own choices.
2. Once or twice this week, take a few minutes to do this relaxation exercise

# Intro to Mindfulness: Mind Power

## Lesson Outline

- Our minds boss us around all the time—we obey our thoughts like a worker obeying a mean supervisor.

- Our reactions to others also boss us around—we react on automatic pilot and do not always behave in our best interests.

- Mindfulness is a chance to take back our power.

- With mindfulness, we're training ourselves to determine when to listen to our mind, and when to ignore its advice.

- We can develop habits of mind that lead to more happiness and emotional freedom.

- To do this, we need to be able to observe the mind and begin to understand how it works. Mindfulness helps us to do that.

## Lesson

Do you know how Tesla developed a self-driving car? The early design had 8 cameras, 12 sound sensors, and a radar system. All this stuff was designed to help the car drive itself on autopilot without crashing into stuff. When working right, the car could drive at the right speed depending on how much traffic was around. It could change lanes, take the correct exit ramp from a highway, and park itself when you're at your destination. But sometimes, the autopilot system needs help. One guy was driving on autopilot and the car warned him that he needed to turn off autopilot and do the steering himself because the road conditions were dangerous. It asked him 7 times to take the steering wheel, but he ignored all the warnings.

Guess what happened?

(*Students answer.*)

Yeah, the car crashed. Sometimes autopilot works, sometimes it doesn't. We live a lot of our lives on autopilot, and a lot of the time it works—but sometimes it doesn't.

Mindfulness takes us off autopilot. Mindfulness is a way of quieting our mind, paying attention to what's true in this moment, and being wise about when we need to take ourselves off autopilot. Some of our habits shouldn't be trusted. To make good choices and be happy, we have to take ourselves off autopilot.

> **Mindfulness is the process of paying attention to what's happening right now, in our own experience, in a curious and open way.**

Do you ever notice how bossy your mind is? We have a thought and we just believe it totally. Or we have an emotional reaction inside, and then we say or do something based on that reaction. An image of a candy bar floats into our mind, and next thing we know, we're marching down to the market or vending machine to buy it.

Does anyone notice that about your mind?

Yeah, well me too. I try hard to be mindful when I teach because I'm smarter—and nicer!—when I'm mindful. I'll give you an example. If I'm not mindful and someone in class is acting out, I might respond in a way that's impatient or harsh. (*Determine the level of self-disclosure appropriate for your group.*) Sometimes autopilot brings out the worst in me, not the best.

Let me ask you a few more questions. Raise your hand if:

— You ever said something you wish you could take back?

— Did something you later regretted?

— Noticed your mind thinking about something over and over, and it wouldn't stop?

— Couldn't fall asleep because your mind kept spinning, or your body felt restless?

— Had trouble focusing in class, or spaced out when your teacher called on you?

— Notice that some days certain things bug you, but other days you're totally fine?

— How about this: Raise your hand if sometimes your mind gets really focused and you're just in the zone—right there with something you love for as long as you want, and it's almost effortless? That feels good, right?

Okay. One more question: Is your mind always trustworthy? Should we always obey or listen to what our mind says to do?

Part of how we begin to decide when to trust our mind is to get familiar with our inner life, to learn how it works. When we're familiar with it, we don't get bossed around so much. To get familiar with our own mind, we need to study it. We need to be able to use our awareness to actually look at and observe our own mind. That's what mindfulness is all about. We settle down until we get quiet inside, and then we discover the world inside of us. We can learn when to obey our minds and when to disobey.

**Practice: Mindfulness of the Body**

So, to start out we need to settle the mind and body a little, or it's going to be hard to observe clearly what's happening. When our mind is all stirred up, it's like trying to look through a telescope to see the moon—

but the telescope is shaking a lot. You'd never see the moon clearly if the telescope was shaking.

So, we're going to begin by listening to the bell and settling into a relaxed body. I'll walk you through the steps of a little relaxation and focusing technique. This method is a very powerful thing to do all on its own, and we'll begin our practice this way each lesson.

✦ First, let yourself sit in a comfortable and relatively upright position in your chair. You don't have to be uptight about it, but just have a sense that the spine is gently extended up toward the sky. Feet can just rest on the ground about hip width apart. Your hands can be folded in your lap or placed palms down on each leg.

✦ If it feels all right to you, let your eyes close. (If not, just gaze down at the ground in front of you.) I'll have my eyes open some of the time to stay aware of the room, so you can just totally relax.

✦ In a moment, I'm going to ring the bell, and I want you to listen to the sound totally and completely. See if you can put all of your attention into hearing the sound from the beginning, through the middle, and all the way to the end. When you can't hear the sound at all anymore, quietly raise your hand.

✦ (*Ring bell; allow it to ring until it's silent.*) Notice how you feel right now.

✦ The next thing we are going to do is to relax. To do this, we're going to notice something that is happening all the time but that we rarely pay attention to—gravity. Right now, bring some awareness to this subtle downward force that is always acting on the body. Let the body get heavy. Feel the points that are clearly touching the ground and let them take the weight of your body.

✦ You can even repeat "relax, relax" a few times silently to yourself. Let any excess tension present in your body drain down and out.

✦ Take a few deep breaths, and when you exhale, see if you can feel any amount of ease or relaxation in your whole body.

✦ As the body settles, simply be aware of your whole body sitting. This is mindfulness of the body.

✦ Now, with this more relaxed awareness, I want you to spend the next minute or so noticing what's happening in your body. As you are being aware, what do you notice?

✦ You don't have to see anything special. In fact, our experience is usually very ordinary. That's fine. If you get stuck, you can prompt yourself with a simple question: What am I aware of right now?

✦ After a minute, I'll ring the bell to signal the end of the period. See if you can listen to its sound again from the moment you hear it until the ringing fades out completely.

*(Ring bell.)*

✦ When you're ready, you can let your eyes open slowly. Notice how you feel. Notice how it feels in the room right now. Maybe move your hands or feet; look around the room.

 **Discussion Questions**

— What did you notice? How did that feel? How many people noticed that you felt more relaxed? Did anyone have the opposite reaction where you actually got more anxious?

— Do we make our best decisions when we're really agitated? Do you think being relaxed might help us listen to our own wisdom and make good choices?

— How else might this practice be useful in your life? *(Offer some suggestions.)*

*(If someone got more anxious, it's important to normalize this response. You might share: "Sometimes when we're real busy, we don't notice our stress, but then when we relax, it comes rushing into our awareness. That's not a problem at all. In fact, mindfulness is designed to deal with that. We'll talk more about that in future lessons.")*

**PRACTICE ROUND 2**

*(Repeat similar instructions from the first sitting. This time, do it for two to four minutes, depending on what feels appropriate.)*

How was this round different than the first? Did you notice how much things can change, even in just a couple of minutes? That's part of what we're learning. How when something is happening, it can kind of feel like it's forever? But the truth is that things change a lot.

 **Take-Home Practice**

1. As a reflection, study your mind to see when it's bossing you around and when you feel like you're making your own choices.

2. Once or twice this week, take a few minutes to do this relaxation exercise.

 **Journal Suggestions**

1. What surprised you about this lesson?
2. What did you learn about how your mind works?
3. When do you feel most relaxed? When do you feel most anxious or agitated?
4. In what ways can relaxation benefit you?

 **Teacher Notes**

(Teacher Notes for this lesson apply to all three versions of the introductory lesson.)

In many ways, the first lesson is the most important lesson of the curriculum you will teach. The more you are able to create a genuine connection with the kids and establish the relevance of this practice, the more likely they are to participate in a wholehearted and open-minded way. As such, we recommend that you do your best to engage the students in honest, authentic conversation. Try to open their minds to the possibility that there is something of great value they can learn here, something that has the potential to serve them for the rest of their lives.

As any good teacher knows, first impressions are key. Whether you are a classroom teacher, school guidance counselor, or an outside provider, how you set the tone and create the container for this first mindfulness lesson will determine the trajectory of future lessons. Decide how you want to set up the room and what you require of them for participation. Make this clear and stick to it. For example: Are the lights on or off? How are the chairs in the room arranged? Are their desks cleared of all materials? Cell phones off? And so forth.

Finally, the essential part of the opening lesson is giving the students a taste of stillness. As much as possible, try to give them an experience of the room being still and quiet. This often happens when you ask them to close their eyes and listen to the sound of the bell carefully. We want to help their nervous systems recognize that it's possible to slow down, and be still and relaxed. The taste of that inner quiet usually creates an intrinsic motivation for the practice.

 **Science Supplement**

(The Science Supplement for this lesson applies to all three versions of the introductory lesson.)

The practice of mindfulness is hypothesized to develop specific skills. In one prominent model of mindfulness, Tang, Hölzel, and Michael Posner (2015) suggested that the practice confers its benefits through three core skill sets. They argue that mindfulness develops self-regulation through the skills of emotion regulation, attention control and self-awareness.

Mindfulness develops emotion regulation. As James Gross (2002), a leading researcher on emotion regulation, wrote: ". . . emotions do not force us to respond in certain ways, they only make it more likely we will do so. This malleability permits us to regulate our emotions. When afraid, we may

run, but do not always do so. When angry, we may strike, but do not always do so. And when amused, we may laugh, but do not always do so. How we regulate our emotions matters: Our well-being is inextricably linked to our emotions" (p. 281). A range of evidence—psychological, behavioral, and neurobiological—supports the claim that mindfulness enhances emotion regulation.

Mindfulness may also deliver its benefits through enhancement of attentional control. The regulation of attention is important to virtually all tasks—reading, studying, writing, listening, even playing sports. Mindfulness practice is a training in *metacognitive* awareness: an awareness of experiences *as* phenomenal experiences. Vision, hearing, sensation, emotion, thought—all of these can be known as experience. Metacognitive awareness is opposed to cognitive fusion, wherein we have experiences, but do not appreciate that they are mediated by processes of thinking, feeling, and perceiving. In practicing mindfulness, we're learning to select an object of attention, sustain connection with that object, disengage from competing stimuli, and return the attention when we notice that we've become "cognitively fused" with competing stimuli (typically verbal thinking). These skills are relevant for academic accomplishment specifically, and goal-directed behavior more generally.

Lastly, mindfulness may confer benefits through the development of self-awareness skills. Self-awareness includes present-moment awareness of somatic and emotional cues. It also refers to decreases in self-referential thinking and greater flexibility in the ideas we have about ourselves.

Although the research is in the early phase, neural correlates have been identified for each of these three mechanisms. By "neural correlates" we mean that brain imaging techniques have identified changes in the structure or activity of the brain that are associated with mindfulness practice. Here is the conclusion from Tang, Hölzel, & Posner's (2015) article in *Nature Reviews Neuroscience:*

"Knowledge of the mechanisms that underlie the effects of meditation is therefore still in its infancy. However, there is emerging evidence that mindfulness meditation might cause neuroplastic changes in the structure and function of brain regions involved in regulation of attention, emotion and self-awareness . . . If supported by rigorous research studies, the practice of mindfulness meditation might be promising for the treatment of clinical disorders and might facilitate the cultivation of a healthy mind and increased well-being."(p. 222)

When you're teaching students about mindfulness, you do not necessarily need to explain these concepts, but they can inform your understanding and shape how you present mindfulness.

**REFERENCES & FURTHER READING**

Chiesa, A., Calati, R., & Serretti, A. (2011). Does mindfulness training improve cognitive abilities? A systematic review of neuropsychological findings. *Clinical Psychology Review, 31,* 449–464.

Gross, J. J. (2002). Emotion regulation: Affective, cognitive, and social consequences. *Psychophysiology, 39,* 281–291.

Kashdan, T. B. & Rottenberg, J. (2010). Psychological flexibility as a fundamental aspect of health. *Clinical Psychology Review, 30,* 865–878.

Tang, Y. Y., Hölzel, B. K., & Posner, M. I. (2015). The neuroscience of mindfulness meditation. *Nature Reviews Neuroscience, 16,* 213–225.

# Intro to Mindfulness: Mind Power

## Key Points

♦ Our minds boss us around all the time. We obey our thoughts like a worker obeying a mean supervisor.

♦ Our reactions to others' behaviors also boss us around. We react on autopilot, and do not always behave in our best interests.

♦ Mindfulness is a chance to take back our power.

♦ With mindfulness, we're training ourselves to determine when to listen to our mind, and when to ignore its advice.

♦ We can develop habits of mind that lead to more happiness and emotional freedom.

♦ To do this, we need to be able to observe the mind and begin to understand how it works. Mindfulness helps us to do that.

> **DEFINITION:** *Mindfulness* is the process of paying attention to what's happening right now, in our own experience, in a curious and open way.

## Practice Instructions

♦ Sit in a posture that is comfortable yet upright, feet on the floor and hands in your lap.

♦ Let your eyes close, or gaze down at the ground in front of you.

♦ Feel the weight of gravity in your body. Notice its heaviness and where it touches the ground. If you like, say "relax, relax" silently inside.

♦ Take a few deep breaths, noticing any ease or relaxation on the exhalation.

♦ As your body settles, become aware of your whole body sitting. Feel the sensations of sitting.

♦ Sit like this for a few minutes, noticing whatever happens in your body.

♦ When you're ready, let your eyes open and look around the room.

 ## Take-Home Practice

1. As a reflection, study your mind to see when you feel like it's bossing you around and when you feel like you're making your own choices.

2. Once or twice this week, take a few minutes to do this relaxation exercise.

 ## Journal Suggestions

1. What surprised you about this lesson?

2. What did you learn about how your mind works?

3. When do you feel most relaxed? When do you feel most anxious or agitated?

4. In what ways can relaxation benefit you?

# INTRO TO MINDFULNESS: A USER MANUAL FOR THE MIND

## The Basics

This lesson is one of our three possible introductory lessons. It describes mindfulness as a tool for training our minds, learning, and accomplishing one's goals in life. It can also be adapted to introduce the cultivation of positive qualities like heartfulness, gratitude, and generosity. While the practice described here is very similar to each of the other introductory lessons, the framing is different and may be more (or less) appropriate for your group of adolescents.

---

**LEARNING OBJECTIVES**

1. To define mindfulness.
2. To demonstrate the sitting posture for mindfulness practice.
3. To practice mindfulness of the body by relaxing and feeling gravity.

---

**LESSON 1.2 IN BRIEF: A SYNOPSIS**

## Intro to Mindfulness: A User Manual for the Mind

1.  **Would you know how to use a super-advanced technology with no manual?**
This class will be about how to train our minds. Imagine you received a piece of technology from 100 years in the future. Without a manual or anyone to teach you, how useful is the technology? The human mind is a kind of "technology." How much time do we spend learning to use our minds?

2.  **Make a case for mindfulness.**
How well do we know how to use our minds? Raise your hand if you:

◆ Ever said something you wish you could take back? Did something you later regretted?

◆ Felt like your mind kept thinking about something that's bothering you, and it wouldn't stop?

◆ Couldn't fall asleep because your mind kept spinning, or your body felt restless?

◆ Had trouble focusing in class, or spaced out when your teacher called on you?

◆ Were in a bad mood but didn't know why, and couldn't get out of it?

◆ Notice that some days certain things bug you but other days you're totally fine?

- If sometimes your mind gets really focused and you're just in the zone—right there with something you love, for as long as you want, and it's almost effortless.

Our minds are like untrained puppies, running all over the place. Some athletes use mindfulness to train their minds, just like they train their bodies. Mindfulness practice is like a user manual for the mind.

**3. Define Mindfulness.**

If we want to learn how to use our minds better, we need to be able to observe them. **Mindfulness** is the process of paying attention to what's happening right now, in our own experience, in a curious and open way. Mindfulness takes us off autopilot; helps us quiet our mind and pay attention; supports better choices and more happiness. Invite students to join you in an experiment to observe and train their own minds.

## Mindfulness of Body: Practice Instructions

Do about one minute of practice to begin.

- Sit in a posture that is comfortable yet upright, feet on the floor and hands in your lap.

- Let your eyes close, or gaze down at the ground in front of you.

- Ring the bell, putting all of your attention into hearing.

- Begin to let your body relax by feeling the weight of gravity. Notice its heaviness and where it touches the ground. If you like, say "relax, relax" silently inside.

- Take a few deep breaths, noticing any ease or relaxation on the exhalation.

- As your body settles, become aware of your whole body sitting. Feel the sensations of sitting.

- Sit like this for a few minutes, noticing whatever happens in your body.

- Ring the bell, listening to the entire sound.

- When you're ready, let your eyes open and look around the room.

Discuss what the students noticed. Time permitting, practice again for another two to three minutes.

 **Discussion Questions**

- What did you notice? How did that feel? How many people noticed that you felt more relaxed? Did anyone have the opposite reaction where you actually got more anxious?

- Raise your hand if you noticed sensations in your body? What sensations did you feel?

- If we want to train our mind, the first step is starting to learn what it's doing by observing it—how it feels, what it's thinking, how it moves. There's nothing that's supposed to happen and you can't do this wrong. We're just learning to slow down and look.

- Any ideas about how might this practice be useful in your life? (*Offer some suggestions*)

 **Take-Home Practice**

1. Next time you feel like your mind is being unruly, running all over the place, try this out for a little bit—could be just 30 seconds, or a few minutes. What's the effect?
2. Observe other people. Ask yourself if their mind is any different than yours inside. How many people do you think have trained their mind well? Can you tell? How?
3. Once or twice this week, take a few minutes to do this relaxation exercise.

# Intro to Mindfulness: A User Manual for the Mind

## Lesson Outline

— Would you know how to use an advanced technology from the future if you didn't have a manual and no one showed you how to use it?

— Our minds are the most advanced technology on the planet, but we spend very little time learning how to actually use them.

— Mindfulness practice is like finding the user's manual to your mind.

— Through mindfulness, we understand more about ourselves and about how to be happy.

— The first step is learning how to observe our own mind.

## Lesson

Today is the first in a series of classes on how to train our minds. Imagine you gave someone from a hundred years ago a smartphone, who'd never seen a telephone, much less a computer. Would they know how to use it?

*(Students answer.)*

Not so much, right? Well what if I told you that you had in your possession, right now, the most advanced piece of technology ever created on this planet? More advanced than anything we can possibly build right now. But I didn't give you any instruction manual, no user guide—nothing. How useful would that be to you?

*(Students answer.)*

I'm going to propose that each of us in this room already has that piece of technology; and it's light years ahead of our most advanced computers. Anyone know what it is?

*(Students answer.)*

That's right, it's your own mind. Even the most advanced artificial intelligence programs we're building, while they can compute a lot faster in certain ways, can't do even some of the most basic things that we can do. And the things they can do are actually modeled after our brains!

So, let's see how well we really know how to operate these things! Let me ask you a few more questions. Raise your hand if you:

— Ever said something you wish you could take back?

— Did something you later regretted?

— Felt like your mind kept thinking about something that's bothering you over and over, and it wouldn't stop?

— Couldn't fall asleep because your mind kept spinning, or your body felt restless?

— Had trouble focusing in class, or spaced out when your teacher called on you?

— Were in a bad mood but didn't know why, and couldn't get out of it?

— Notice that some days certain things bug you, but other days you're totally fine?

— How about this: Raise your hand if sometimes your mind gets really focused and you're just in the zone—right there with something you love for as long as you want, and it's almost effortless.

So, what's going on here? How well do we really know how to use these things? *(Point to your head.)* Sometimes it seems like our mind will do what we want, but other times it won't listen to us at all! I mean, if it's *your mind*, you should be able to get it to do what you want, right?

*(Depending on the class, you can include references to philosophical or scientific studies of consciousness, and the fact that self-awareness is still kind of a mystery that we don't really understand.)*

A lot of the time, our mind behaves like a little puppy that's not trained. Anyone ever been around a young puppy? What does it do?

*(Students answer.)*

Yeah, it runs around all over the place doing whatever *it* wants to do, chewing on everything, peeing everywhere. Ever feel like your mind is running all over the place and getting you into trouble? Thinking about food, or that person you like, then worrying about stuff, then listening to the teacher for a second, then back to lunch . . . Sometimes that's not such a big deal, but other times it gets us into trouble, and sometimes it's straight up exhausting!

Now what if there were an instruction manual for how to use this technology called the human mind? What if I could show you how to *train* your own mind? There are some pretty cool examples today of how training your mind can help you do great things. For example, how many people here like sports? Anyone watch basketball? Anybody know what Michael Jordan, Kobe Bryant, and Steph Curry all have in common, besides the fact that they've all won the NBA Championship multiple times?

*(Students answer.)*

Yeah—they train hard. They trained their bodies over and over and over again. How many times do you think a professional basketball player at the top of their game has practiced a free-throw?

*(Students answer.)*

And that training is part of what makes them so good at their sport. But that's not the only thing they have in common. *They've also trained their minds: They all practice mindfulness.* They've all got a kind of training manual for how to stay in the zone. They learned from a mindfulness coach how to stay focused and steady under pressure.

Does anyone know what mindfulness is?

*(Students answer.)*

Mindfulness practice is a form of mental training. It's like having an instruction manual for the mind, so we can actually learn how to use our mind better. Imagine what would it be like if you could train your mind to stay focused and do what you want more of the time? How might that be helpful?

*(Students answer.)*

If we want to learn how to use our mind better, to train it, *first* we need to be able to observe our mind! Mindfulness helps us to do that. It's a way of quieting the mind, paying attention to what's true in this moment, so we can get smarter about how to use our minds and train ourselves. It gives us a way to learn how be more alert, balanced, and clear, so we can be on point and in the flow, and so we don't get yanked around by every passing thought or emotion.

> **Mindfulness is the process of paying attention to what's happening right now, in our own experience, in a curious and open way.**

## Practice: Mindfulness of the Body

Today we're going to learn the first steps of mindfulness practice. It's the first step of the user manual, like learning your basic foot position in basketball, or how to play a G chord on the guitar. If we want to train our minds, the first thing we need to do is learn how to slow things down and settle a bit. When our mind is running all over the place like that puppy, it can't learn anything.

I'm going to introduce a little relaxation and focusing method. This method is a very powerful thing to do all on its own, and we'll be adding pieces to it as the lessons progress.

✦ First, let the body be in a comfortable and relatively upright position in your chair. You don't have to be uptight about it, but just have a sense that the spine is gently extended upward toward the sky. Feet can just rest on the ground about hip width apart. You can fold your hands in your lap, or place them palms down on your legs.

✦ If it feels all right to you, you can close the eyes. (If not, just gaze down at the ground in front of you.) I'll have my eyes open some of the time to stay aware of the room, so you can just totally relax.

✦ In a moment, I'm going to ring the bell, and I want you to listen to the sound totally and completely. See if you can put all of your attention into hearing the sound from the beginning, through the middle, and all the way to the end. When you can't hear the sound at all anymore, quietly raise your hand.

✦ (Ring bell; allow it to ring until it's silent.) Notice how you feel right now.

✦ The next thing we are going to do is to relax. To do this, we're going to notice something that is happening all the time but that we rarely pay attention to—gravity. Right now, bring some awareness to this subtle downward force that is always acting on the body. Let the body get heavy. Feel the points that are clearly touching the ground, and let them take the weight of your body.

✦ You can even repeat "relax, relax" a few times silently to yourself. Let any excess tension present in your body drain down and out.

✦ Take a few deep breaths, and when you exhale, see if you can feel even a little bit of relaxation move through your whole body.

✦ As the body settles, simply be aware of the whole body sitting. This is mindfulness of the body—being aware of, and feeling the sensations of your body sitting.

✦ Now, with this more relaxed awareness, I want you to spent the next minute or so noticing what's happening in your body. As you sit quietly, what do you notice?

✦ You don't have to see anything special. In fact, our experience is usually very ordinary. That's fine. If you get stuck, you can prompt yourself with a simple question: What am I aware of right now?

✦ In a bit, I'll ring the bell to signal the end of the period. See if you can listen to its sound again from the moment you hear it until the ringing fades out completely.

(Ring bell.)

✦ When you're ready, you can let your eyes open slowly. Notice how you feel. Notice how it feels in the room right now. Maybe move your hands or feet; look around the room.

 **Discussion Questions**

— What did you notice? How did that feel? How many people noticed that you felt more relaxed? Did anyone have the opposite reaction where you actually got more anxious?

— Raise your hand if you noticed sensations in your body. What sensations did you feel?

— If we want to train our mind, the first step is starting to learn what it's doing by observing it—how it feels, what it's thinking, how it moves. There's nothing that's supposed to happen, and you can't do this wrong. We're just learning to slow down and look.

— Any ideas about how this practice might be useful in your life? (*Offer some suggestions.*)

*(If someone got more anxious, it's important to normalize this response. You might share: "Sometimes when we're really busy, we don't notice our stress but then when we relax, it comes rushing into our awareness. That's not a problem at all. In fact, mindfulness is designed to deal with that. We'll talk more about that in future lessons.")*

 ## Take-Home Practice

1. Next time you feel like your mind is being unruly, running all over the place, try this out for a little bit—could be just 30 seconds, or a few minutes. What's the effect?
2. Observe other people. Ask yourself if their mind is any different than yours inside. How many people do you think have trained their mind well? Can you tell? How?
3. Once or twice this week, take a few minutes to do this relaxation exercise.

 ## Journal Suggestions

1. Did anything surprise you about this lesson? What did you learn about your mind?
2. In what ways can mental training help you in your life?

3. If your mind were super well-trained, what would you do? What would you use it for?
4. In what ways can relaxation benefit you?

 ## Teacher Notes

See introductory lesson version 1.1.

 ## Science Supplement

See introductory lesson version 1.1.

In 2012, Google Brain was founded on the principle that artificial neural networks could learn by trial and error in a manner similar to the human brain. Though this idea was present in the 1940s during the early age of computing, it has reemerged in recent decades with new force as the power of computers has increased to match the demands required for this kind of machine learning. The scale and pace of learning of artificial intelligence (AI) was demonstrated when Google Brain switched their Google Translate software from the previous model to an AI-based system using neural networks. As Lewis-Kraus (2016) reported in *The New York Times Magazine*, "The A.I. system . . . demonstrated overnight improvements roughly equal to the total gains the old one had accrued over its entire lifetime [of 10 years] (p. 40).

**REFERENCES & FURTHER READING**
Lewis-Kraus, G. (2016, Dec. 18) The great A.I. awakening. *The New York Times Magazine, 14.*

# Intro to Mindfulness: A User Manual for the Mind

**1.2**

## Key Points

- Would you know how to use an advanced technology from the future, if you didn't have a manual and no one showed you how to use it?

- Our minds are the most advanced technology on the planet, but we spend very little time learning how to actually use them.

- Mindfulness practice is like finding the user's manual to your mind. We use it to train our mind just like we train our body for a sport.

- Through mindfulness, we understand more about ourselves and about how to be happy.

- The first step is learning how to observe our own mind.

## Practice Instructions

> **DEFINITION:** *Mindfulness* is the process of paying attention to what's happening right now, in our own experience, in a curious and open way.

- Sit in a posture that is comfortable yet upright, feet on the floor and hands in your lap.

- Let your eyes close, or gaze down at the ground in front of you.

- Feel the weight of gravity in your body. Notice its heaviness and where it touches the ground. If you like, say "relax, relax" silently inside.

- Take a few deep breaths, noticing any ease or relaxation on the exhalation.

- As your body settles, become aware of your whole body sitting. Feel the sensations of sitting.

- Sit like this for a few minutes, noticing whatever happens in your body.

- When you're ready, let your eyes open and look around the room.

 ## Take-Home Practice

1. Next time you feel like your mind is being unruly, running all over the place, try this out for a little bit—could be just 30 seconds, or a few minutes. What's the effect?

2. Observe other people. Ask yourself if their mind is any different than yours inside. How many people do you think have trained their mind well? Can you tell? How?

3. Once or twice this week, take a few minutes to do this relaxation exercise.

 ## Journal Suggestions

1. Did anything surprise you about this lesson? What did you learn about your mind?

2. In what ways can mental training help you in your life?

3. If your mind were super well-trained, what would you do? What would you use it for?

4. In what ways can relaxation benefit you?

# INTRO TO MINDFULNESS: STRESS AND WELL-BEING

## The Basics

This lesson is one of our three possible introductory lessons. It takes a distinctive approach to describing mindfulness by emphasizing our relationship with the mind as central to happiness in life. While the practice described here is very similar to each of the other introductory lessons, the framing is different and may be more or less appropriate for your group of adolescents.

---

**LEARNING OBJECTIVES**

1. To define mindfulness.
2. To demonstrate the sitting posture for mindfulness practice.
3. To practice mindfulness of the body by relaxing and feeling gravity.

---

**LESSON 1.3 IN BRIEF: A SYNOPSIS**

## Intro to Mindfulness: Stress and Well-Being

**1. How happy are human beings? What would we need to do improve life on earth?**

These lessons are about understanding our minds. How many would say that things on the planet are in great shape? People are exceptionally happy? Some are happy, but life is challenging?

If we want to be happier and improve things on the planet, what do we need to do? We need to work both externally (on systemic issues) and internally (on our mind, how we handle things).

**2. Make a case for mindfulness.**

We each have a relationship with our mind for our entire life. What's it like? Raise your hand if you:

♦ Ever said something you wish you could take back? Did something you later regretted?

♦ Felt like your mind kept thinking about something over and over, and it wouldn't stop?

♦ Couldn't fall asleep because your mind kept spinning, or your body felt restless?

♦ Had trouble focusing in class, or spaced out when your teacher called on you?

♦ Were in a bad mood but didn't know why, and couldn't get out of it?

♦ Notice that some days certain things bug you but other days you're totally fine?

♦ If sometimes your mind gets really focused and you're just in the zone—right there with something you love, for as long as you want, and it's almost effortless?

We're going to learn some ways to understand our mind. Improving our relationship with our mind can make us happier, help us to get along better with others, and accomplish our goals in life.

### 3. Define Mindfulness.

If we want to understand our mind, we need to be able to observe it. **Mindfulness** is the process of paying attention to what's happening right now, in our own experience, in a curious and open way. It takes us off autopilot; helps us quiet our mind and pay attention; supports better choices and more happiness. Invite students to join you in an experiment to observe and train their own minds.

## Mindfulness of Body: Practice Instructions

Do about two to three minutes of practice.

- Sit in a posture that is comfortable yet upright, feet on the floor and hands in your lap.

- Let your eyes close, or gaze down at the ground in front of you.

- Ring the bell, putting all of your attention into hearing.

- Begin to let your body relax by feeling the weight of gravity. Notice its heaviness and where it touches the ground. If you like, say "relax, relax" silently inside.

- Take a few deep breaths, noticing any ease or relaxation on the exhalation.

- As your body settles, become aware of your whole body sitting. Feel the sensations of sitting.

- Sit like this for a few minutes, noticing whatever happens in your experience.

- You might notice sounds, sensations in your body, thoughts and images, emotions.

- Ring the bell, listening to the entire sound.

- When you're ready, let your eyes open and look around the room.

 **Discussion Questions**

- How many people were able to feel the weight of their body?

- Raise your hand if you noticed other sensations in your body? What sensations?

- How many people felt more relaxed during the exercise?

- Did anyone have the opposite reaction where you actually got more anxious?

- What else did you notice?

- Any ideas about how might this practice be useful in your life? *(Offer some suggestions)*

Our whole life is composed of these different kinds of experiences: sensory input (body sensations, sights, sounds, smells, tastes), emotions, thoughts, and images. Is there anything outside of this that you can experience? During our time together, we'll be learning how to understand and relate to all of these experiences, so that we don't stress as much.

 **Take-Home Practice**

1. Next time you feel like your mind is being unruly, running all over the place, try this out for a little bit—could be just 30 seconds, or a few minutes. What's the effect?

2. Observe other people. Ask yourself if their mind is any different than yours, inside. How many people do you think have trained their mind well? Can you tell? How?

3. Once or twice this week, take a few minutes to do this relaxation exercise.

# Intro to Mindfulness: Stress and Well-Being

## Lesson Outline

- Life has both happiness and challenges.
- If we want to be happier and improve things on the planet, we need to work both externally (on systemic issues) and internally (on our mind, how we handle things).
- We each have a relationship with our mind for our entire life.
- Improving our relationship with our mind can make us happier, help us to get along better with others, and help us accomplish our goals in life.
- If we want to understand our mind, we need to be able to observe it.

## Lesson

Today is the first in a series of classes we'll be doing on the human mind. Between lessons, I'll ask you to do some short experiments to make our discussions more real and practical.

I want to start off with a little poll. Looking around at the world, how many of you would say that things on the planet are great, that everything is in good shape?

(*Students answer.*)

Right—not so many! What about human beings? How many of you would say that people as a whole are *exceptionally* happy?

(*Students answer.*)

Okay, things aren't looking so good. Let's take a different angle: How many of you would say that some happiness is available to people, but life also has a lot of challenges—some of them quite intense?

(*Students answer.*)

Yes, more takers on that one. So, the world situation could be a lot better. We can be a little happy, and then things get hard. Let's keep going. When you look around at the planet, what kinds of challenges are we facing?

(*Students answer. If you want, you can write their answers up on the board and group them by internal and external, adding those category labels at the end of the brainstorm.*)

Yes (*summarize and/or add a few: finances, racism, disease, war, famine*), these are some of the main issues confronting us as individuals and as a society today. And there are all the *internal* challenges we face— sadness, anger, worry, frustration, and fear, among many others.

So, how many of you think it's possible for us to do better as a species? Raise your hand if you think we could make certain changes that would make us happier in life.

If we want to suffer less as a species, what would we need to do? How would we work on it?

(*Students answer.*)

Yeah—the bottom line is that we're going to have to work *both* externally and internally. Externally, we're going to have to push for changes on all kinds of different fronts systemically, from the criminal justice system, to climate change, to things as basic as making sure all human beings have clean drinking water. There is a lot of work to be done to make the world more just and equitable. Some of you are already very involved with these issues, which is great.

Internally, we're going to have to look at our own mind and behavior. Because even if we got external circumstances just the way we wanted them, the mind still has this way of not being content. Has anybody experienced that, in yourself or in those around you? Everything can be going all right, but we're still stressing. Do you know what I'm talking about?

(*Students answer.*)

Yes. Good examples. So, I want to propose something and see if we agree. Each of us, no matter who we are or where we are, is going to have a *relationship with our own mind* for the rest of our life. Where you live, what you do, and who you do it with will certainly change, but through it all, your mind is a constant. Anyone disagree with that?

(*Students answer. Explore if anyone disagrees.*)

**This mind is with us for life.** Yet how much time do you spend in school studying how we relate to our mind? Have you had any courses on how the mind works, how to handle your thoughts and emotions, how to relate to the internal challenges of life?

Not so much, right? In school, we mostly use the mind to learn other things—to absorb information and build skills. But we rarely look at the mind itself— why it gets stressed, what makes it peaceful or joyful, what makes it agitated. So, do you think it would be worthwhile to spend some time looking at these issues, trying to understand our mind better?

(*Students answer.*)

Well, what's it like in here? (*Point to your head.*) Let me ask a few more questions. Raise your hand if you:

— Ever said something you wish you could take back?

— Did something you later regretted?

— Felt like your mind kept thinking about something that's bothering you over and over, and it wouldn't stop?

— Couldn't fall asleep because your mind kept spinning, or your body felt restless?

— Had trouble focusing in class, or spaced out when your teacher called on you?

— Were in a bad mood but didn't know why, and couldn't get out of it?

— Notice that some days certain things bug you but other days you're totally fine?

— How about this: Raise your hand if sometimes your mind gets really focused and you're just in the zone—right there with something you love for as long as you want, and it's almost effortless?

What I'm going to teach you in these lessons can help with a lot of that. We're going to learn some ways to look at our own mind. And we're going to experiment with tools that can help us have a better relationship with it. When we have a good relationship with our own mind, we can handle challenges better, get along well with others (and their minds!), and work for some of the external changes we've been talking about in a more balanced and sustainable way.

Our primary tool for this is something called "mindfulness." **It's a way of quieting the mind, paying attention to what's happening right now in our own experience in a curious and open way.** It gives us a way to learn how be more alert, balanced, and clear, so we can be on point and in the flow, and so we don't get yanked around by every passing thought or emotion.

## Practice: Mindfulness of the Body

If we want to learn about our mind we need to be able to observe it. How can you work on something if you don't even know what it is, right? It's weird, but many of us have never spent time paying real attention to our mind and body.

So today I'm going to introduce a little relaxation and focusing method. This method is a very powerful thing to do all on its own, and we'll be adding pieces to it as the course progresses. We're going to begin by listening to the bell, and settling into a relaxed body. Then I'll point out a few things you might notice to look directly at what makes up our experience.

◆ First, let the body be in a comfortable and relatively upright position in your chair. You don't have to be bolt upright like it's some military exercise, but just sense that the spine is upright and settled. Your feet are on the ground; your hands can be folded in your lap or palms down on your legs.

◆ Let your eyes close, or just relax the lids by looking downward—whichever feels better.

◆ In a moment, I'm going to ring the bell, and I want you to listen to the sound totally and completely. See if you can put all your attention into hearing the sound from the beginning, through the middle, and all the way to the end. When you can't hear the sound at all anymore, quietly raise your hand.

◆ (*Ring bell; allow it to ring until it's silent.*) Notice how you feel right now.

◆ Next, we're going to relax our bodies. I want you to bring your attention to something that's happening all the time, which we rarely pay attention to—gravity. Feel the weight of your body and let it get heavy. Feel the points that are touching the chair or the ground, and let them take the weight of your body.

◆ You can even silently repeat the word "relax, relax" a few times to yourself. See if you can let any extra tension in your body drain down and out.

◆ As your body settles, try to become aware of the whole body sitting—this is mindfulness of the body.

◆ Now, with this more relaxed awareness, I want you to spend a minute or two noticing what's happening in your experience. As you are being aware, what do you notice?

◆ (*Leave some silence, then offer a few things the students might notice.*) You might notice sounds, or sensations in your body. You might notice thoughts or images in your mind, or emotions. Feel your body sitting, and notice whatever you can about your experience.

◆ In a bit, I'll ring the bell to signal the end of the period. See if you can listen to its sound again from the moment you hear it until the ringing fades out completely.

(*Ring bell.*)

◆ When you're ready, you can let your eyes open slowly. Notice how you feel. Notice how it feels in the room right now. Maybe move your hands or feet; look around the room.

### DISCUSSION

Okay. Let's talk about that a little bit. How many people were able to feel the weight of your body? (*Show of hands.*) How many people felt more relaxed during the exercise? (*Show of hands.*)

So, that's kind of interesting right there. We're already learning something about how to work with our mind. Feeling the sensations of the body sitting can help us to relax. Now, when you paid attention to your inner experience, what did you notice?

(*Depending on the time, engage in a discussion and elicit information from the students, or simply ask for a show of hands to see how many people noticed or felt each distinct category of experience.*)

So, our whole life is composed of these different kinds of experiences: sensory input (body sensations, sights, sounds, smells, tastes); emotions, thoughts, and images. Is there anything outside of this that you can experience? Interesting, isn't it?

Here's the last point for today: Our inner experience is kind of like a band or orchestra. It can make any kind of music, just as we can have an almost infinite variety of experiences. And yet, all the orchestra's sounds come from a limited number of instruments. Classical orchestras have around 100. Rock and hip-hop use a lot fewer—sometimes as few as 3-6. So, we have these 4 "instruments" for our internal experience: sensations, emotions, thoughts, and images. During our time together, we'll be learning more about how to understand and relate to all these experiences so that we don't stress as much.

*(You can end by practicing once more, time permitting.)*

 **Take-Home Practice**

1. Can you find or think of any experience (past, present, or future) that isn't some mixture of these four things: sensory input, emotions, thoughts, and images?

2. Once or twice this week, take a few minutes to do this relaxation exercise.

3. Can you begin to get comfortable with the fact that there is a part of your mind that can simply witness and observe all this occurring? A part that doesn't get caught up in any of it but just knows it's happening?

 **Journal Suggestions**

1. What situations can you think of where the relaxation exercise could be helpful?

2. When do you feel most relaxed? When do you feel most anxious or agitated?

3. What did you learn about how your mind works?

4. Was there anything that surprised you?

 **Teacher Notes**

See introductory lesson version 1.1.

 **Science Supplement**

See introductory lesson version 1.1.

# Intro to Mindfulness: Stress and Well-Being

**1.3**

## Key Points

◆ Life has both happiness and challenges.

◆ If we want to be happier and improve things on the planet, we need to work both externally (on systemic issues) and internally (on our mind, how we handle things).

◆ We each will have a relationship with our mind for our entire life.

◆ Improving our relationship with our mind can make us happier, help us to get along better with others, and help us accomplish our goals in life.

◆ If we want to understand our mind, we need to be able to observe it.

## Practice Instructions

◆ Sit in a posture that is comfortable yet upright, feet on the floor and hands in your lap.

◆ Let your eyes close, or gaze down at the ground in front of you.

◆ Feel the weight of gravity in your body. Notice its heaviness and where it touches the ground. If you like, say "relax, relax" silently inside.

◆ Take a few deep breaths, noticing any ease or relaxation on the exhalation.

◆ As your body settles, become aware of your whole body sitting. Feel the sensations of sitting.

◆ Sit like this for a few minutes, noticing whatever happens in your experience.

◆ When you're ready, let your eyes open and look around the room.

**DEFINITION:** *Mindfulness* is the process of paying attention to what's happening right now in our own experience in a curious and open way.

 ## Take-Home Practice

1. Can you find or think of any experience (past, present, or future) that isn't some mixture of these four things: sensory input, emotions, thoughts, and images?

2. Once or twice this week, take a few minutes to do this relaxation exercise.

 ## Journal Suggestions

1. What situations can you think of where the relaxation exercise could be helpful?

2. When do you feel most relaxed? When do you feel most anxious or agitated?

3. What did you learn about how your mind works?

4. Was there anything that surprised you?

# OUR BENDABLE BRAINS: MINDFULNESS OF SOUND

## The Basics

This lesson introduces students to the concept of neuroplasticity and the idea that our brains can learn and strengthen. It also introduces the practice of mindfulness of sound as a way of settling and training the mind.

---

**LEARNING OBJECTIVES**

1. To define neuroplasticity and understand the brain's ability to change.
2. To give present-moment attention to the experience of hearing, returning the attention if and when the attention strays.

---

**2**

---

**LESSON 2 IN BRIEF: A SYNOPSIS**

## Our Bendable Brains: Mindfulness of Sound

**1. Check in & review: Who practiced at home? What experiences or questions came up?**
Review the definition of mindfulness and its purpose or benefits.

**2. Introduce neuroplasticity.**
Discuss how the brain learns: It can change its shape and function. Give an example (London taxi cab experiment). Define neuroplasticity, the brain's ability to form new neural connections. We are always shaping our brain by how we use our attention. We learn information or exercise our bodies in school, but we don't spend time developing our minds themselves.

**3. Mindfulness strengthens focus and attention.**
Has anyone ever told you to "pay attention"? Has anyone ever taught you how? Mindfulness can teach us how to focus and pay attention better. Today, we'll learn mindfulness of sound, which is one way to strengthen our ability to focus and pay attention.

### Practice Instructions

◆ Sit in a posture that is comfortable yet upright, feet on the floor and hands in your lap.

◆ Let your eyes close, or gaze down at the ground in front of you.

◆ Feel the weight of gravity in your body. Notice its heaviness and where it touches the ground. If you like, say "relax, relax" silently inside.

◆ Take a few deep breaths, noticing any ease or relaxation on the exhalation.

- As your body settles, become aware of your whole body sitting. Feel the sensations of sitting.

- Ring the bell, putting all of your attention into hearing.

- Sit like this for a few minutes, noticing whatever happens in your experience.

- When you're ready, let your eyes open and look around the room.

 ### Discussion Questions

- How many people were able to notice when they stopped hearing the bell?

- How many people's minds wandered while listening to the bell, maybe thinking about something else? Raise your hand if you were able to bring it back?

- What other sounds did you hear at the end?

- Did your mind wander more or less without the bell?

It's normal for our minds to wander: That's what we do all day long. Exercise for the mind is *noticing* that it's gone off into random thoughts, and bringing it back. That process of noticing and returning is how we train our minds to pay attention and begin to strengthen these new neural networks.

 ### Take-Home Practice

1. Can you find or think of any experience (past, present or future) that isn't some mixture of these four things: sensory input, emotions, thoughts, and images?

2. Once or twice this week, take a few minutes to do this relaxation exercise.

# Our Bendable Brains: Mindfulness of Sound

## Lesson Outline

— Mindfulness can make our brains stronger, even changing their shape and how they work.

— Different studies show how the brain grows and changes shape and function.

— Our brain's malleability is called "neuroplasticity."

— When we use our attention, we're training our brain.

— We spend a lot of time learning information or exercising our bodies in school, but we don't spend time developing our minds themselves.

— Mindfulness can teach us how to focus and pay attention better.

— We usually train our minds to jump from one thing to another. Mindfulness of sound is one way to strengthen our ability to focus and pay attention.

## Lesson

*(Organize the room for mindfulness, and engage the students in a transitional activity. Then, restate the hook or theme from your introductory lesson. Here are three examples, depending on which introductory lesson you chose.)*

During our first class, we talked about:

— (1.1) how mindfulness can give us back our power. It can help us learn when to listen to our mind, and when to disobey it!

— (1.2) how practicing mindfulness is like having an instruction manual for our mind, that it can teach us how to use our mind better.

— (1.3) how mindfulness can help us to understand our minds better so we can be happier.

Today, we're going to take a closer look at the way our mind works, and how we can use it better. First, does anyone remember how we defined mindfulness?

*(Students answer.)*

That's right, we said that **mindfulness is paying attention to what's happening right now, in our own experience, in a curious and open way.**

And we said that the first step of this training was learning how to relax and settle into our body, so we could start to observe our mind. Did anyone take some time to practice mindfulness of the body? How did that work for you? What did you notice? *(Students answer. If they're not forthcoming, try polling. Here are a few suggestions.)*

— How many people felt at least a little more relaxed or at ease when they did it?

— How many people felt sleepy?

— How many people noticed their mind wandering? And were able to bring your attention back to just feeling the sensations of your body sitting?

Today, I want to talk about some of the ways that mindfulness works to make our minds stronger, and teach you another technique to settle your body and sharpen your mind.

Check this out: There was a study on people training to be taxi cab drivers in London, England, who had to memorize the maze of London city maps with more than 25,000 streets. And you know what they found? The *volume* of a certain part of their brains actually got larger! Studies with adults show that mindfulness practice thickens parts of the brain associated with

**2**

awareness, reflection, and feeling things (insula, prefrontal cortex, somatosensory cortex).

So, our brains can get stronger and grow, kind of like muscles. Their shape or structure changes, *and the very way they function can change*. In other words, our brains are **malleable**. Does anyone know what that word means?

*(Students answer.)*

Yeah, it means that you can bend or shape something, kind of like clay or soft plastic. The word for this property of our brains is called "neuroplasticity." One of the ways our brain works is by sending signals down pathways called neural networks. When you do something a lot, the brain remembers it. It's kind of like walking through a grassy field over and over again; soon, a trail develops. Or, you can think about it like taking a new route to school: Once you've done it a few times you remember how to go that way. In our brain, if we do something a lot, it gets etched in. In neuroscience they say, "Neurons that fire together wire together."

So, we spend a lot of time learning information in school, developing intelligence, and strengthening our bodies through sports or exercise. But we don't spend much time learning how to use our mind itself.

Raise your hand if you ever heard a teacher or an adult say, "Pay attention." Keep your hand raised if anyone ever showed or taught you *how* to pay attention. Right. How many people find it hard to pay attention sometimes? Maybe you're trying to do your homework, and you keep reading the same paragraph over and over?

Our minds can wander a lot, because we haven't taught them how to rest and stay with one single thing. In fact, most of what we are doing each day is training them *not* to stay on one thing. Our cell phones, tex-

ting, Facebook, Twitter, and video games all train the mind to move quickly and jump around from one thing to another. We're strengthening those patterns in our minds.

Mindfulness is mental training, and one of the things it does is strengthen our brain's ability to focus. So let's do some practice. Each day we'll practice being mindful of one thing. Today we're going to use sound to help strengthen our minds.

## Practice: Mindfulness of Body and Sound

Let's start the same way we did last time, with our posture and the sound of the bell.

✦ Let your body sit in a comfortable and relatively upright position in your chair. Remember, you don't have to be uptight, but just have a sense that the spine is extended upward. Feet are on the ground, hands in your lap.

✦ If it feels all right to you, gently close your eyes, or else gaze down at the ground.

✦ When you hear the sound of the bell, listen completely. Put all of your attention into hearing the sound from the beginning, through the middle, and all the way to the end. When you can't hear the sound at all anymore, quietly raise your hand.

✦ (*Ring bell; allow it to ring until it's silent.*) Notice how you feel right now.

✦ Try to notice the relaxing effects of gravity. Bring awareness to that downward force that's always here in the body. Let your body get heavy; feel the points that are touching the ground, and let them take the weight of your body.

✦ If you like, you can say "relax, relax" a few times silently to yourself. Let any tension in your body drain down and out.

✦ Take a few deep breaths, and when you exhale, see if you can feel any relaxation or ease. As your body settles, become aware of the whole body sitting.

2

In a moment, I'm going to ring the bell again. Keeping your eyes closed, let all your attention go to the sound, listening from the first moment as closely as you can until the moment it ends. See if your mind wanders or any thoughts come while you're listening. (*Ring bell.*)

✦ Notice how you feel. Keeping your eyes closed, see if you can notice any other sounds. Just let your attention be wide open, listening to the sounds around you.

(*Wait about 30 to 60 seconds, then ring the bell.*)

✦ When you're ready, you can let your eyes open slowly. Notice how you feel. Notice how it feels in the room right now.

 ## Discussion Questions

— How many people were able to notice when they stopped hearing the bell?

— How many people's minds wandered while listening to the bell, maybe thinking about something else? Raise your hand if you were able to bring it back?

— What other sounds did you hear at the end?

— Did your mind wander more or less without the bell?

It's totally normal for our minds to wander. Remember, that's kind of what we do all day long, jumping from one thing to the next. The exercise for the mind is *noticing* that it's gone off into random thoughts, and bringing it back. That process of noticing and returning is how we train our minds to pay attention and begin to strengthen our brains.

 ## Take-Home Practice

1. Take five minutes to practice mindfulness of the body. See if you can use the feeling of gravity and a few deep breaths to help yourself relax.

2. Pay attention to the sounds around you. Take a few minutes (on the bus, walking, at home) and listen to all the sounds come and go around you. Whenever your mind wanders, bring it back to hearing.

3. Put on a favorite song or album and listen mindfully. See if you can notice something new about the track that you've never heard before.

 ## Journal Suggestions

1. How was it for you to practice mindfulness today? Did you feel calm, relaxed, agitated, frustrated?

2. You're learning a tool to train your mind. Are there specific things you'd like to train your mind to be able to do? What?

3. What questions do you have about mindfulness?

**ALTERNATE ACTIVITY**

If you have more time, you could play one or more pieces of music and ask students to listen for particular instruments, or to shift their attention from one sound/instrument to another.

 ## Teacher Notes

Using a singing bowl or resonant chime with a long ringing sound is ideal for this activity. The real, live vibration in the room has the natural tendency to capture the students' attention. Be sure to comment on any palpable settling or quiet in the room. It's important to help students be aware of the physiological changes they experience, as well as to reinforce the recognition that they played an active role in affecting those shifts through the power of their attention.

**Science Supplement**

## MEDITATION AND CHANGES IN THE STRUCTURE OF THE BRAIN

Sometimes sharing recent scientific findings can support learning and motivation to practice mindfulness. Depending on the student group and the teacher's preferences, research can be integrated into lessons. Here, we summarize some of the findings on mindfulness and brain change.

Research has documented numerous clinical benefits for mindfulness and meditation practices. When there's evidence for the effectiveness of a practice, the next question is, "Okay, but how does it work?" Understanding the "mechanism of change"—how it works—is an important scientific question. When we can understand how something works, it gives more control to distill the "active ingredients" from what's not beneficial or even harmful, like the side effects of a medication. It may even help to make the intervention—in this case, mindfulness—more powerful.

The dominant view within neuroscience is that changes in behavior, cognition, or emotion always involve associated neurobiological changes. One implication of this framework is that the benefits of mindfulness practice must somehow be related to changes in the function and/or structure of the brain.

An important study was published by Kalina Christoff (Fox, et al., 2014) and her colleagues. In that article, she asked the question, *"Is meditation associated with altered brain structure?"* This research is significant because it mathematically synthesizes the findings from numerous prior studies. This kind of synthesis is known as a meta-analysis. The findings from a single study are always shaped by the particular subjects included in that study and other features of the research design. But aggregating many studies in a meta-analysis has the advantage of examining a specific question across different study samples and research designs.

The authors were interested in brain *morphology,* which is the study of the structure, shape, and composition of the brain. Scientists are interested in morphology because there is a link between morphology and the capacities of the brain. This is important—because if brain changes weren't related to behavior and subjective well-being, then we wouldn't care so much about the brain.

The authors approached the subject cautiously and were "conservative" in their work: They wanted to be careful not to *overestimate* the effects of meditation on the brain. Despite this cautious approach, the researchers identified several brain regions that evidenced structural changes resulting from meditation practice. These areas include the rostrolateral prefrontal cortex, sensory cortices and insular cortex, hippocampus, anterior and midcingulate, orbitofrontal cortex, superior longitudinal fasciculus, and the corpus callosum.

Surveying these brain regions, (Fox et al., 2014) note that meditation appears to engage high-order brain regions. The authors speculate how changes in the insula might be related to superior bodily and emotional awareness, and changes in the orbitofrontal cortex could plausibly provide meditators more freedom to evaluate the present situation rather than relying exclusively on prior learned associations. Hippocampal degeneration has been found in a number of psychiatric and neurologic diseases. The association between meditation and hippocampal volume could represent a mechanism whereby meditation alleviates symptoms of depression and anxiety, and helps manage stress.

Now, there's an important caveat here. As we say, *correlation is not causation.* That means that while two things can be associated (meditation and brain changes) this does not necessarily mean that meditation *causes* brain changes. Here is what Fox (2014) writes: "Evidence for meditation practice as the causative factor in structural brain change remains tenuous, and much further work is needed before such a relationship is either established or disconfirmed. Several regions show consistent differences in advanced practitioners vs. meditation-naïve controls, but the possibility remains that pre-existing brain structure heterogeneities explain the observed group differences." (p. 65–66).

## MEDITATION AND BRAIN FUNCTION

While this subject is too large and complex to be covered here, it is important to know that much of the neuroscientific interest in mindfulness and meditation has been about understanding how the brain *functions*—and how different parts of the brain interact in real time. Christoff's group (Fox et al., 2016) conducted a review of 78 studies on meditation and brain function—how the brain works—rather than how it's composed. They write:

> "Many have understandably viewed the nascent neuroscience of meditation with skepticism, but recent years have seen an increasing number of high-quality, controlled studies that are suitable for inclusion in meta-analyses and that can advance our cumulative knowledge of the neural basis of various meditation practices. With nearly a hundred functional neuroimaging studies of meditation now reported, we can conclude with some confidence that different practices show relatively distinct patterns of brain activity, and that the magnitude of associated effects on brain function may have some practical significance"(p. 225).

Clearly, there's substantial enthusiasm for this realm of research. However, it is important not to let our enthusiasm for mindfulness outpace the evidence. Fox, Christoff, et al. (2016) conclude:

> "The only totally incontrovertible conclusion, however, is that much work remains to be done to confirm and build upon these initial findings"(p. 225).

## NOTES ON THE LONDON TAXI AND BUS DRIVERS AND BRAIN CHANGES

The researchers compared bus drivers—who take the same routes—and taxi drivers, who need to find new ways to navigate from one location to another. Therefore, we would expect taxi drivers to engage brain regions associated with spatial navigation or memory more than the bus drivers, who don't need to imagine new routes. Maguire, Woollett, & Spiers (2006) studied this issue. Here is one of their important findings: "We found that compared with bus drivers, taxi drivers had greater gray matter volume in mid-posterior hippocampi and less volume in anterior hippocampi. Furthermore, years of navigation experience correlated with hippocampal gray matter volume only in taxi drivers, with right posterior gray matter volume increasing and anterior volume decreasing with more navigation experience. This suggests that spatial knowledge, and not stress, driving, or self-motion, is associated with the pattern of hippocampal gray matter volume in taxi drivers"(p. 1091).

2

### REFERENCES & FURTHER READING

Fox, K. C., Nijeboer, S., Dixon, M. L., Floman, J. L., Ellamil, M., Rumak, S. P., . . . & Christoff, K. (2014). Is meditation associated with altered brain structure? A systematic review and meta-analysis of morphometric neuroimaging in meditation practitioners. *Neuroscience & Biobehavioral Reviews, 43,* 48–73.

Fox, K. C., Dixon, M. L., Nijeboer, S., Girn, M., Floman, J. L., Lifshitz, M., . . . & Christoff, K. (2016). Functional neuroanatomy of meditation: A review and meta-analysis of 78 functional neuroimaging investigations. *Neuroscience & Biobehavioral Reviews, 65,* 208–228.

Maguire, E. A., Woollett, K., & Spiers, H. J. (2006). London taxi drivers and bus drivers: A structural MRI and neuropsychological analysis. *Hippocampus, 16,* 1091–1101.

# Our Bendable Brains: Mindfulness of Sound

## Key Points

+ Mindfulness can make our brains stronger, even changing their shape.

+ Our brain's ability to grow and change is called "neuroplasticity."

+ We spend a lot of time learning information or exercising our bodies in school, but we don't spend time developing our minds themselves.

+ Mindfulness of sound is one way to strengthen our ability to focus and pay attention.

> **DEFINITIONS:** *Neuroplasticity* is the brain's ability to change and form new neural connections throughout life. A neural network is a set of interconnected neurons working together in a circuit to transmit information in the brain or nervous system.

**2**

## Practice Instructions

+ Sit in a posture that's comfortable yet upright, feet on the floor and hands in your lap.

+ Let your eyes close, or gaze down at the ground in front of you.

+ Feel gravity and the weight of the body. Notice its heaviness and where it touches the ground. If you like, say "relax, relax" silently inside.

+ Take a few deep breaths, noticing any ease or relaxation on the exhalation.

+ Become aware of your whole body sitting. Feel the sensations of sitting.

+ Put all of your attention on the experience of hearing.

+ Listen to the different sounds you hear; notice how they come and go.

+ When you're ready, let your eyes open and look around the room.

 ## Take-Home Practice

1. Take five minutes to practice mindfulness of the body. See if you can use the feeling of gravity and a few deep breaths to help yourself relax.

2. Take a few minutes (on the bus, walking, at home) and pay attention to hearing sounds. Listen to sounds come and go. Whenever your mind wanders, bring it back to hearing.

3. Put on a favorite song or album and listen mindfully. See if you can notice something new about the track that you've never heard before.

 ## Journal Suggestions

1. How was it to practice mindfulness today? Did you feel calm, relaxed, agitated, frustrated?

2. You're learning a tool to train your mind. Are there specific things you'd like to train your mind to be able to do? What?

3. What questions do you have about mindfulness?

# GETTING (BACK) ONLINE: MINDFULNESS OF BREATHING

## The Basics

This lesson introduces basic brain concepts as a way to frame the practice of mindful breathing.

**LEARNING OBJECTIVES**
1. To explain the different parts of the brain.
2. To learn and practice mindfulness of breathing using "anchor words."

**LESSON 3 IN BRIEF: A SYNOPSIS**

**3**

## Getting (back) Online: Mindfulness of Breathing

**1. Check in & review:**
Who practiced at home? What experiences or questions came up?

**2. Discuss the role of thoughts and emotions in life.**
Can we control these? What it's like when they get out of control? What are the effects?

How is it possible that we can get "kicked offline" in our own brain? Discuss the analogy with Wi-Fi: If it goes down, we need to reset our router. It's the same with our brain.

**3. Explore basic neurobiology and its evolution.**
Getting kicked offline is a wiring issue. Discuss evolution of the brain, its older capacities (physical and social desires, relating to the environment) and its newer capacities (thinking, reflection, planning). Discuss the benefits and drawbacks (when older parts take over, newer parts can ruminate in unhelpful ways) and the idea of these parts "talking" to each other.

**4. Mindfulness of breathing is like resetting the router.**
Define mindfulness again. Mindfulness of breathing is like hitting the "reset" button, bringing newer parts of the brain back online. It gives us an anchor, a place from which to watch the storms go by.

### Practice Instructions

✦ Sit in a posture that is comfortable yet upright, feet on the floor and hands in your lap.

✦ Let your eyes close, or gaze down at the ground in front of you.

- Feel the weight of gravity. Notice its heaviness, where it touches the ground. "Relax, relax."
- Take a few deep breaths, noticing any ease or relaxation on the exhalation.
- As your body settles, become aware of your whole body sitting. Feel the sensations of sitting.
- Bring your attention to your anchor, the spot where you can feel your breathing most clearly.
- Feel the sensations of breathing in and out. Anytime your mind wanders, gently bring it back.
- When you're ready, gently let your eyes open.

 **Discussion Questions**

- How many people were able to feel their breath?
- How many people used [name each: belly, chest, nose] as the anchor spot?

- What did it feel like there? What sensations let you know you were breathing in? What was different between the in-breath and the out-breath?
- Did anyone notice thoughts or emotions? Could you come back to your anchor?
- Any ideas for how this practice could support you in life—here at school, or at home?

See if you can notice when your brain goes offline. Take a few mindful breaths to reset the system.

 **Take-Home Practice**

1. Practice mindfulness of breathing at least twice before our next lesson.
2. If something gets you angry or upset this week, remember there are different parts of your brain at work. Do two minutes of mindfulness practice. Can you balance the emotions in the old brain with the mindful awareness in the new brain?

3

# Getting (back) Online: Mindfulness of Breathing

## Lesson Outline

- When we're upset, we can't control our thoughts and feelings; cognitive control goes "offline."
- Thoughts and feelings are wired to the rest of our body and will follow what's happening in our biology.
- Our brain has many parts, some older and some newer.
- When the newer parts and the older parts stop "talking" to each other, we can get hijacked by challenging emotions.
- Mindfulness is one way to make the newer parts of the brain stronger and help them "talk" to the older parts of the brain.
- Today we'll learn the next basic step of mindfulness practice: mindful breathing.
- Mindfulness of breathing gives us an anchor to watch the storms go by.

## Lesson

*(Organize the room for mindfulness and engage the students in a transitional activity.)*

So, we've been learning more about how to train our minds, to make them stronger and clearer. I'm curious, did anyone remember to use mindfulness between our last lesson and today? *(Show of hands.)* When did you practice? How'd it go?

*(Students answer.)*

Cool. So today we're going to build on this. I want to start with a simple question: Can we control what our mind and body think and feel? Think about your day. Do you choose each thought or emotion you have?

*(Students answer.)*

Sure, it's a mix. Sometimes, we can choose to think or feel something intentionally, but a lot of the time our thoughts and feelings aren't up to us. Sometimes that's okay, like if we're just daydreaming on the bus or something. **But other times, they can get out of control.** We can get hijacked by our thoughts, or feelings in ways that aren't so cool. Can anyone give me an example?

*(Students answer.)*

Yeah, when we're really stressed, maybe if someone lied to us, or when we feel really hurt or angry. In these situations, we can't just will ourselves to think or feel differently about what's happening. It's like if your internet connection goes down: You're not Googling anything until you get back online. When we're tripping on something, we lose the ability to think clearly and make good decisions. So, why is that? I mean, how do we manage to get kicked offline in our own brain?

*(Students answer.)*

Basically, it's a wiring issue. If you unplug your modem, the Wi-Fi goes down, right?

Same with our thoughts and feelings. They're not just floating out there on their own. **Thoughts and feelings are connected to the rest of our mind, brain, and body.** When we get triggered or upset, the wiring inside starts working in a different way. Our whole biology is having the reaction—not just our thoughts—and *that's* what we need to understand and work with.

3

I want to talk a little bit about the wiring in here (point to your head). Our brain is incredibly complex; it has different parts, which evolved over time, with many different functions. Some scientists spend their entire lives studying just one part of the brain.

One way of breaking it down is saying that there are older parts, and newer parts. Anybody want to guess what some of the older parts of our brain are responsible for?

*(Students answer.)*

Right, good answers. The *older aspects of our brain* do a lot of the same things that the brains of other animals do:

— *Basic physical desires*: Getting food and shelter.
— *Basic social desires*: Being close with family, figuring out where we stand socially in relation to others, mating, raising kids, competing for resources.
— *Basic responses to the environment*. We like some things and dislike other things. We are drawn toward some things and avoid others.

Okay. What about the *newer parts of our brain?* What do you think is going on there?

*(Students answer.)*

Good answers again. Hundreds of thousands of years ago, what became the human brain evolved some new abilities, including:

— Being able to imagine the future. *(Students can give examples. A simple one is building alternate worlds like they do in online gaming.)*
— Being capable of complex planning and goal-directed behavior. *(Students can give examples. A simple one is building an iPhone.)*

— Becoming self-conscious in a way that more primitive animals are not. *(Students can give examples. A simple one is "imagining the person you want to be when you grow up.")*

Scientists believe that the older parts of the brain and the newer parts of the brain need to be "talking" to each other in order to regulate our emotions and behavior. When they're not talking to each other, there can be problems—we can wind up feeling out of control or behaving in ways we regret. When we're freaked out, those newer capacities of thought can ruminate on stuff that's not helpful, imagining our worst fears and getting us really down.

So, we want to train our brains so that the different parts are friends—not ignoring each other—and we want to strengthen some of the newer parts of our brain so they can really get the attention of the older parts of our brain.

Taking some mindful breaths in the heat of the moment is like resetting your Wi-Fi—it helps you get back online by activating some of the newer parts of the brain, and helping those newer parts talk to some of the older parts.

Today we're going to add the next step in mindfulness training: Once we relax and become aware of our body, we learn to be mindful of our breathing. Remember, **mindfulness is the process of paying attention to what's happening in a curious and open way.** So we learn to feel and pay attention to our breathing in a curious and open way.

Mindful breathing can help us to calm down in the moment and it gives us a way to strengthen mindfulness over time. The breath is also neutral. It's not a strong emotion, it's not something to hate or love. It's just there, all day, every day, breathing in, breath-

3

ing out. So, we can use it for mindfulness anytime we want. Okay, let's do some practice together.

## Practice: Mindfulness of Breathing

◆ Let the body be comfortable and upright, feeling your spine. Feet on the ground, hands on your lap. Let your eyes close (or look down at the ground in front).

◆ When you hear the sound of the bell, listen with all of your attention until the end.

◆ Sense the relaxing effects of gravity. Feel that downward force in your body, and let your body get heavy. Feel the points that are touching the ground, letting them take the weight of the body.

◆ If you want, you can repeat "relax, relax" a few times silently to yourself. Let any tension in your body drain out.

◆ As your body settles, feel the sensations of your whole body sitting.

◆ Now let's take two deep breaths together. As you breathe, see where you feel your breath most clearly. It might be at your nose or mouth, in your chest, or down in your belly. Try each place out.

◆ Let your breath return to normal, and pick one spot to see if you can continue to feel the sensations of breathing in and breathing out. (*Leave some silence.*)

◆ Our breathing can be an "anchor" because it steadies our attention, just as an anchor keeps a boat from drifting off at sea.

◆ It might help to put your hand there wherever you feel the breath the most, on your belly, chest, or in front of your nose. See if you can let your attention begin to settle with the sensations of breathing there. As you breathe in, feel those sensations of breathing in. As you breathe out, feel the sensations of breathing out.

◆ When your mind drifts away from the anchor and into planning, worrying, or remembering, gently bring it back to the anchor of the sensations of breathing. Don't worry if you have to do that again and again. You're not doing it wrong. (*Let the students*

*practice with the breathing for at least a minute or two, depending on how quiet they are.*)

(*Ring bell.*)

◆ When you're ready, you can let your eyes open; take a moment to look around the room.

 **Discussion Questions**

— How many people were able to feel their breath?

— How many people used their abdomen or belly as the anchor spot? How about the chest? Anyone feel it most at the nose or nostrils?

— What did it feel like there? What sensations let you know you were breathing in? What was different between the in-breath and the out-breath?

— Did anyone notice some thoughts or emotions? Were you able to just let them go by and come back to your anchor?

— Any ideas for how this practice could support you in life—here at school, or at home?

Over the next few days, try to see if you can notice when your emotions or reactions kick the rest of your brain offline. Try taking a few mindful breaths to see if you can reset the system. The more we understand this mind, the less it'll hijacked us and the more equipped we are to make wise choices.

 **Take-Home Practice**

1. Take some time to practice mindfulness of breathing twice before our next lesson.
2. If something gets you angry or upset this week, see if you can remember that there are different parts of your brain at work. Do a minute or two of mindfulness practice and see if you can balance your inner state.

**Journal Suggestions**

1. What surprised you about this lesson?
2. How did it feel to practice mindfulness of breathing? What did you enjoy about it? What didn't you enjoy about it?
3. Are there any things you learned today that could help you with school or things at home? What?

 **Teacher Notes**

It can take time for students to develop the ability to feel their breathing. In the beginning, many of them may focus more on the *idea* of breathing in and breathing out rather than the *felt experience*. Help the students to identify the actual sensations they experienced. The more clearly they understand what it is you are inviting them to notice and feel, the easier it will be for them to practice.

 **Science Supplement**

Meditation research is maturing. The initial questions of "does this practice work?" is yielding to more sophisticated questions, such as: How do the practices compare to each other in terms of effectiveness and the mechanism through which they work? Tania Singer (Lumma, Kok, & Singer, 2015), a brain scientist at Max Planck Institute in Germany, has done important research comparing and contrasting different meditation practices. In one study, she examined the cardiovascular effects of three types of meditation practice: breath meditation, loving-kindness meditation, and awareness of thought meditation. The research participants did each practice on a daily basis for three months. As the scientists predicted, heart rate and subjective effort were higher during loving-kindness meditation and awareness of thoughts meditation, when compared to breathing meditation. Here are Singer's conclusions:

"Overall the current study showed that not all types of meditation are equally relaxing when comparing three different types of meditation. Furthermore, the study showed that with training participants enjoy the mental exercises more and experience it as less effortful on a subjective level, while at the same time training the two types of more complex meditations comes with an increase in sympathetic activation, suggesting heightened mastery and concentration needed with increasing expertise. Such findings are important, because they show that different types of meditation should be recommended for different purposes. Breathing meditation was perceived as the least effortful exercise and also had the lowest heart rate, which makes it suitable for an easy to learn exercise for meditation novices"(p. 44).

Focused attention meditations, such as mindfulness of breathing, have been linked to activations in regions linked with cognitive control: dorsolateral prefrontal cortex, anterior cingulate cortex, and premotor cortex. Deactivations were identified in key nodes of the default mode network (discussed later in the curriculum) including the posterior cingulate cortex. These data may help explain the salutary effects of mindfulness of breathing.

**REFERENCES & FURTHER READING**

Fox, K. C., Dixon, M. L., Nijeboer, S., Girn, M., Floman, J. L., Lifshitz, M., . . . & Christoff, K. (2016). Functional neuroanatomy of meditation: A review and meta-analysis of 78 functional neuroimaging investigations. *Neuroscience & Biobehavioral Reviews, 65*, 208–228.

Goldin, P. R., McRae, K., Ramel, W., & Gross, J. J. (2008). The neural bases of emotion regulation: Reappraisal and suppression of negative emotion. *Biological Psychiatry, 63*, 577–586.

Lumma, A. L., Kok, B. E., & Singer, T. (2015). Is meditation always relaxing? Investigating heart rate, heart rate variability, experienced effort and likeability during training of three types of meditation. *International Journal of Psychophysiology, 97*, 38–45.

Ochsner, K. N., Ray, R. D., Cooper, J. C., Robertson, E. R., Chopra, S., Gabrieli, J. D., & Gross, J. J. (2004). For better or for worse: Neural systems supporting the cognitive down- and up-regulation of negative emotion. *NeuroImage, 23*, 483–499.

Wager, T. D., Davidson, M. L., Hughes, B. L., Lindquist, M. A., & Ochsner, K. N. (2008). Prefrontal-subcortical pathways mediating successful emotion regulation. *Neuron, 59*, 1037–1050.

3

## Getting (back) Online: Mindfulness of Breathing

### Key Points

♦ When we're upset, we can't control our thoughts and feelings; our thinking goes "offline."

♦ Our thoughts are wired to our whole body, and will follow what's happening in our biology.

♦ Our brain has many parts, some older and some newer.

♦ When the older parts take over, we can get hijacked by thoughts and emotions.

♦ Mindfulness is one way to make the newer parts of the brain stronger, so we don't get hijacked by the older parts as easily.

♦ Mindfulness of breathing gives us an anchor to watch the storms go by.

> **DEFINITION:** An *"anchor spot"* is the place that we feel our breath most clearly; we can bring our minds back to that spot when they wander.

### Practice Instructions

♦ Sit in a posture that is comfortable yet upright, feet on the floor and hands in your lap.

♦ Let your eyes close, or gaze down at the ground in front of you.

♦ Feel the weight of gravity on the body. Notice its heaviness and where it touches the ground. If you like, say "relax, relax" silently inside.

♦ Take a few deep breaths, noticing any ease or relaxation on the exhalation.

♦ As your body settles, become aware of your whole body sitting. Feel the sensations of sitting.

♦ Bring your attention to your anchor, the spot where you can feel your breathing most clearly.

♦ Feel the sensations of your body breathing in and out. Anytime your mind wanders, gently bring it back to the breathing.

♦ When you're ready, gently let your eyes open.

###  Take-Home Practice

1. Take some time to practice mindfulness of breathing at least twice before our next lesson.

2. If something gets you angry or upset this week, see if you can remember that there are different parts of your brain at work. Do a minute or two of mindfulness practice and see if you can balance the emotions running in the old brain with the awareness supported by mindfulness in the new brain.

###  Journal Suggestions

1. What surprised you about this lesson?

2. How did it feel to practice mindfulness of breathing? What did you enjoy about it? What didn't you enjoy about it?

3. Are there any things you learned today that could help you with school or things at home? What?

3

# IMPULSES AND PATIENCE

## The Basics

This lesson explores the experience of impulses, the role of mindfulness in noticing an impulse, and the value of mindful breathing to help soothe the mind and make good decisions.

> **LEARNING OBJECTIVES**
> 1. To understand the difference between impulsive action and mindful action.
> 2. To understand the role of self-control in long-term goal achievement.
> 3. To learn mindful breathing practices and their relevance to soothing the mind during intense impulses.
> 4. To learn a mental noting technique where the use of words is paired with a specific attentional focus.

## LESSON 4 IN BRIEF: A SYNOPSIS

**4**

## Impulses and Patience

**1. Check in & review:**
Who practiced at home? What experiences or questions came up?

**2. Discuss impulses.**
Ever acted impulsively and regretted it? What's that like? To achieve our goals, we need to have patience and self-control. For that, we need to be able to recognize our impulses.

Discuss the marshmallow experiment. What would you have done at age five? If I gave you five $100 bills and agreed to give you another $500 in 6 months, if you didn't spend them, could you do it? Studies have shown that higher self-control brings better health, less addiction, and higher earnings.

**3. Discuss impulse control.**
What skills do you need to resist the marshmallow? To be mindful of the *impulse* itself and the craving. If it could talk, what would craving say? We can learn to be aware of our impulses, so that we have more choice over which ones we follow. During this practice, anytime you notice an impulse (to open your eyes, to scratch an itch, for the bell to ring), see if you can pause, breathe, and relax.

### Practice Instructions

◆ Sit in a posture that's comfortable yet upright, feet on the floor and hands in your lap.

- Let your eyes close, or gaze down at the ground in front of you.

- Feel gravity and the weight of your body. Notice its heaviness and where it touches the ground. If you like, say "relax, relax" silently inside.

- Take a few deep breaths, noticing any ease or relaxation on the exhalation.

- Become aware of your whole body sitting, then bring your attention to your breathing.

- Find your anchor spot and feel the sensations of breathing in and breathing out.

- You can silently label the breath with a soft mental note, "breathing in . . . breathing out . . ."

- If your mind drifts off, just notice, and bring it back to your anchor.

- When you feel an impulse—to move, open your eyes, and so on—first notice the impulse. Then say silently, "Pausing, pausing." Next, feel the sensations of your breathing.

- When you're ready, let your eyes open and look around the room.

 **Discussion Questions**

- What impulses did you notice? What did the impulses feel like?
- What happened when you used the breathing to soothe your mind during a strong impulse?
- How could this be useful to you in your daily life?

 **Take-Home Practice**

1. When you find yourself in the middle of a strong impulse, notice it and see what it's like to do just 20 seconds of mindful breathing.

2. Start to notice how relaxation can help with making wise choices. If you regret a certain choice, look back on it and try to remember how your body and mind felt in that moment.

## Impulses and Patience

### Lesson Outline

- Achieving our goals depends on self-control; mindfulness can help us develop self-control.

- Delayed gratification is an expression of self-control (the "marshmallow experiment").

- To resist an impulse, first, one must become aware (mindful) of that impulse.

- Mindful breathing can be a resource when an impulse threatens to overwhelm us.

- Mental noting—a technique of silently saying words in one's mind—can be useful in focusing the attention on the breath and helping calm the mind.

### Lesson

(*Organize the room for mindfulness and engage the students in a transitional activity.*)

Raise your hand if you remembered to use mindfulness between our last lesson and today? (*Show of hands.*) How did it go? What helped? Was there a time that you tried to use mindfulness but it didn't help?

(*Students answer.*)

Today, I want to talk about our impulses, how to notice them, and how to pause with mindfulness so that we can get what we really want—not what our impulses tell us in the moment. To get what we really want in life, we need to have patience and self-control. And to develop self-control, we need to learn to recognize impulses.

How many people have acted on an impulse to do or say something and it's gotten you in trouble?

Yeah, we all do that. Part of mindfulness is about developing more choice even when we're having intense feelings. But to decide if we should act on our impulse, we have to be aware of that impulse first, right?

Let me tell you about a research study. It's been called The Marshmallow Test. The experiment was simple. A psychologist at Stanford University would take a child age 5 to 6, put him or her into an empty room with just a table and a chair in it. He asked the child to sit in the chair and placed one marshmallow on the table. Then, he told the child he was going to leave the room and come back in 15 minutes. The child could eat the marshmallow if they wanted to. But if it was still on the table when he returned, he told the child that they would get a second marshmallow.

Imagine yourself at age five. What would you have done? (*Ask rhetorically.*)

Now imagine for a minute another version of this test. I'm not really going to do this, but what would happen if today, right now, I gave you five marked $100 bills. The test is that if you still have these same five $100 bills in six months, I will give you $500 more. I'm not going to ask you to share your answer to either test. But just imagine what would happen for you.

The researcher at Stanford found that 2 out of 3 of the five-year-olds could resist the temptation and get the second marshmallow. Years later, the researchers looked at how the kids were doing—and the ones who were able to wait were doing much better than the ones who ate the first marshmallow immediately.

Bigger studies have found that those higher in self-control grow up to be healthier, have lower rates of

4

addiction, make more money, and get in less trouble with the police.

So, what skills do you need to resist the marshmallow?

*(Students answer.)*

Right. You need mindfulness to become aware of the impulse and the wanting. If a craving could talk, it would say something. Let's say we want the marshmallow—sitting there, in that room alone, what is the craving saying in your mind?

*(Students answer.)*

Yeah, it would probably be saying eat that marshmallow, and this bad feeling of craving will go away. Does that make sense? So, sometimes we may want to obey the craving, but sometimes not. In order to choose, we need mindfulness.

When we notice an impulse, we can become aware of it and pause. We can practice breathing mindfully and relaxing. Some of our bad decisions come when we're rushed, stressed out, and operating on automatic. Mindful breathing helps us pause, relax and make better choices.

In a minute, we're going to do our mindfulness practice. During that time, you'll probably have some impulses. Like, maybe you'll want to scratch an itch, or to open your eyes and look around. Or maybe you'll want the bell to ring early because you're bored. Or maybe you'll think about eating something delicious and want to go get it. When you feel these impulses, see if you can pause, breathe and relax.

## Practice

So, we'll begin as we usually begin, by establishing mindfulness of the body.

♦ Let the body be comfortable and upright, feeling your spine. Feet on the ground, hands on your lap. If it feels all right to you, gently close your eyes.

♦ When you hear the sound of the bell, listen with all of your attention all the way to the end.

♦ Sense the relaxing effects of gravity. Feel that downward force in your body and let your body get heavy. Feel the points that are touching the ground, letting them take the weight of the body.

♦ If you want, you can repeat "relax, relax" a few times silently to yourself. Let any excess tension present in your body drain down and out.

♦ Take a few deep breaths, and when you exhale, see if you can feel a ripple of relaxation across the whole body.

♦ As your body settles, feel the sensations of your whole body sitting.

♦ Now, bring the awareness to the breathing specifically. Choose a place where you feel the breath most clearly—either the belly, chest, or nose.

♦ The breath is neutral. It's not a strong emotion, it's not something we hate or love. It's just there, continually, all day, every day, breathing in, breathing out. We can find it anytime we remember.

♦ Bring your attention to the spot where you feel your breath easiest—your anchor in your belly, chest, or nose. Just like an anchor keeps a boat from drifting off, we use our breath to anchor our mind.

♦ When your mind drifts away from the anchor and into planning, worrying or remembering, direct your mind back to the anchor of the sensations of breathing. Don't worry if you have to do that again and again. You're not doing it wrong.

♦ When you notice a strong impulse—maybe you want to move your body—this is an opportunity to practice. First, just notice that this is an impulse. Then, silently, calmly make a note to yourself in your own mind. Silently say, "pausing, pausing." Then feel your breath and silently say, "breathing" with each breath.

♦ Turn to your breath to soothe your mind when

you find yourself caught in an impulse. Really feel the breath. You can silently say "breathing in" as you inhale, "breathing out" as you exhale.

✦ We'll do this for a couple of minutes.

*(Ring bell.)*

✦ When you're ready, you can let your eyes open slowly. Notice how you feel.

## Discussion Questions

— How did that go for you?

— What impulses did you notice? What did the impulses feel like?

— What happened when you used the breathing to soothe your mind during a strong impulse?

— How could this be useful to you in your daily life?

## Take-Home Practice

1. When you find yourself in the middle of a strong impulse, notice it and see what it's like to do just 20 seconds of mindful breathing.
2. Start to notice how relaxation can help with making wise choices. If you regret a certain choice, look back on it and try to remember how your body and mind felt in that moment.

## Journal Suggestions

1. What surprised you about this lesson?
2. What role do impulses play in your life?
3. In what area(s) of your life do you want more control of impulses?

## Teacher Notes

It can be helpful to go over how to use the labeling technique with your students. Be sure it's clear that the intention is to keep most of their attention focused on the sensations of breathing rather than the words "in" and "out." You can use the example of pointing at the clock. Everyone seeing your fingers understands its meaning and looks at the clock. A mental label functions in the same way: It is meant to *point* our attention to the object, in this case the feeling of an inhalation or exhalation.

## Science Supplement

One of the leading researchers on self-control, Roy Baumeister (Baumeister, Vohs, & Tice, 2007), writes:

"Every day, people resist impulses to go back to sleep, to eat fattening or forbidden foods, to say or do hurtful things to their relationship partners, to play instead of work, to engage in inappropriate sexual or violent acts, and to do countless other sorts of problematic behaviors—that is, ones that might feel good immediately or be easy but that carry long-term costs or violate the rules and guidelines of proper behavior. What enables the human animal to follow rules and norms prescribed by society and to resist doing what it selfishly wants? Self-control refers to the capacity for altering one's own responses, especially to bring them into line with standards such as ideals, values, morals, and social expectations, and to support the pursuit of long-term goals . . . Self-control has attracted increasing attention from psychologists for two main reasons. At the theoretical level, self-control holds important keys to understanding the nature and functions of the self. Meanwhile, the practical applications of self-control have attracted study in many contexts. Inadequate self-control has been linked to behavioral and impulse-control problems, including overeating, alcohol and drug abuse, crime and violence, overspending, sexually impulsive behavior, unwanted pregnancy, and smoking. It may also be linked to emotional problems, school underachievement, lack of persistence, various failures at task performance, relationship problems and dissolution, and more."(p. 351)

Baumeister (2007) highlights the centrality of self-control in a successful human life. Terrie Moffitt (Moffitt, et al., 2011)—an influential researcher at Duke University, published a groundbreaking study on self-control that concluded this way: "Differences between individuals in self-control are present in early childhood and can predict multiple indicators of health, wealth, and crime across three decades of life in both genders . . . Our findings imply that innovative policies that put self-control center stage might reduce a panoply of costs that now heavily burden citizens and governments."(p. 2697)

Regulating oneself is thus a critical capacity for human beings. We can first examine how self-regulation functions in our life and how it fails. There are certain conditions under which self-regulation is most likely to fail. In these circumstances, we need to take extra care to be mindful and support healthy choices.

Neuroscientist Todd Heatherton (Heatherton & Wagner, 2011), writes that the most common conditions under which self-regulation fails are: (1) when we're in a bad mood, (2) when minor indulgences snowball into full-blown binges, (3) when we're overwhelmed by immediate temptations or impulses, (4) when control itself is impaired—such as self-regulatory depletion. We want to highlight the fourth point on that list—self-regulatory depletion. Baumeister has formulated the strength model of self-regulation. He suggests that self-regulatory capacity is akin to a muscle. Muscles fatigue. Self-regulation strength can be depleted too: There is finite pool of self-regulatory energy. Repeated exertions of self-regulation draw down that pool of energy—and make it more difficult to subsequently regulate oneself. If you give a person a task that requires a lot of self-control and then afterwards test them by asking if they want a candy bar, they're more likely to say "yes" to the candy, even if they want to say "no."

Perhaps you might have noticed that after emotionally intense episodes, it's more difficult to make wise choices. Again, here is Gailliot and Baumeister (2007):

". . . Recent evidence has indicated that some brain and cognitive processes likewise consume substantial amounts of energy—indeed, some far more than others. The "last-in, first-out rule" states that cognitive abilities that developed last [in our evolutionary development] are the first to become impaired when cognitive and physiological resources are compromised. Self-control, as a relatively advanced human capacity, was probably one of the last to develop and hence may be one of the first to suffer impairments when resources are inadequate."(p. 334–335)

So, what do we do? Fortunately, just as we can exercise muscles to get stronger, we can exercise self-regulatory capacities too—we can expand our pool of self-regulatory energy. Research suggests that acts of self-regulation strengthen our long-term capacity to regulate ourselves in the future. *Mindfulness meditation is one way we can practice this.*

This framework highlights why it's harder to regulate urges at certain moments, and to cultivate compassion for ourselves when the strength of the impulse overrides our pool of self-regulation energy.

## WANTING, LIKING, AND COMPULSIVITY

Self-regulation requires energy because the mechanisms of "wanting" have a prominent place in our brain. Resisting our "wants" requires strength. Kent Berridge (Berridge & Robinson, 2016), a leading neuroscientist, describes the difference between "wanting" and "liking."

"Rewards are both 'liked' and 'wanted,' and those two words seem almost interchangeable. However, the brain circuitry that mediates the psychological process of 'wanting' a particular reward is dissociable from circuitry that mediates the degree to which it is 'liked.' Incentive salience or 'wanting,' a form of motivation, is generated by large and robust neural systems that include mesolimbic dopamine. By comparison, 'liking,' or the actual pleasurable impact of reward consumption, is mediated by smaller and fragile neural systems, and is not dependent on dopamine."(p. 670)

This highlights the way in which equanimity can sometimes require us to move against evolutionary pressures—the mechanisms for wanting are robust and they keep us feeling like something is missing. Part of mindfulness practice is developing equanimity with wanting. This allows us to come home to the present moment in such a way that nothing feels like it's missing.

**REFERENCES & FURTHER READING**

Baumeister, R. F., Vohs, K. D., & Tice, D. M. (2007). The strength model of self-control. *Current Directions in Psychological Science, 16*, 351–355.

Berridge, K. C. & Robinson, T. E. (2016). Liking, wanting, and the incentive-sensitization theory of addiction. *American Psychologist, 71*, 670–679.

Gailliot, M.T ., Baumeister, R. F., DeWall, C. N., Maner, J. K., Plant, E. A., Tice, D. M., . . . & Schmeichel, B. J. (2007). Self-control relies on glucose as a limited energy source: Willpower is more than a metaphor. *Journal of Personality and Social Psychology, 92*, 325–336.

Heatherton, T. F. & Wagner, D. D. (2011). Cognitive neuroscience of self-regulation failure. *Trends in Cognitive Sciences, 15*, 132–139.

Moffitt, T. E., Arseneault, L., Belsky, D., Dickson, N., Hancox, R. J., Harrington, H., . . . & Sears, M. R. (2011). A gradient of childhood self-control predicts health, wealth, and public safety. *Proceedings of the National Academy of Sciences, 108*, 2693–2698.

**4**

# Impulses and Patience

## Key Points

♦ Achieving our goals depends on self-control; mindfulness helps us develop self-control.

♦ Delayed gratification is an expression of self-control (the "marshmallow experiment").

♦ To resist an impulse, one first must become aware (mindful) of that impulse.

♦ Mindful breathing can be a resource when an impulse threatens to overwhelm us.

♦ Mental noting—a technique of silently saying words in one's mind—can be useful in focusing the attention on the breath and helping calm the mind.

## Practice Instructions

♦ Sit in a posture that's comfortable yet upright, feet on the floor and hands in your lap.

♦ Let your eyes close, or gaze down at the ground in front of you.

♦ Feel gravity and the weight of your body. Notice its heaviness and where it touches the ground. If you like, say "relax, relax" silently inside.

♦ Take a few deep breaths, noticing any ease or relaxation on the exhalation.

♦ Become aware of your whole body sitting, then bring your attention to your breathing.

♦ Find your anchor spot and feel the sensations of breathing in and breathing out.

♦ You can silently label the breath with a soft mental note, "breathing in . . . breathing out . . ."

♦ If your mind drifts off, just notice, and bring it back to your anchor.

> **DEFINITION: An *impulse* is the urge to act, to do or say something.**

♦ When you feel an impulse—to move, open your eyes, and so on—first notice the impulse. Then say silently, "Pausing, pausing." Next, feel the sensations of your breathing.

♦ When you're ready, let your eyes open and look around the room.

###  Take-Home Practice

1. When you find yourself in the middle of a strong impulse, notice it and see what it's like to do just 20 seconds of mindful breathing.

2. Start to notice how relaxation can help with making wise choices. If you regret a certain choice, look back on it, and try to remember how your body and mind felt in that moment.

###  Journal Suggestions

1. What surprised you about this lesson?

2. What role do impulses play in your life?

3. In what area(s) of your life do you want more control of impulses?

---

↓ Printable PDF available for download at http://wwnorton.com/mindschls

# SOAKING IN THE GOOD: A HEARTFULNESS LESSON

## The Basics

This lesson teaches students to use mindfulness to strengthen positive experiences in their lives. It introduces the concept of the "Negativity Bias" and describes how mindfulness can counterbalance our hypersensitivity to the negative.

---

**LEARNING OBJECTIVES**

1. Understand threat detection and the negativity bias.
2. Introduce the possibility of using mindfulness to help savor what's good in life.
3. Learn the practice of directing attention toward goodness and feeling the effects of this in your body.

---

**LESSON 5 IN BRIEF: A SYNOPSIS**

## Soaking in the Good: A Heartfulness Lesson

**1. Check in & review:**
Who practiced at home? What experiences or questions came up?

**2. Introduce negativity bias and discuss evolution.**
Ever noticed how hard it is to stop thinking of something bad that happened? Or to stop worrying about something bad that hasn't happened? Why? Connect this to survival of our ancestors in the wild, giving examples, such as assuming that a dead branch might be a snake.

Point out that we're descended from people who assumed that things were dangerous. How did that help our ancestors? What's different today? How can this hinder us?

**3. Discuss negativity bias.**
Define the negativity bias, and discuss Rick Hanson's quote, "Your brain is like Velcro for negative experiences but Teflon for positive ones." (Bring in examples; have them repeat the quote). Is this true in your life? Is it easier to think of bad stuff or good stuff?

We can use mindfulness to enhance our ability to enjoy and savor the good, slowly shifting the tendency of the negativity bias. This isn't about denying the stuff that's difficult; it's about finding balance and enjoying the good parts of life.

## Practice Instructions

◆ Sit in a posture that's comfortable yet upright, feet on the floor and hands in your lap.

◆ Let your eyes close or gaze down at the ground in front of you.

◆ Feel gravity and the weight of your body. Notice its heaviness and where it touches the ground. If you like, say "relax, relax" silently inside.

◆ Take a few deep breaths, noticing any ease or relaxation on the exhalation.

◆ Become aware of your whole body sitting. Feel the sensations of sitting.

◆ Think of something positive in your life: anything that makes you happy.

◆ Think of an image or a word that represents that good thing. Focus on that and notice how it feels in your body. Soak in any good feelings that come.

◆ Repeat this one or two more times.

◆ Take a few moments to end by feeling your breathing and letting this settle in.

◆ When you're ready, let your eyes open and look around the room.

 ### Discussion Questions

**Polling questions** (for quieter groups):

◆ How many people were able to conjure up a positive image?

◆ How many people felt at least a little bit good thinking of it?

◆ Raise your hand if you noticed yourself smiling?

◆ Raise your hand if you felt warm or happy inside?

◆ How many people felt relaxed or at ease?

◆ How many people found it easy to pay attention to the good thing?

◆ How many people noticed their mind wander?

◆ Did anyone notice the negativity bias come in and start worrying about something?

**Open questions** (for talkative groups)

◆ What did you notice? How did that feel?

◆ Could this practice be useful in your life? When? How? (Offer some suggestions)

◆ Can anybody think of a time or an activity, maybe when you were younger, that you naturally "savored" and really enjoyed? What was it?

◆ What's something in your life today that feels good, which you could savor more?

◆ What is optimism and pessimism? What is realism? Which is better? Are there strengths or shortcomings to each?

 ### Take-Home Practice

Rick Hanson talks about training our brains to soak up the positive, by pausing for at least 20 seconds to be mindful of anything good and really take it in.

1. This week, soak in the positive. Take 20 seconds (or more) anytime you feel good, to really be with it.

2. Try to notice and savor at least *three* things each day. Pay attention to small things, like a good meal; big things, like the people you love.

5

## Soaking in the Good: A Heartfulness Lesson

### Lesson Outline

— Bad stuff seems to stick in our minds more than good stuff.

— Why do we tend to focus on the negative?

— This habit tied to our evolutionary need for survival (ancestors who were more fearful avoided danger, survived, and passed on those genes).

— How does this affect our lives today? (We're not under threat in the same way).

— Reflect on your life: is it easier to notice what's wrong or what's going well?

— We can use mindfulness to increase our ability to notice and savor goodness.

— Let's practice that by calling to mind something good and savoring it.

### Lesson

*(Organize the room for mindfulness and engage the students in a transitional activity.)*

When something bad happens, ever notice how hard it is to stop thinking about it? Or maybe nothing's happened yet, but you're worried about something bad happening, and your mind gets fixated on it. How many people know what I'm talking about?

Today I want to talk about why that happens, and how we can use mindfulness to do something different. The answer is in our own biology and evolution as a species. So, these bodies and nervous systems: What were the conditions like when we evolved? What was life like for our ancestors tens of thousands of years ago?

*(Students answer.)*

Yeah, things were pretty rough. We were always on the lookout for danger. Basically, our brains and nervous systems are finely tuned to *detect and avoid danger* because our survival depended on this ability for so much of our history. We were on the lookout for people or animals who might harm us. Here's a simple example to illustrate this. Tell me what you see in this photo?

ROCK FORMATION IN FRANCE
PERCEIVED AS A FACE
*Source: Public domain*

Obviously, we're looking at rocks here, but do you see a "face" there too? This isn't an accident. Our minds are highly conditioned to recognize patterns—particularly patterns that suggest something nearby might be alive and could attack or eat us!

5

If you think about it, this is a pretty good strategy. If I'm walking through the forest and I assume a lot of the dead branches I see are snakes, are my chances of survival going to increase or decrease?

(Students answer.)

Yes, they are definitely going to increase. If I never assume that the branches are snakes, and then one time the branch turns out to be a snake, what happens?

(Students answer.)

Yeah, trouble! So, what's this have to do with all of us here today? Well, on a real level, we can say that all of us sitting in this classroom right now are the descendants of humans who had this bias! The ones that didn't have this bias ingrained wouldn't be the ones passing down their genes.

But what's happened is that the way we experience stress and emotions is still running on that same survival wiring of our ancient ancestors.

Scientists call this the "negativity bias." And while it's fantastic for avoiding snakes, it's not always so great for being alive in the 21st century. What are some of the problems with the brain's negativity bias in the context of modern life?

(Students answer.)

We are hypersensitive to threat and overemphasize the negative or problematic aspects of our experience. Who in the room has had the experience of a problem literally taking over their life? Right—that's the negativity bias at work. To counteract the bias in our minds, it can be helpful to remember this simple saying from the psychologist Rick Hanson (2009):

"Your brain is like Velcro for negative experiences and Teflon for positive ones."(p. 41) (*If needed, explain Teflon is what they make nonstick frying pans out of. Have them imagine putting butter in a hot skillet and they'll get the idea.*)

So—negative experiences are like Velcro, or Teflon?

(Students answer.)

And positive ones? (*Students answer.*)

Let's test this out. I want you to think of something specific that's been on your mind lately that's a big deal for you. Just let the first thing come to mind. (*Allow some time.*)

Okay, raise your hand if you thought of something difficult, hard or negative? Raise your hand if you thought of something good, or positive? Notice how much more readily we think of the hard stuff? If we tried to make two lists—one of all the tough stuff in our lives, the other of all the good stuff—which do you think would be easier to write?

That's the negativity bias at work! Our minds are primed to notice and fixate on the things that we perceive as dangerous—even if they're not actually life-threatening, we're still using that same basic wiring.

## Practice: Savoring the Good

The question is, how can we use mindfulness to make the positive ones stick rather than slide away? How can we incline our mind toward the positive? We're not trying to deny the negative or pretend that we don't have challenges. We're simply reminding ourselves of all the goodness that's already here.

The answer is that we need to soak up the positive in much the same way a sponge soaks up water. "Soaking up" means to really savor a positive experience—being mindful of what goes well, what we're grateful for, the people we love, and letting ourselves really feel it. When we can do this, over time, our minds start to notice the good, nourishing things in our life as much as the bad ones.

To help us train this ability, we are going to practice using mindfulness to soak up the positive. It's like bathing in feelings of goodness.

Let's begin, as usual, by settling into mindfulness of the body.

✦ Find your posture—comfortable and upright. Let your eyes close (or gaze down).

✦ When you hear the sound of the bell, listen with all of your attention to the end of the tone.

✦ Sense the relaxing effects of gravity. Feel that downward force in your body and let your body get heavy. Feel the points that are touching the ground, letting them take the weight of the body. Let any tension in your body drain out.

✦ Take a few deep breaths, feeling any ease or relaxation that comes, as you exhale. If you want you can repeat "relax, relax" a few times silently to yourself.

✦ As your body settles, feel the sensations of your whole body sitting.

✦ Bring your attention to your anchor, and feel the sensations of breathing.

✦ Now, I want you to think of something positive in your life. It could be a person or an event or an achievement. It can really be anything— as long as it really makes you happy. See if there is an image that comes to mind that represents that.

✦ See that image in your mind's eye; make it as clear as possible. When the image fades away, bring it back.

✦ If it feels natural, bring a tiny smile to your face.

✦ Perhaps there is one word that represents all that goodness. Say that word to yourself silently a few times.

✦ Next, feel any effects in your body. Thinking of the image or saying the word is like ringing a bell; feeling the effects is like hearing the sound ringing through your body.

✦ Let yourself soak up any pleasant sensations that come: any relaxation, warmth, lightness. Maybe a smile or some good feeling inside.

✦ If the feeling starts to fade, recall the image or word again, like "ringing the bell."

✦ Let the image dissolve and fade away.

✦ (If there's time, move on to a second positive item and repeat.)

✦ To finish, let's take a few moments to feel our breathing.

(Ring the bell.)

✦ When you're ready, let your eyes open slowly. Notice how you feel; notice how it feels in the room right now.

 **Discussion Questions**

**Polling questions** (for quieter groups):

— How many people were able to picture / think of a positive image?

— How many people felt at least a little bit good thinking of it?

— Raise your hand if you noticed yourself smiling?

— Raise your hand if you felt warm or happy inside?

— How many people felt relaxed or at ease?

— How many people found it easy to pay attention to the good thing?

— How many people noticed their mind wander?

— Did anyone notice the negativity bias come in and start worrying about something?

**Open questions** (for talkative groups)

— What did you notice? How did that feel?

— Could this practice be useful in your life? When? How? (Offer some suggestions)

— Can anybody think of a time or an activity, maybe when you were younger, that you naturally "savored" and really enjoyed? What was it?

— What's something in your life today that feels good, which you could savor more?

— What is optimism and pessimism? What is realism? Which is better? Are there strengths or shortcomings to each?

 ## Take-Home Practice

Rick Hanson, the psychologist who said, "Your brain is like Velcro for negative experiences and Teflon for positive ones," talks about training our brains to soak up the positive by pausing for at least 20 seconds to be mindful of anything good and really take it in.

1. This week, soak in the positive. Take 20 seconds (or more) anytime you feel good to really be with it.
2. Try to notice and savor at least THREE things each day. Pay attention to small things, like a good meal; big things, like people you love.

 ## Journal Suggestions

1. Is it easier for you to think of negative things or positive things?
2. Did you have any resistance to thinking about something good and feeling it? What thoughts or fears got in the way?
3. What's one thing you'd like to savor more in your life? How would this affect you? Would it affect those around you? If so, how?

You may want to use a singing bowl, a stringed instrument, or a drop of food dye in a glass of water, to provide a visual example of the concept of "savoring" or "resonating."

Draw a picture of a time you felt really good inside. Draw what was happening around you (where were you, who was there, what was happening). Draw how you felt inside.

Think of a time when you felt really good, really happy. Write down everything you can remember about that time (where you were, what you noticed, saw, heard, felt). This could be in sentences, or it could just be words and phrases like a mind map. How does it feel to do this?

 ## Teacher Notes

Note that some students may have some difficulty with this activity and may find their minds getting sucked into things that are negative or hard. If and when this happens, first be sure to normalize their experience. Point out how the very thing their mind is doing—focusing on the hard stuff—is an example of the negativity bias. Then, give them another practice to do that can help to bring their attention out of that difficult memory / thought / experience. You could have them draw, focus on sounds, or do some heartfulness practice.

 ## Science Supplement

### EARLY RESEARCH ON THE NEGATIVITY BIAS AND WHY IT EXISTS

In 2001, Roy Baumeister and his colleagues wrote an influential article describing the "negativity bias." They titled the article "Bad is Stronger than Good." Here is the summary of their article:

"The greater power of bad events over good ones is found in everyday events, major life

5

events (e.g., trauma), close relationship outcomes, social network patterns, interpersonal interactions, and learning processes. Bad emotions, bad parents, and bad feedback have more impact than good ones, and bad information is processed more thoroughly than good. The self is more motivated to avoid bad self-definitions than to pursue good ones. Bad impressions and bad stereotypes are quicker to form and more resistant to disconfirmation than good ones . . . Hardly any exceptions (indicating greater power of good) can be found. Taken together, these findings suggest that bad is stronger than good, as a general principle across a broad range of psychological phenomena."(p. 323)

There is an old Russian saying: "A spoonful of tar can spoil a barrel of honey, but a spoonful of honey does nothing for a barrel of tar." Why would this be so? Are we all just pessimists? The researchers hypothesize that the negativity bias serves evolutionary functions.

"From our perspective, it is evolutionarily adaptive for bad to be stronger than good. We believe that throughout our evolutionary history, organisms that were better attuned to bad things would have been more likely to survive threats and, consequently, would have increased probability of passing along their genes. As an example, consider the implications of foregoing options or ignoring certain possible outcomes. A person who ignores the possibility of a positive outcome may later experience significant regret at having missed an opportunity for pleasure or advancement, but nothing directly terrible is likely to result. In contrast, a person who ignores danger (the possibility of a bad outcome) even once may end up maimed or dead. Survival requires urgent attention to possible bad outcomes, but it is less urgent with regard to good ones. Hence, it would be adaptive to

be psychologically designed to respond to bad more strongly than good."(p. 325)

## POSITIVE PSYCHOLOGY AND HUMAN FLOURISHING

Within psychology, this pattern of the negativity bias has been repeated—the emphasis of research has been on bad rather than good. In some ways, this makes sense: Public health measures are more interested in mitigating suffering than promoting flourishing. Nevertheless, in 2000, Seligman and Csikszentmihalyi marked the formal beginning of "positive psychology." In that paper, they argued that psychology was failing to produce "knowledge of what makes life worth living." Positive psychology is the study of the factors that promote flourishing of people and groups.

Shelly Gable and Jonathan Haidt (2005), prominent people involved in positive psychology, have written:

"The science of psychology has made great strides in understanding what goes wrong in individuals, families, groups, and institutions, but these advances have come at the cost of understanding what is right with people. For example, clinical psychology has made excellent progress in diagnosing and treating mental illnesses and personality disorders. Researchers in social psychology have conducted groundbreaking studies on the existence of implicit prejudice and negative outcomes associated with low self-esteem. Health psychology has shown us the detrimental effects that environmental stressors have on our physiological systems. And cognitive psychology has illuminated the many biases and errors involved in our judgments. These are all important findings in our field, but it is harder to locate corresponding work on human strengths and virtues (p. 103) . . . The recent movement in positive psychology

5

strives toward an understanding of the complete human condition, an understanding that recognizes human strengths as clearly as it does human frailties and that specifies how the two are linked." (p. 109)

## NEGATIVITY BIAS IN THE BRAIN

The negativity bias can be analyzed at the psychological and behavioral level, but is also evident from the activity of our brains. For example, threat is detected more quickly and evokes stronger brain responses than positive cues. Leanne Williams and her colleagues (Williams, et al., 2009) documented some of these effects. They write:

"The group distinguished by a Negativity Bias showed heightened startle responses, and elevated heart rate during conscious and nonconscious fear perception. Those with a Negativity Bias were also distinguished by enhanced activation in neural fear circuitry; brainstem, amygdala, medial prefrontal cortex and anterior cingulate. For conscious fear, Negativity Bias was distinguished by activation in the dorsal medial prefrontal cortex and anterior cingulate, and for nonconscious fear in the ventral medial prefrontal cortex. This profile suggests that traits of negativity bias are associated with hypersensitivity to fear cues of potential danger, from the earliest automatic timescales of emotion processing." (p. 812)

Savoring the good counters the negativity bias and our tendency to perceive threat everywhere—we may even percieve threat when it's safe to relax and enjoy the goodness in our lives!

Recent research (Yaun et al. 2015) has suggestion that adolescents are may be especially *susceptible* to negativity bias as they evidence hypersensitivity to emotional events more generally:

"Adolescents are more emotionally sensitive to negative stimuli compared to adults, regardless of the emotional intensity of the stimuli, possibly due to the immature prefrontal control system over the limbic emotional inputs during adolescence."(p. 1)

## REFERENCES & FURTHER READING

Baumeister, R. F., Bratslavsky, E., Finkenauer, C., & Vohs, K. D. (2001). Bad is stronger than good. *Review of General Psychology*, 5(4), 323–370.

Gable, S. L. & Haidt, J. (2005). What (and why) is positive psychology? *Review of General Psychology*, 9(2), 103–110.

Hanson, R. (2009). *The practical neuroscience of Buddha's brain: Happiness, love and wisdom*. New Harbinger Publications.

Seligman, M. E. & Csikszentmihalyi, M. (2000). Special issue: Positive psychology. *American Psychologist*, 55(1), 5–14.

Williams, L. M., Gatt, J. M., Schofield, P. R., Olivieri, G., Peduto, A., & Gordon, E. (2009). "Negativity bias" in risk for depression and anxiety: Brain–body fear circuitry correlates, 5-HTT-LPR and early life stress. *NeuroImage*, 47(3), 804–814.

Yuan, J., Ju E., Meng X., Chen X., Zhu S., Yang J., & Li H. (2015). Enhanced brain susceptibility to negative stimuli in adolescents: ERP evidences. *Frontiers in Behavioral Neuroscience*, 9:98.

5

# Soaking in the Good: A Heartfulness Lesson

## Key Points

◆ Bad stuff seems to stick in our minds more than good stuff.

◆ We tend to focus on the negative due to our evolutionary need for survival. Those who were more fearful avoided danger, survived, and passed on those genes.

◆ Today, we're not under threat in the same way, but this pattern is still at play.

◆ Reflect on your life: Is it easier to notice what's wrong, or what's going well?

◆ Our brains are like "Velcro for negative experiences and Teflon for positive ones."

◆ We can use mindfulness to increase our ability to notice and savor the good.

## Practice Instructions

◆ Sit in a posture that's comfortable yet upright, feet on the floor and hands in your lap.

◆ Let your eyes close, or gaze down at the ground in front of you.

◆ Feel gravity and the weight of your body. Notice its heaviness and where it touches the ground. If you like, say "relax, relax" silently inside.

◆ Take a few deep breaths, noticing any ease or relaxation on the exhalation.

◆ Become aware of your whole body sitting. Feel the sensations of sitting.

◆ Think of something positive in your life: anything that makes you happy.

> **DEFINITION:** *Negativity bias* **refers to our tendency as humans to give more psychological and emotional weight to** *bad* **experiences than** *good* **ones.**

◆ Think of an image or a word that represents that good thing. Focus on that, and notice how it feels in your body. Soak in any good feelings that come.

◆ Repeat this one or two more times.

◆ Take a few moments to end, by feeling your breathing and letting this settle in.

◆ When you're ready, let your eyes open and look around the room.

 ## Take-Home Practice

1. Anytime you feel good, take 20 seconds or more to really feel it; soak in the good.

2. Try to notice and savor at least three things each day: pay attention to small things, like a good meal; big things, like people you love.

 ## Journal Suggestions

1. Is it easier for you to think of negative things or positive things?

2. Did you have any resistance to thinking about something good, and feeling it? What thoughts or fears got in the way?

3. What's one thing you'd like to savor more in your life? How would this affect you? Would it affect those around you? If so, how?

# MINDFULNESS OF EMOTIONS

## The Basics

Emotions figure prominently in the lives of adolescents. The lesson provides an empowering context to understand emotion and to help undercut myths and self-critical notions about emotion. It introduces the formal practice of mindfulness of emotion.

---

**LEARNING OBJECTIVES**

1. To understand the significant role emotion plays in our lives.
2. To identify some myths or assumptions about emotions.
3. To detect emotions as sensations in the body.

---

**LESSON 6 IN BRIEF: A SYNOPSIS**

## Mindfulness of Emotions

**1. Check in & review:**
Who practiced at home? What experiences or questions came up?

**2. Introduce topic of emotions.**
Read list and invite students to consider which of these they've felt in the last week, or ever.

**3. Connect emotions with our goals and needs in life.**
Invite an example of something someone wants; trace it back to wanting to *feel* a certain way. Invite an example of something someone doesn't want; trace it to not wanting to *feel* a certain way. Emotions are a big deal in our life.

**4. Discuss the myths we have about emotions.**
What stories and beliefs do we have about our feelings from our society or culture? Discuss these:

◆ You're supposed to feel happy. Do everything "right" and you'll feel good all the time.

◆ Emotions are permanent.

◆ Emotions are your fault. Or, they're someone else's fault.

◆ We're stuck the way we are; our emotional patterns can't change.

Emotions are information about something that matters to us, but we need to slow down and get

| HAPPY | ANGRY | DEPRESSED | PEACEFUL | GRATEFUL | SPECIAL |
|---|---|---|---|---|---|
| EXCITED | SAD | LONELY | DOUBTFUL | FRIGHTENED | DISAPPOINTED |
| RESTLESS | ANXIOUS | JEALOUS | CURIOUS | BORED | GUILTY |
| WORRIED | EAGER | HATEFUL | ALONE | STRONG | LOVING |
| ENVIOUS | EMBARRASSED | JOYFUL | MISCHIEVOUS | SERIOUS | ASHAMED |

**6**

that information before we act. Being mindful of an emotion is about observing it as an experience of sensation in our body, so that we have more choice about how to respond.

## Practice Instructions

- Sit in a posture that is comfortable yet upright, feet on the floor and hands in your lap.

- Let your eyes close, or gaze down at the ground in front of you.

- Feel the weight of gravity. Notice its heaviness, where it touches the ground. "Relax, relax."

- As your body settles, become aware of your whole body sitting. Feel the sensations of sitting.

- Picture someone you love, seeing their face in your mind. Pay attention to your belly, chest, and face. When you think of this person, do the sensations in your body change?

- What if we heard a loud sound suddenly? How would your body feel?

- There are emotional circuits in the body that have sensations when we feel emotion. Let's pay attention to these emotional circuits and see what else we can feel. *(Ring bell.)*

### DISCUSS:
- How did your body feel when you pictured someone you care about?

- When you imagined a loud sound, did you feel anything in your body?

- Did anyone have trouble being aware of emotion in your body?

### PHYSICAL VS. EMOTIONAL SENSATIONS
There's a difference between physical sensation and emotional sensations. The sensations from tapping on my chest are different from sensations I feel when startled by a loud sound. We're learning to pay attention to the *emotional sensations*.

## Practice Round 2:

- Tune into the body and be aware of any emotional sensations in the body.

- The sensations may be pleasant, unpleasant, or neutral. They may be intense or weak. They may be moving a lot like a lava lamp or they may not be moving much.

- You might know what you're feeling—happiness or anxiety or something else—or you might not know what you're feeling. All that is totally okay.

- If you're enjoying this, you're having emotional sensations. If you're bored or can't wait for this to end, you're also having emotional sensations. Whatever is there—pleasant or unpleasant—can you be aware?

- Attend to emotional sensations; notice if they get stronger, weaker, or stay the same.

- There's no need to try to feel peaceful. Just paying attention is enough. *(Ring the bell.)*

- When you're ready, let your eyes open slowly.

 ## Discussion Questions

- How was this round different than the first?

- Did you notice how much things can change, even in just a couple of minutes?

- What else did you notice?

 ## Take-Home Practice

1. When something emotional is going on this week, see if you can do two minutes of mindfulness practice and tune in to the emotional sensations in the body.

2. When something really good happens this week, notice how the body feels.

6

# Mindfulness of Emotions

## Lesson Outline

- Emotion is at the center of our lives and what we value—when we hope for something, we're hoping to *feel* a certain way.

- We all carry certain assumptions and common myths about emotions.

- It's normal to feel difficult emotions. What we feel isn't our *fault*, but how we negotiate and respond to our emotions is our *responsibility*.

- We can be mindful of emotions and this can help us navigate our emotional life with more skill and freedom.

## Lesson

*(Organize the room for mindfulness and engage the students in a transitional activity.)*

Today we're going to look at what mindfulness can teach us about our emotions. I'm going to read a list of emotions, and as you listen, I want you to consider which of these you've felt—today, this week, or ever.

Emotions are a big deal in our lives. Sometimes, we don't even notice how important they are. I want to do a quick experiment. Think about something that you want. Picture it in your mind. Who's willing to share something they want?

*(Call on a student; let them name something).*

Why do you want that? What would it mean, or give you, if you had it?

*(Student answers.)*

*(Help the students trace their wish for that thing back to a wish to feel a particular way. For example, if an adolescent says, "a nice car," show them how they're looking to feel a particular way when driving, or that a car provides the freedom to have particular experiences that are pleasant.)*

Okay, different question: What's something you *don't* want?

*(Hear from one or two students and help them to see how avoidance of certain things is a way of avoiding unpleasant or difficult feelings.)*

We want things because we want to feel a particular way. Feelings are at the center of our lives. Love, joy, humor, sadness, anger, fear—these experiences are such an important part of being human.

But there are a lot of myths about emotion. *(Have a discussion with the students about what myths we inherit about emotions. You might give them one example and then ask them for others, or give them a prompt like, "What are the myths about what emotions are okay for one gender to feel but maybe not for another gender? And let them answer).*

| | | | | | |
|---|---|---|---|---|---|
| HAPPY | ANGRY | DEPRESSED | PEACEFUL | GRATEFUL | SPECIAL |
| EXCITED | SAD | LONELY | DOUBTFUL | FRIGHTENED | DISAPPOINTED |
| RESTLESS | ANXIOUS | JEALOUS | CURIOUS | BORED | GUILTY |
| WORRIED | EAGER | HATEFUL | ALONE | STRONG | LOVING |
| ENVIOUS | EMBARRASSED | JOYFUL | MISCHIEVOUS | SERIOUS | ASHAMED |

Here are some myths that I see often:

**1. Myth: You're supposed to feel happy. Do everything right, and you'll feel good all the time.**

When someone asks you, "How are you doing?" do you ever feel pressure to say "good" or feel embarrassed to say that maybe life is difficult right now? There can be a cultural pressure to be happy all the time and sometimes it's awkward if you say, "Well, actually I'm struggling right now." It's important to remember that there's no way to engineer a life where you only feel good and never feel bad. In fact, trying to only feel good can make our lives even more difficult, because then we're *afraid* to feel bad.

**2. Myth: Emotions are permanent.**

Ever notice how when you feel down, it seems like you'll always feel that way? Or when you're in a good mood it's as if it will never change? Emotions can feel like they're permanent. Have you ever had any emotion that lasted forever? Of course not. They're just like the weather; one day sunny, the next day cloudy.

**3. Myth: Emotions are your fault.**

Have you ever had an emotional reaction—maybe sadness or anger or embarrassment—and then blamed yourself for feeling the way you did? We attach so much meaning to the feelings we experience and believe that our emotions say something deeply about who we are. But your emotional life is *not* a commentary on who you are. It's simply a pattern of feeling arising in the moment. That pattern arises out of a million causes outside of us: our family history, the evolutionary and genetic history of the human species, the events of the past day, or month or life. We experience emotion—pleasant and unpleasant— because we're human.

**4. Myth: Emotions are someone else's fault.**

Sometimes we blame other people for our emotions. "You made me angry." The things we do and say can

affect one another, but can anyone actually *make* you feel something? That's a lot of power! Our emotional reactions depend on a lot of other factors than what someone else said or did: our mood that day, what we're wanting or expecting, and—this is a big one— the stories we tell ourselves about what something means.

**5. Myth: You can't change your emotional patterns.**

While it's important not to blame ourselves or others for the feelings we have, our emotional patterns can be changed. With mindfulness practice, we can learn to have a different relationship with our feelings. We become less intimidated by our feelings. It starts to feel more and more safe inside. Do you know how it feels when you're in a really safe place or with people you totally trust—and you feel really safe? We can feel safe like that on the inside too.

**Key Point:** Generally, emotions try to get us to react or do something. They're information from our body and mind trying to help us. If our emotions could talk, they would often yell "Do this" or "Do that." Mindfulness is different. We're trying to pay attention to the feeling without *immediately* or *automatically* obeying what the emotion tells us to do. Instead of listening to what they tell us to do, we see them as information about what's important to us. **Then, when we're clearer inside, we choose how we want to respond and what's needed to take care of the situation.**

> Mindfulness isn't about being passive. We can practice feeling our feelings *first* and then decide how to move forward in our lives.

6

## Practice: Mindfulness of Emotions

So, we're going to do this practice twice. We'll begin with mindfulness of the body.

✦ Let the body be in a comfortable and relatively upright position in your chair. Let your eyes close (or gaze down in front of you).

✦ When you hear the sound of the bell, listen with all of your attention through to the end.

✦ Sense the relaxing effects of gravity. Feel that downward force in your body and let your body get heavy. Feel the points that are touching the ground, letting them take the weight of the body. Let any tension in your body drain out.

✦ Take a few deep breaths, feeling any ease or relaxation that comes, as you exhale. If you want you can repeat "relax, relax" a few times silently to yourself.

✦ As your body settles, feel the sensations of your whole body sitting.

✦ Bring your attention to your anchor, and feel the sensations of breathing.

✦ Now, let's examine an emotion as a feeling in our body.

✦ As a way of tuning into the emotion in the body, picture someone you love. Really get a clear picture of their face. Now, as you think about that person, pay attention to your belly, chest and face. When you think of that person, did the sensations in your body change?

✦ What if all of a sudden we heard a loud sound? I would feel something in my chest. You might feel it in your chest or somewhere else in your body. Can you imagine those sensations?

✦ These are the emotional circuits of the body. When we feel love or joy or fear or anger, the body has sensations. It's like there are circuits in the body that feel emotion. Let's take a minute to pay attention to these emotional circuits.

*(Ring the bell. Then discuss their experience as follows.)*

✦ How did your body feel when you pictured someone you care about? When you imagined a loud sound, did you get a feeling in your body of fear or something like that?

✦ Did anyone have trouble being aware of emotion in your body?

✦ There's a difference between physical sensation and emotional sensations. If I tap on my chest, I have some sensations. If I heard a loud sudden noise, I would also have sensations in my chest but they would feel different from the tapping. Those are the emotional sensations I'm talking about. Does that make sense?

### PRACTICE ROUND 2:

All right, let's try it again for a few minutes. *(Ring the bell to begin.)*

✦ Tune into the body and be aware of any emotional sensations in the body.

✦ Those sensations may be pleasant or unpleasant or neutral. They may be intense or weak. They may be moving a lot like a lava lamp or they may not be moving much.

✦ You might know what you're feeling—happiness or anxiety or something else—or you might not know what you're feeling. All of that is totally okay.

✦ If you're really enjoying this, you're probably having emotional sensations. If you're bored or you can't wait for this to end, you're *also* having emotional sensations. Whatever is there—pleasant or unpleasant—can you be aware?

✦ As you attend to emotional sensations, notice if they are getting stronger, weaker or staying the same.

✦ There's no need to try to feel peaceful. Trust that your awareness is doing good work—just paying attention is enough.

*(Ring the bell.)*

✦ When you're ready, let your eyes open slowly.

6

**Discussion Questions**

— How was this round different than the first?

— Did you notice how much things can change, even in just a couple of minutes?

— What else did you notice?

 **Take-Home Practice**

1. When something emotional is going on this week, see if you can do two minutes of mindfulness practice and tune in to the emotional sensations in the body.

2. When something really good happens this week, notice how the body feels.

 **Journal Suggestions**

1. What surprised you about this lesson?

2. What did you learn about how your emotions work?

3. What do you want to understand better about your emotions?

 **Teacher Notes**

It's important to make clear the distinction that being mindful of an emotion doesn't mean that we don't take action. Sometimes it's very important for us to act on our emotions: to set a limit with someone, to speak up, to advocate for our own or others' needs. Being mindful of emotions can help break the tendency to act on them impulsively and automatically. (Of course, in situations of grave physical danger one acts immediately and without forethought.) You might engage students in a discussion about what conditions make us most effective in advocating for change: being swept up in and driven by an emotion, or feeling its potency with clear awareness?

 **Science Supplement**

How is emotion defined scientifically? One of the leading emotion researchers, James Gross of Stanford University (2014), characterized emotions as "multifaceted, whole-body phenomena that involve loosely coupled changes in the domains of subjective experience, behavior, and central and peripheral physiology." This means that emotions manifest in the body and have effects on our inner life and our outer behavior. It is thought that our emotions reflect our evolutionary history. Emotions have evolved across evolutionary time as tendencies to adapt and respond to threats and opportunities. Our emotional habits are designed to help us meet challenges and respond to our world to keep us safe. A lot of the time, emotions work for us—but sometimes, they work against us.

Our skill in emotion regulation has many important implications for our lives. To return to the work of Terrie Moffitt (Moffitt, et al., 2011), she studied a group of 1,000 people over the course of decades. She concludes the following:

"Differences between individuals in self-control are present in early childhood and can predict multiple indicators of health, wealth, and crime across 3 decades of life in both genders . . . Our findings imply that innovative policies that put self-control center stage might reduce a panoply of costs that now heavily burden citizens and governments . . . For example, by adulthood, the highest and lowest fifths of the population on measured childhood self-control had respective rates of multiple health problems of 11% vs. 27%, rates of polysubstance dependence of 3% vs. 10% rates of annual income under $20,000 (in New Zealand dollars) of 10% vs. 32%, rates of offspring reared in single-parent households of 26% vs. 58%, and crime conviction rates of 13% vs. 43% . . . Thus, interventions in ado-

**6**

lescence that prevent or ameliorate the consequences of teenagers' mistakes might go far to improve the health, wealth, and public safety of the population"(p. 2697).

It is possible that mindfulness may be one such intervention to support the self-regulation of adolescents. Emotion regulation researchers have been very interested in mindfulness. In one notable review of the subject, Chambers and colleagues (2009) write: "Mindful emotion regulation represents the capacity to remain mindfully aware at all times, irrespective of the apparent valence or magnitude of any emotion that is experienced. It does not entail suppression of the emotional experience, nor any specific attempts to reappraise or alter it in any way. Instead, mindfulness meditation involves a systematic retraining of awareness and nonreactivity, leading to defusion from whatever is experienced, and allowing the individual to more consciously choose those thoughts, emotions, and sensations they will identify with, rather than habitually reacting to them. In this way, it erodes the automatic process of appraisal that gives rise to disturbing emotions in the first place. At the same time, mindful emotion regulation encourages the practitioner to increasingly perceive the awareness that underlies all mental phenomena. As this occurs, a number of positive emotions or qualities emerge, which reinforce the capacity for mindfulness, and leads in turn to increasing levels of openness"(p. 569).

## FIVE KINDS OF EMOTION REGULATION

James Gross (2014) identifies five methods of emotional regulation. First, and perhaps most familiar to us, is that we change the situation. An example of "situation modification" would be moving to a different seat on a train to avoid hearing the sound of someone chewing gum next to us. Next time, we might even choose a car on the train where there are very few people, thereby minimizing the possibility of running into another loud gum-chewer. This is "situation selection," where we anticipate situations that are more or less likely to create emotional demands. Without knowing it, we are doing this much of the time—and it's generally effective.

To continue with the example, if we sat next to the loud chewer, and chose not to get up to switch seats, perhaps because all the other seats were occupied, we might still try to regulate our emotions by directing our attention in a particular way. This is a mode of emotion regulation known as "attentional deployment." Certain aspects of mindfulness practices can be considered a form of attentional deployment. Typically, during an intense emotional experience, the attention is directed to the content of our thoughts. We try to solve or resolve the emotion by thinking (often thinking a lot!). While some types of thinking and problem solving might be helpful, often the thinking can devolve into unhelpful obsessive forms of thought, such as rumination.

In working with emotions, we will often be directed to attend not to the content of our thought, but to the landscape of experience itself. We temporarily put down the world of meaning and interpretations and rest the attention with direct experience. We move out of the story of the emotion, and connect with our moment-to-moment experience of the emotion. Often, we direct the attention to the bodily experience of emotion and cultivate equanimity and acceptance of the emotional sensations. The capacity to tune into the bodily experience of emotion is tremendously valuable in navigating emotional challenges.

The fourth form of emotion regulation is known as "cognitive reappraisal." Even if there were no other seats available, and we couldn't focus attention away from the story of the emotion, the presence of the loud chewer need not doom us to frustration. Frustration and annoyance depend on certain appraisals of the situation—the meanings we give to a particular event.

This is an important realization. It means that

6

we can reappraise situations in ways that modulate our emotional responses. Cognitive reappraisal has received a good deal of attention from scientists. Recent data has confirmed the value of reappraisal as an adaptive emotion regulation strategy because it promotes positive emotion and weakens negative emotion, but without the maladaptive aspects of suppressing emotion. A recent meta-analysis on the brain regions involved in reappraisal finds that the strategy engages several areas of the brain implicated in cognitive control, including the posterior parietal lobe, the dorsomedial, dorsolateral, and ventrolateral prefrontal cortex. The same research found that cognitive reappraisal was most consistently associated with reductions in the bilateral amygdala, regions especially important in the detection of and monitoring of emotionally significant experience, especially aversive or fear-generating stimuli.

The fifth mode of emotion regulation is known as "response modulation." Response modulation is a strategy to influence the physiological or experiential conditions once the emotion has fully arisen. An example would be choosing to exercise. We might go for a run because we know it eases anxiety or worry. We might take a deep pause as the students complete an assignment on their own. Alternatively, we might speak with a loved one or close friend about our experience as a way of modulating our emotional experience. We usually think about regulating emotion as something we only do alone, but part of the value of close relationships is that others can help us regulate our emotional experience simply through their compassionate listening. We probably all know the experience of speaking with an empathic person about some difficulty we're experiencing, and almost as if magically, at the end of the conversation, we feel much better. In addition to exercise or speaking with a confidante, mindfulness practice can function as a form of response modulation. Specifically, mindfulness can be used to de-escalate the states of hyperarousal that are part of many difficult emotions.

## REFERENCES & FURTHER READING

Brown, K. W., Ryan, R. M., & Creswell, J. D. (2007). Mindfulness: Theoretical foundations and evidence for its salutary effects. *Psychological Inquiry, 18*, 211–237.

Buhle, J. T., Silvers, J. A., Wager, T. D., Lopez, R., Onyemekwu, C., Kober, H., . . . & Ochsner, K. N. (2014). Cognitive reappraisal of emotion: A meta-analysis of human neuroimaging studies. *Cerebral Cortex, 24*, 2981–2990.

Chambers, R., Gullone, E., & Allen, N. B. (2009). Mindful emotion regulation: An integrative review. *Clinical Psychology Review, 29*, 560–572.

Davidson, R. J. (2012). *The emotional life of your brain: How its unique patterns affect the way you think, feel, and live —and how you can change them.* New York: Penguin Books.

Gross, J. J. (2014). Ed. *Handbook of emotion regulation, second edition.* New York: The Guilford Press.

Moffitt, T. E., Arseneault, L., Belsky, D., Dickson, N., Hancox, R. J., Harrington, H., . . . & Sears, M. R. (2011). A gradient of childhood self-control predicts health, wealth, and public safety. *Proceedings of the National Academy of Sciences, 108*, 2693–2698.

**6**

# Mindfulness of Emotions

## Key Points

♦ Emotion is at the center of our lives and what we value—when we hope for something, we're hoping to *feel* a certain way.

♦ We all carry certain assumptions and common myths about emotions.

♦ It's normal to feel difficult emotions. What we feel isn't our *fault*, but how we negotiate and respond to our emotions is our *responsibility*.

♦ We can be mindful of emotions, and this can help us navigate our emotional life with more skill and freedom.

## Practice Instructions

♦ Sit in a posture that's comfortable and upright; feet on the floor and hands in your lap.

♦ Let your eyes close, or gaze down at the ground in front of you.

♦ Feel gravity and the weight of your body. Notice where your body touches the ground.

♦ Take a few deep breaths, noticing any ease or relaxation on the exhalation.

♦ Become aware of your whole body sitting.

♦ Take a few more moments to feel the sensations of breathing in and breathing out.

♦ How are you feeling right now? Notice any emotions as sensations in your body.

♦ Notice how these emotional sensations change, get more or less intense.

♦ Come back to your breathing anytime you get lost or need a break.

♦ When you're ready, let your eyes open. and look around the room.

 ## Take-Home Practice

1. When something emotional is going on this week, see if you can do two minutes of mindfulness practice and tune into the emotional sensations in the body.

2. When something really good happens this week, notice how the body feels.

 ## Journal Suggestions

1. What surprised you about this lesson?

2. What did you learn about how your emotions work?

3. What do you want to understand better about your emotions?

**6**

Printable PDF available for download at http://wwnorton.com/mindschls

# CHANGING THE CHANNEL: HEARTFULNESS PRACTICE

## The Basics

This lesson introduces the practice of heartfulness, with a focus on kindness and a mention of other positive mind states like gratitude and generosity. Learning to place the attention on these qualities helps to make us happier and can rebalance the heart and mind when we are upset or overwhelmed.

---

**LEARNING OBJECTIVES**

1. To recognize the capacity to shift attention from one object to another.
2. To explain how mindfulness strengthens our ability to choose where we put our attention.
3. To define "heartfulness practice."

---

**LESSON 7 IN BRIEF: A SYNOPSIS**

## Changing the Channel: Heartfulness Practice

**1. Check in & review:**
Who practiced at home? What experiences or questions came up? Review the negativity bias.

**2. "Changing the channel" experiment: Move attention from hands to feet.**
How useful would it be if we could "change the channel" in our mind when stuck on something?

Have students close their eyes; move attention consciously from hands to feet, feeling sensations. Choosing where we put our attention is a skill that we can develop. You can "change the channel" from hands to feet because you use them daily and know where they are. The same is true for states of mind. When we know how to "find" a state of mind, we can put our attention there at will.

**3. Introduce heartfulness.**
If you spend enough time intentionally feeling an emotion, it becomes your default. "Heartfulness" practice is a kind of mindfulness that makes our hearts stronger. Today, we'll focus on kindness, the warm feeling you get with a good friend of a favorite relative.

## Practice Instructions

◆ Sit in a posture that's comfortable yet upright, feet on the floor and hands in your lap.

◆ Let your eyes close, or gaze down at the ground in front of you.

**7**

- Feel gravity and the weight of your body. Notice where your body touches the ground.

- Take a few deep breaths, noticing any ease or relaxation on the exhalation.

- Become aware of your whole body sitting.

- Take a few more moments to feel the sensations of breathing in and breathing out.

- Picture someone you like who you see regularly. Notice how you feel inside.

- Send this person kind wishes, repeating three or four simple wishes silently:

  *"May you be happy . . . May you be healthy . . . May you be peaceful . . ."*

- Any time you get lost, come back to their image and the phrases.

- You can do this for additional people, one at a time.

- When you're ready, let your eyes open and look around the room.

 **Discussion Questions**

- How many of you were able to picture someone else in your mind?

- How many of you couldn't visualize the person, but you were still able to have a sense of them?

- How many people used the phrases I suggested? Did anyone use their own? What were they?

- How did you feel doing this? What did you notice?

 **Take-Home Practice**

1. Try this practice at home at least once or twice before our next lesson.
2. Notice any acts of kindness that you or others do. How does it feel to notice that?
3. Next time you feel stuck, try "changing the channel." Put your mind on kind thoughts.

**7**

# Changing the Channel: Heartfulness Practice

## Lesson Outline

- At times, we'd like to be able to change the channel in our mind, just like on a TV.

- Attention is a skill that can be trained.

- With practice, we can choose where we put our attention.

- Most of us have some unproductive mental habits, paying attention to things that don't bring us much happiness.

- We can strengthen positive mind states like kindness and gratitude, training our attention to go there at will, just like changing the channel.

## Lesson

*(Organize the room for mindfulness and engage the students in a transitional activity.)*

Anyone remember to use mindfulness between our last lesson and today? *(Show of hands).* When did you practice?

*(Students answer.)*

Today I want to teach you another powerful tool for building happiness and mental strength *(reference any theme or hook you have been using: mind-power, reducing stress, and so on.)* Remember the negativity bias? Who can tell me what that is?

Right, our minds are like Teflon for positive stuff, Velcro for the negative. We talked about soaking in the good stuff, but what about when you're really stuck on something harsh, replaying some thought, memory, or worry—like a bad song or TV show? How useful would it be if you could change the channel in your own mind, just like you might flip to a different song or different TV station? *(You may want to actually bring in a remote control.)*

> Today I want to teach another practice that can help us learn how to change the channel in our own mind. It's similar to mindfulness, and it's called "heartfulness."

First, let's do a little experiment together, just for a minute or two. Let your eyes close. I want you to put your attention into your hands. See if you can become aware of any sensations you feel in your hands right now. They might feel warm or cool, moist or dry. Maybe you notice heaviness, or even a little tingling.

Now I want you to put your mindful attention down into your feet. Without moving, see if you can become aware of any sensations in your feet. Just feel whatever you feel there—the softness of your socks or the pressure of your shoes. Maybe the hardness of the floor. It might feel warm or tingly. Just notice any sensations you feel there.

Okay, now go ahead and open your eyes.

- Raise your hand if you were able to feel any sensations in your hands?

- Raise your hand if you were able to feel any sensations in your feet?

Nothing too special, right? Feel your feet, feel your hands—no big deal.

Check this out, though: In a certain way, you just changed the channel. You were able to *intentionally* move your attention from one place to another. It's totally ordinary, but it has some pretty big implica-

7

tions. We can move our attention, and that also means we can train our minds to strengthen the ability to *choose* what we focus on.

Can anyone think of some ways that this could be helpful in your life, being able to choose what you pay attention to and keeping your mind there?

*(Examples: dealing with distraction, studying, job interviews, learning, and so forth.)*

Being able to *choose* where we put our attention is actually a skill—and it's a skill we learn with mindfulness. Every time your mind wanders off and you choose to bring it back to your breathing you're strengthening that capacity to choose where you put your attention.

We use our hands and feet intentionally every single day, almost all day long. We consciously *place our attention there* many, many times a day, so it's easy to put our mind there at will.

The more you put your attention somewhere, the more easily you can find that spot and feel it. And this holds true for *states of mind* as much as it does for *parts of our body*. So the more time you spend, say, feeling an uplifting emotion like gratitude or kindness, the easier it is for you to feel that emotion.

That means when you're tripping on something, or if you're having a hard time and need a break, if you've practiced putting your attention on kindness, you can "change the channel" in your mind to that station. You could spend some time thinking more positive thoughts and feeling kind—just like you could put your attention in your feet and spend some time feeling the sensations there.

And if you spend enough time putting your attention on an emotion (positive or negative), eventually it becomes your default. When nothing else is going on, your mind just goes back there to feeling whatever you've trained it to feel.

We call this aspect of mindfulness "heartfulness practice," because we're consciously, intentionally making our hearts stronger.

Okay. Let's do some practice with this. Today we're going to focus on kindness—that natural feeling of warmth you get when you see a good friend or spend time with a favorite relative. One of the ways to practice heartfulness is to use phrases or thoughts.

So, we'll start with some mindfulness, and then we'll visualize seeing a person in our life that makes us happy. Then we'll practice sending some kind thoughts together, placing our attention on kindness and strengthening our ability to feel that positive emotion. Sometimes, people associate kindness with weakness, but as we'll see, kindness comes from strength—and kindness makes us stronger.

## Practice

+ Find your posture—comfortable and upright. Let your eyes close (or gaze down).
+ When you hear the sound of the bell, listen with all of your attention through to the end of the tone.
+ Start feeling the relaxing effects of gravity. Let your body get heavy. Feel the points that are touching the ground and let them take the weight of your body.
+ Take a few deep breaths, feeling any ease or relaxation that comes, as you exhale.
+ Let any excess tension in your body drain down and out, into the ground.
+ As your body settles, feel the sensations of your whole body sitting.

### HEARTFULNESS
+ Next, think of someone you care about who naturally makes you smile. Choose someone you see *regu-*

7

*larly.* Try to see their face, their image, in your mind. Maybe picture them doing something they enjoy. They're feeling happy. See their face, see them smiling. If you can't actually picture them, just have a sense of what it feels like to be around them.

✦ Notice how it feels, imagining how it is to be with them. Notice the emotional sensations you feel inside as you see them.

✦ Now, let's start to send some good wishes to them. This isn't a prayer—and there's nothing magical about this. We're literally practicing kindness. I'll say some phrases out loud, and I want you to repeat them silently, one at a time. You can use the same words or your own—just remember to keep them simple and use the same three or four phrases. If you want, you can put one hand on your heart, or just continue to sit.

> – *"May you be happy." (Leave some space between each phrase.)*
> – *"May you be safe."*
> – *"May you be peaceful."*

✦ Repeat the phrases in your mind, silently sending thoughts of goodwill.

✦ "May you be happy." . . . "May you be safe.". . . "May you be peaceful."

✦ If you notice the mind is lost in thinking, that's okay. See if you can gently let go, come back to their image, and start offering these kind wishes again.

*(Depending on how much time you have and how settled your group is, you may end here or continue by choosing another person.)*

✦ Now let their image fade in your mind, and just come back to sitting.

*(Ring the bell)*

✦ When you're ready, let your eyes open. Notice how you feel, how it feels in the room.

 **Discussion Questions**

– How many of you were able to picture someone else in your mind?

– How many of you couldn't actually visualize the person, but you were still able to have a sense of them—remembering what it feels like to be around them?

– How many people tried out the phrases I suggested?

– Did anyone use their own? Anyone want to share one or two of their phrases?

– How did you feel doing this? What did you notice?

 **Take-Home Practice**

1. Try this practice at home at least once or twice before our next lesson.
2. Notice any acts of kindness that you or others do. How does it feel to notice that?
3. Next time you feel stuck, try "changing the channel." Put your mind on kind thoughts.

 **Journal Suggestions**

1. How did it feel to practice heartfulness? What did you like about it? What didn't you like?
2. Do you know anyone in your life whose default "inner channel" is a negative mood or emotion? What's it like to be around them?
3. What about the opposite? Do you know anyone in your life whose default "inner channel" is a positive mood or emotion? What's it like to be around them?
4. What's your default mental channel? If you reflect on it now, what mood or emotion does your mind tend to go to when nothing else is happening?

**7**

## ALTERNATE ACTIVITIES

The following exercises can be used for students who have trouble with this practice, or who require more engagement:

— Write the names of five people to whom you want to send kind wishes. Write the phrases for each of them.

— Write down two or three kind things others have done for you. How's that feel?

— Write two or three kind things you've done. How's that feel?

— Make a list of any kind things that happened to you in the past week; write as many as you can. Make another list of any acts of kindness that you did. Last, write down as many kind things as you can imagine doing the rest of today.

— Draw a picture of how it feels when someone else is kind to you. When you're kind?

— Draw a picture of how you and/or the person you're sending heartfulness to might feel when doing this practice.

— Practice saying the phrases silently, but moving your lips while you say them.

 ## Teacher Notes

One of the most common difficulties students will have with this activity is feeling sad because they thought of someone who has died, or who is no longer present in their life (they left, moved away, are in jail . . .). When you teach this lesson, you may want to emphasize that it's important to choose someone who is alive and who we see on a regular basis when first learning heartfulness. Over time, once we've learned how to put our attention on kindness, we can send good wishes to others who may not be around if we want.

If a student grows sad or has a hard time, normalize the emotions they feel. *"It's natural for us to feel sad when we think about someone we miss."* Assure them that it's okay to feel however they feel: sad, angry, hurt, numb . . . Remind them of some tools for mindfulness of emotions to feel the sadness without getting overwhelmed by it (naming the emotion, feeling their breath, feeling the emotional sensations). You can also ask them what they appreciated or loved about that person, as a way of bringing out the positive aspects of their memory.

Another common challenge with heartfulness practice is students "not feeling" anything. It's important to point out that the practice is one of strengthening our *intention* to be kind by repeating these wishes. Sometimes we will feel emotional effects, at other times we won't. The practice can still have positive impacts on our well-being and mental habits regardless of whether or not we feel anything. To emphasize this, you can point out how much of our day we spend thinking about meaningless or stressful things. Wouldn't it be better to have thoughts of kindness going through your mind?

 ## Science Supplement

The researcher Cendri Hutcherson (Hutcherson, et al., 2008) gives a poignant description of the place of belonging and social connection in human life. She writes, "As a species whose survival depends on the ability to build mutually beneficial relationships with others, human beings have a deep-seated need to feel connected, to be trusted and loved, and to trust and love in return. Feeling connected to others increases psychological and physical well-being and decreases the risk of depression and physical ailments. A sense of connectedness also increases empathetic responding as well as acts of trust and cooperation, which tend to have mutually reinforcing effects: They beget trust and cooperation in return . . . How can we increase feelings of connection at an automatic

7

level, most crucially toward those individuals not yet within our circle of trust? A growing psychological literature has focused on decreasing antisocial behaviors or implicit prejudice. These interventions typically involve efforts to raise awareness about the negative consequences of such prejudice, or exposure to individuals from the disliked, stereotyped group toward whom one holds a positive attitude. However, Western science has only recently begun to recognize the benefit not just of counteracting negative, antisocial emotion, but also of fostering positive prosocial emotions and behaviors. Even when highlighting the important role of positivity in counteracting implicit negativity, most studies leave unanswered the question of how to generate such positivity in the first place" (p. 720).

The researchers then suggest that loving-kindness meditation (LKM), or heartfulness practice, might enhance social connection. They found that just seven minutes of LKM increased the sense of social connection and positivity toward unknown people and this effect was observed on both explicit and implicit levels.

More research attention has been directed at mindfulness practice compared with LKM. In 2015, researchers conducted a systematic review of all available studies examining loving-kindness practice. Twenty-four studies including 1759 people demonstrated that LKM increased daily positive emotions. Another meta-analysis analyzed 22 studies including LKM and compassion practice. These practices were moderately effective in reducing depressive symptoms, increasing mindfulness, compassion and self-compassion. Positive emotions were increased compared to a relaxation training. The authors acknowledge that results were inconclusive for some outcomes, and more research needs to be conducted.

## HEARTFULNESS & CLINICAL CONDITIONS
Hofmann (Hofmann, et al., 2011) examined the potential for kindness-based practice for clinical conditions such as anxiety or depression. They conclude in this way:

"In sum, existing research studies suggest that LKM and compassion meditation are highly promising practices for improving positive affect and for reducing stress and negative affect such as anxiety and mood symptoms. We hypothesize that LKM may be particularly useful for targeting interpersonal problems such as anger control issues, whereas both compassion meditation and LKM may be particularly useful for treating depression and relationship problems, such as marital conflicts, or counteracting the challenges among caregiving professionals or nonprofessionals who must provide long-term care to a relative or friend"(p. 1131).

## LOVING-KINDNESS & POSTTRAUMATIC STRESS DISORDER (PTSD)
Mindfulness has been explored as a way to improve symptoms of PTSD in a recent study in the *Journal of the American Medical Association*. More recently, loving-kindness or heartfulness practice has been explored as a component of treatment for PTSD for veterans by Kearney and colleagues (2013). This was a pilot study with 12 sessions, assessing feasibility of preliminary measures of effectiveness. Attendance was high with 74 percent attending nine or more classes. A large effect was found for PTSD symptoms at three-month follow-up and a medium effect size was found for depression at three-month follow-up. Increases in self-compassion seemed to account for some of these positive effects.

In our experience, heartfulness, self-compassion, and other positive-emotion focused practices can be a very important adjunct to mindfulness practice.

**7**

## REFERENCES & FURTHER READING

Galante, J., Galante, I., Bekkers, M. J., & Gallacher, J. (2014). Effect of kindness-based meditation on health and well-being: A systematic review and meta-analysis. *Journal of Consulting and Clinical Psychology, 82*, 1101–1114.

Hofmann, S. G., Grossman, P., & Hinton, D. E. (2011). Loving-kindness and compassion meditation: Potential for psychological interventions. *Clinical Psychology Review, 31*, 1126–1132.

Hutcherson, C. A., Seppala, E. M., & Gross, J. J. (2008). Loving-kindness meditation increases social connectedness. *Emotion, 8*, 720–724.

Kearney, D. J., Malte, C. A., McManus, C., Martinez, M. E., Felleman, B., & Simpson, T. L. (2013). Loving-kindness meditation for posttraumatic stress disorder: A pilot study. *Journal of Traumatic Stress, 26*, 426–434.

Polusny, M. A., Erbes, C. R., Thuras, P., Moran, A., Lamberty, G. J., Collins, R. C., . . . & Lim, K. O. (2015). Mindfulness-based stress reduction for posttraumatic stress disorder among veterans: A randomized clinical trial. *JAMA, 314*, 456–465.

Zeng, X., Chiu, C. P., Wang, R., Oei, T. P., & Leung, F. Y. (2015). The effect of loving-kindness meditation on positive emotions: a meta-analytic review. *Frontiers in Psychology, 6*, 1693.

7

# Changing the Channel: Heartfulness Practice

## Key Points

- At times, we'd like to be able to change the channel in our mind, just like on a TV.

- Attention is a skill. With practice, we can choose where we put our attention.

- Most of us have some unproductive mental habits, such as paying attention to things that don't bring us much happiness.

- We can strengthen positive mind states like kindness by training our attention.

## Practice Instructions

> **DEFINITION:** *Heartfulness practice* is using mindfulness to strengthen our hearts by focusing on a positive emotion like kindness; repeating kind thoughts is one way of doing this.

- Sit in a posture that's comfortable yet upright, feet on the floor and hands in your lap.

- Let your eyes close or gaze down at the ground in front of you.

- Feel gravity and the weight of your body. Notice where your body touches the ground.

- Take a few deep breaths, noticing any ease or relaxation on the exhalation.

- Become aware of your whole body sitting.

- Take a few more moments to feel the sensations of breathing in and breathing out.

- Picture someone you like who you see regularly. Notice how you feel inside.

- Send this person kind wishes, repeating three or four simple wishes silently:

    – *"May you be happy . . . May you be healthy . . . May you be peaceful . . ."*

- Any time you get lost, come back to their image and the phrases.

- You can do this for additional people, one at a time.

- When you're ready, let your eyes open and look around the room.

 ## Take-Home Practice

1. Try this practice at home at least once or twice before our next lesson.

2. Notice any acts of kindness that you or others do. How's it feel to notice that?

3. Next time you feel stuck, try changing the channel by putting your mind on kind thoughts.

 ## Journal Suggestions

1. How did it feel to practice heartfulness? What did you like about it? What didn't you like?

2. Do you know anyone in your life whose default "inner channel" is a negative mood or emotion? What's it like to be around them?

3. What about the opposite? Do you know anyone in your life whose default "inner channel" is a positive mood or emotion? What's it like to be around them?

4. What's your default mental channel? If you reflect on it now, what mood or emotion does your mind tend to go to when nothing else is happening?

7

**LESSON 8**

# BEING AT HOME IN OUR BODIES: BODY SCAN

## The Basics

The body scan—moving the attention systematically through the body—is a core mindfulness practice. It can be done lying down, although this may not be feasible or appropriate in certain contexts.

---

**LEARNING OBJECTIVES**

1. To understand the body as a home.
2. To identify individual and cultural ideas and beliefs about the body.
3. To appreciate the value of non-judgmental awareness of the body and its sensations.
4. To learn the practice of the body scan.

---

**LESSON 8 IN BRIEF: A SYNOPSIS**

### Being at Home in Our Bodies: Body Scan

**1. Check in & review:**
Who practiced at home? What experiences or questions came up?

**2. The body is our home.**
How important is your body? Is there anything in life that *doesn't* involve our body? We focus on our bodies a lot: how they look, what we do or don't like about them. What are some ways that society judges our bodies (Size, shape, skin color . . .)? Our body is personal, but we see it through the lens of society.

**3. We can have a kind relationship with our body.**
How can we free ourselves from society's ideas about our bodies? What would it mean to be kind to your body? What would it look like to have a good relationship with it?

**4. What is sensation?**
There's a practice that can transform our relationship with our body, learning to feel and observe sensations mindfully, without judgment. What is a sensation? Rub your palms together—what do you feel? As we move our attention through our body, we'll be mindful of any sensations we feel.

## Practice Instructions

- Sit in a posture that's comfortable and upright, feet on the floor and hands in your lap.

- Let your eyes close, or gaze down at the ground in front of you.

- Feel gravity and the weight of your body. Notice where your body touches the ground.

- Take a few deep breaths, noticing any ease or relaxation on the exhale.

- Be aware of your whole body sitting, feeling the sensations of breathing in and breathing out.

- Scan your attention through your body part by part.

- Notice any sensation (or blankness) in each part with openness and curiosity.

- Your head, face, neck, shoulders, arms, through the rest of your body, one part at a time.

- When you're ready, let your eyes open and look around the room.

 ## Discussion Questions

- How did that go? How do you feel now?

- Did anyone have the sense of just accepting your body as it is? Not judging it?

- Were there parts of your body where it was hard to feel sensations? What part was the hardest to feel? What part of your body was the easiest to feel?

- What did it feel like? Soft, tense, cool, warm, and so on.

 ## Take-Home Practice

1. Sometime this week, especially if you're feeling stressed, take a few minutes to do a body scan: for 3 minutes, 10, or 20. See how you feel before and after the body scan.

2. Try to notice your body during school. When do you get tense, when is your body relaxed?

**LESSON 8 IN DETAIL: A SAMPLE SCRIPT**

# Being at Home in Our Bodies: Body Scan

## Lesson Outline

– The body is our home—we live our lives here.

– We spend a lot of time focusing on our bodies, and have assumptions and ideas about them that we inherit from our culture or society.

– What would it be like to have a non-judgmental, kind relationship with one's own body?

– Systematically moving the attention through the body helps us have a different relationship with it.

## Lesson

*(Organize the room for mindfulness and engage the students in a transitional activity. Then begin with a reference to the last lesson you completed, an overview statement or inquiry into how things have been going, or about triumphs and difficulties applying mindfulness.)*

Our body is kind of like our home. When we think about ourselves, we're often thinking about our body. Any pleasure or pain that we experience, sickness or health, joy, sadness, love or humor—all of it involves our body. Your body lets you know how you're feeling and what you like and what you don't like. Wherever we go, whatever we do, we're here in our own body.

We spend a lot of time focusing on our bodies. We think about what they look like, what we like about our bodies and what we don't like. Plus, our society has lots of judgments too about people's bodies. Take skin color. Throughout much of human history, and to this very day—a lot of people have a lot of ideas

about skin color. Think about all the suffering that's been created because of racist ideas about skin color.

So, our bodies are very personal—they're intimately ours—but we also have many ideas about our bodies from our culture or society.

What are some ideas our culture has about bodies?

*(Engage the students in a discussion of societal ideas of beauty and body-image. You can supplement this with other images, video from the media.)*

What's it feel like to believe these ideas about how our bodies should look, or what they should feel like? How many people ever felt judged (positively or negatively) for what your body looked like? Think about if you ever judged someone else for how their body looked?

So how do we get free from these ideas and beliefs we inherit from our society—all the beliefs we have or other people have? How do we get beneath all that static to see what this body really is, and what it's actually like?

This is important. If we're going to live our entire lives in this body, we want to develop a good relationship with it! What do you think it means, or what would it look like, to have a "kind relationship" with your body?

*(Students answer.)*

Yeah, we need to respect it and treat it well, to care for it, to let go of harsh judgments, to be kind to ourselves. Today I want to introduce you to a practice that can help us learn how to do that. We're going to scan our attention through the body and just observe it without judging. This is about feeling the sensations that are there on the inside. What's a sensation? Who can give me some examples?

(*Students answer.*)

Yes, it's something we can feel directly with our body. I want everyone to rub your two palms together. Feel that softness, that rubbing? Okay, now I want you to clap your hands together once. Feel that hardness, that stinging? These are all sensations: temperature, texture, movement, heaviness or lightness, tingling or aching, itching or tickling.

As we move our attention through our bodies, we're going to be mindful of whatever sensations we feel. No pride, no blame; just being mindful in an open, curious way. Real simple.

## Practice: Body Scan

So, let's begin as usual, by establishing mindfulness of the body.

◆ Find your posture—comfortable and upright. Let your eyes close.

◆ Listen to the sound of the bell with all of your attention, all the way to the end of the tone.

◆ Start feeling the relaxing effects of gravity. Let your body get heavy. Feel the points that are touching the earth and let them take the weight of your body.

◆ Take a few deep breaths, feeling any ease or relaxation that comes, as you exhale. Relaxing, let any excess tension in your body drain down and out into the ground.

◆ As your body settles, feel the sensations of your whole body sitting.

◆ Now, we are going to try scanning our whole body for sensations. You may feel very strong sensations in your body or you might feel weak ones. Anything you feel is fine. In some parts of the body, you might not feel any sensations at all. That's also totally normal. Just be curious no matter what you feel.

◆ So, let's start at the top of your head and your forehead. Pay attention to this area and feel any sensations there.

◆ Pay attention to your eyes. Relax the muscles around your eyes and feel any sensations there.

◆ Pay attention to your cheeks. Your nose. Your mouth. Relax your jaw. Feel any sensations you notice.

◆ Pay attention to your chin. The back of your head. Feel the sensations in your neck and throat.

◆ Then bring your attention to your left shoulder, resting your attention there. Notice your upper left arm, your elbow, and now your lower arm.

◆ Now feel your hands and all five fingers. Notice any sensations in your hands.

◆ Then move your attention to your right shoulder, feel your right upper arm, right elbow, lower arm, hands and fingers. Come back to your back and feel your upper back for any sensations.

◆ Whatever you're feeling, try to be kind and gentle with yourself. We're accepting whatever we're feeling in this moment.

◆ You may not feel anything, or maybe you feel some discomfort or some pressure or tingles or itches. Scan your attention across your back and down your spine and to your lower back.

◆ Now come up to your chest and feel sensations in your chest. Feel your belly. Relax your belly. Take your time, we don't have to rush.

◆ Notice where your body is touching the chair. Does it feel heavy or hard? Now feel your left leg from the hip to the knee. Feel the knee and the calf. Feel the ankle. Feel the foot and all five toes.

◆ Place your attention in your right hip and feel the right thigh, your knee, your calf, and feel your foot including the toes.

◆ Now notice your entire body at once. Keep your attention on your entire body, letting your attention notice everything at once.

**8**

*(Ring the bell.)*

◆ When you're ready, you can let your eyes open slowly. Move your hands or feet or look around the room. Notice how you feel. Notice how it feels in the room right now.

 **Discussion Questions**

— How did that go? How do you feel now?

— Did anyone have the sense of just accepting your body as it is? Not judging it?

— Were there parts of your body where it was hard to feel sensations? What part was the hardest to feel? What part of your body was the easiest to feel?

— Could you feel anything in your face? What part of your face could you feel?

— What did it feel like? Soft, tense, cool, warm, and so on.

— Could you relax your jaw or eyes? What did that feel like?

 **Take-Home Practice**

— Sometime this week, especially if you're feeling stressed, take a few minutes to do a body scan: for 3 minutes, 10, or 20. See how you feel before and after the body scan.

— Try to notice your body during school. When do you get tense, when is your body relaxed?

 **Journal Suggestions**

1. What surprised you about this lesson?
2. What did you learn about your image of your body?
3. In what ways are you kind toward your body and in what ways are you judgmental?

 **Science Supplement**

The researcher Charlotte Markey (2010) has suggested that body image is related to many key aspects of development including puberty, identity, family, peer, and romantic relationships. Significant health concerns, including obesity and eating disorders, are associated with body dissatisfaction. Further, the large number of adolescents affected by body dissatisfaction makes it essential that developmental psychologists direct their attention to this area of research.

In a notable review of body image in adolescents, Grabe (Grabe, et al., 2008) states that body dissatisfaction is extremely common, with about 50 percent of girls and young women reporting dissatisfaction with their bodies. The prevalence of body dissatisfaction is lower in boys, but nevertheless represents a substantial public health burden. Negative perceptions can develop in children as young as seven years old. Body dissatisfaction is a consistent risk factor for eating disorders and predicts low self-esteem, depression, and obesity. There appears to be a link between media consumption—specifically exposure to increasingly thin models of beauty depicted in media. Grabe finds that "media exposure is linked to women's generalized dissatisfaction with their bodies, increased investment in appearance, and increased endorsement of disordered eating behaviors." Further, peer attitudes appear to have strong impacts on an adolescent's sense of body image.

Rachel Andrew and her colleagues (2016) conducted research on *positive* body image among adolescent girls. They outline the current state of knowledge and highlight their findings:

◆ Body image is recognized as a complex construct that affects cognitive, behavioral, and emotional functioning.

◆ The majority of body image research has focused on understanding negative aspects of body image.

◆ Positive body image is broadly described as the

love, respect, and acceptance of one's appearance and physical function, and is distinct from body satisfaction or a lack of negative body image.

✦ Body appreciation has been shown to relate to adaptive psychosocial indicators of well-being including self-esteem, optimism, and self-compassion, and has been shown to protect against media-induced body image disturbance.

✦ Body appreciation may have benefits for girls across a wide range of domains: Findings suggest that fostering body appreciation may be beneficial and protective for girls' health, in terms of decreased dieting, increased physical activity, and protection against alcohol and cigarette use.

✦ Interventions might aim to increase parental or peer awareness of the importance of displaying an accepting and nonjudgmental stance toward their daughters' or friends' appearance and body shape.

✦ Unhelpful thinking styles described in cognitive behavior therapy, such as catastrophizing and black and white thinking, may contribute to an inaccurate and negatively biased perception of body-related messages.

✦ Girls might be trained in mindfulness and acceptance techniques that emphasize observation, but not judgment or modification of thoughts, emotions, or physical sensations.

✦ Increasing self-compassion may be another way to enhance body appreciation. One study has shown self-compassion to protect body appreciation against body image-related threats such as appearance comparison in women. Self-compassion meditation has also been shown to increase body appreciation in adult women.

Although the interest is quite recent, there are reasons to expect relationships between mindfulness and body acceptance.

In a study conducted with adults, Dijkstra and Barelds (2011) ". . . found a positive relation between mindfulness and body satisfaction: As individuals are more mindful, they are more satisfied with their body.

This is consistent with the fact that non-judgment, a central component of mindfulness, is also highly relevant to the construct of body image. We also found that individuals who were more mindful engaged less often in body comparisons. This finding supports the suggestion by Langer and colleagues, who argue that social comparisons are mindless and automatic activities that may be reduced by being more mindful" (p. 421).

### REFERENCES & FURTHER READING

Andrew, R., Tiggemann, M., & Clark, L. (2016). Predictors and health-related outcomes of positive body image in adolescent girls: A prospective study. *Developmental Psychology, 52,* 463–474.

Dijkstra, P. & Barelds, D. P. (2011). Examining a model of dispositional mindfulness, body comparison, and body satisfaction. *Body Image, 8,* 419–422.

Grabe, S., Ward, L. M., & Hyde, J. S. (2008). The role of the media in body image concerns among women: A meta-analysis of experimental and correlational studies. *Psychological Bulletin, 134,* 460–474.

Markey, C. N. (2010). Why body image is important to adolescent development. *Journal of Youth and Adolescence, 39,* 1387–1391.

Langer, E., Pirson, M. & Delizonna, L. (2010). The mindlessness of social comparisons. *Psychology of Aesthetics, Creativity, and the Arts, 4,* 68–74.

# Being at Home in Our Bodies: Body Scan

## Key Points

♦ The body is our home—we live our lives here.

♦ We spend a lot of time focusing on our bodies, and have assumptions and ideas about them that we inherit from our culture or society.

♦ What would it be like to have a nonjudgmental, kind relationship with one's own body?

## Practice Instructions

♦ Sit in a posture that's comfortable and upright, feet on the floor and hands in your lap.

♦ Let your eyes close or gaze down at the ground in front of you.

♦ Feel gravity and the weight of your body. Notice where your body touches the ground.

♦ Take a few deep breaths, noticing any ease or relaxation on the exhalation.

♦ Become aware of your whole body sitting.

♦ Take a few more moments to feel the sensations of breathing in and breathing out.

♦ Scan your attention through your body part by part.

♦ Notice any sensations (or blankness) in each part with openness and curiosity.

♦ Start at your head, then your face, neck, shoulders, arms, continuing down through the rest of your body, one part at a time.

♦ When you're ready, let your eyes open and look around the room.

 **Take-Home Practice**

1. Sometime this week, especially if you're feeling stressed, take a few minutes to do a body scan: for 3 minutes, 10 minutes, or more. See how you feel before and after the body scan.

2. Try to notice your body during school. When do you get tense, when is your body relaxed?

 **Journal Suggestions**

1. What surprised you about this lesson?

2. What did you learn about your image of your body?

3. In what ways are you kind toward your body and in what ways are you judgmental?

↓ Printable PDF available for download at http://wwnorton.com/mindschls

# LESSON 9

# THE MOVIE IN YOUR MIND: MINDFULNESS OF THINKING

## The Basics

This lesson addresses the topic of thinking. It describes two ways of dealing with thinking: putting thoughts to the side—or being mindful of thought itself.

---

**LEARNING OBJECTIVES**

1. To understand the capacity of thinking as natural to being human.
2. To recognize the ways in which thoughts can help us and harm us.
3. To identify thoughts as words and pictures.

---

**LESSON 9 IN BRIEF: A SYNOPSIS**

## The Movie in Your Mind: Mindfulness of Thinking

**1. Check in & review:**
Who practiced at home? What experiences or questions came up?

**2. Thinking can help or harm us. What is the most common mistaken idea about mindfulness?**
How does thinking help us? How does it create problems? Thinking is part of being human (Descartes). A common misconception is that you have to get rid of your thoughts to practice mindfulness. Sometimes people feel embarrassed or upset by their thinking, but it's as natural as hearing. Trying to stop your thoughts is like **trying** to stop hearing sounds.

**3. We each have a movie in our mind.**
We think all the time, like having a narrator in our head. We get mesmerized by our thoughts, like being so engrossed in a movie that you forget it's not real. We can learn to observe the narrator in our mind, and choose which thoughts to listen to and which to ignore. We think in words and pictures. (Experiment: think your name; see your route to school). We can be mindful of thoughts by: labeling them and returning to the breath; or observing them directly.

## Practice Instructions

♦ Sit in a posture that's comfortable and upright, feet on the floor and hands in your lap.

♦ Let your eyes close, or gaze down at the ground in front of you.

♦ Feel gravity and the weight of your body. Notice where your body touches the ground.

- Take a few deep breaths, noticing any ease or relaxation on the exhale.

- Be aware of your whole body sitting, feeling the sensations of breathing in and breathing out.

- First, practice labeling thoughts. Every time a thought arises (a word or picture), make a soft mental note: "thinking." Gently let go and bring your attention back to your breathing.

- Next, practice being mindful of thoughts themselves. Pay attention to any words or images that appear in your mind. Try not to get lost or entangled in their stories; just observe. Notice what happens to them.

- When you're ready, let your eyes open and look around the room.

 **Discussion Questions**

- What was it like to label your thoughts and come back to mindfulness of breathing?

- How about noticing thoughts directly, seeing the pictures and hearing the words in your mind?

- Who had more words than pictures? Who had more pictures than words?

- Which technique was better for you—labeling the thoughts, or noticing them directly?

 **Take-Home Practice**

1. Pay attention to thinking this week. Notice how thoughts and feelings are connected.
2. If you're feeling down, see if you can notice the words and pictures that are going through your mind. Can you just be aware of your thinking, rather than believing it?

# The Movie in Your Mind: Mindfulness of Thinking

## Lesson Outline

- Thinking is totally natural; it's not an "enemy" of mindfulness practice!

- If we don't honor the power of thought, negative thoughts can turn into negative feelings and affect our well-being.

- We are generally spellbound by our inner dialogue.

- Mindfulness lets us clearly observe our thinking and helps us to develop a wise relationship to our thoughts.

## Lesson

*(Organize the room for mindfulness and engage the students in a transitional activity.)*

How are you doing? Any experiences using mindfulness recently? Today, I want to talk about something we all know really, really well . . . thinking. What comes to mind when I say the word "thinking?"

*(Students answer.)*

What's thinking good for?

*(Students answer.)*

Yeah, it can help us plan, figure things out, or get what we want. What about the other side? How can thinking actually stress us out?

*(Students answer.)*

Yeah, thinking cuts both ways—it's so important for our happiness and plans and goals, but sometimes it can cause problems.

Thinking is so central to our lives. Has anyone ever heard of the philosopher Descartes? What's his famous line? "I think therefore I am." The fact that we're thinking is a core aspect of being human. Anyone know what is the biggest mistaken idea people have about mindfulness practice?

*(Students answer.)*

It's that to do silent mindfulness practice, you need to get rid of all your thoughts! But that's not true—if that were true, no one would be able to start practicing mindfulness! Sometimes, when learning mindfulness practice, people get embarrassed or upset that they think. But thinking is as natural as hearing. It wouldn't make sense to believe that we needed to stop hearing sounds in order to do mindfulness, right?

Ever notice how much we think? Sometimes it seems like it's nonstop! Even though thinking is completely natural, we get kind of mesmerized by it. Most of us don't know how spellbound we are by our inner dialogue.

Do you know the experience of watching a movie in a theater, and the movie is so good that you completely forget that you're sitting in a dark room watching light projected onto a blank screen? And it feels like all those imaginary characters are as real as your best friend? Do you know what I'm talking about?

Well, we're kind of living in the movie of our thoughts.

Who's seen a documentary film? Do you know how they sometimes have a narrator and you don't see the

9

narrator, but they are speaking in the background for a lot of the film? It might be someone like Morgan Freeman, with a deep, royal sounding voice.

Well, we've all kind of got a narrator in our head. We're narrating our lives by talking to ourselves in our own heads. You know what I mean (or is it just me!)?

Let's see for ourselves. In a moment, we'll do mindful breathing for 30 seconds. During these 30 seconds, pay attention to every breath as much as possible, and notice the first time you have a thought.

*(Practice mindful breathing briefly, in silence for 30 seconds.)*

Raise your hand if your attention wandered away and got lost in thoughts? Can anyone tell me what their first thought was? *(Students answer.)*

Thoughts can be really important. Sometimes, we remember the past. Sometimes, we plan for the future. We imagine things we want and plan to avoid the things we don't want. Raise your hand if you thought more about the past? More about the future?

Sometimes, thoughts can have negative effects on our mood. If someone is depressed or real anxious and they go to see a therapist, what do you imagine the therapist is going to explore?

*(Students answer.)*

Yeah, one big part of it will be their thoughts. That's the basis of cognitive therapy, which is used a lot. Cognitive therapy says that what we think about ourselves, about others and about the future matters for how we feel. So negative thoughts can turn into negative feelings. Does that make sense? You know what I'm talking about, how our thoughts can get us real down sometimes?

They can get us into trouble and even make us feel badly. Sometimes our thoughts are like BAD advice! Does anyone have an example of when your thoughts have gotten you into trouble? *(Students answer.)*

So, in mindfulness, we're learning to notice our thoughts without acting them out. We want to learn to see our thinking with mindfulness. How do we do this? Well, we think in words and pictures. Let's try an experiment. I want everyone to say your name silently in your own mind.

*(Give them a few moments.)*

Did you hear that? Where did you hear it? Good: so that's one way we think, in words. We also think in pictures. Close your eyes and picture the route you took to get to school today. *(Give them another moment.)* Could you picture that?

So, these are the two main ways we think: in words and in pictures. When we're mindful of thinking, we're being aware of the words and pictures in our mind.

Sometimes, in mindfulness, we just ignore our thoughts. For example, if we're doing mindful breathing and a thought comes up, we can just label it, "thinking," put it aside and come back to our breath. Other times, we can actually pay attention to the thoughts themselves. In other words, the thoughts become the object of our meditation. We're learning to listen to the words and see the pictures without getting caught up in them—like we're seeing the movie but still aware that we're sitting in the theater.

## Practice

So, we'll begin as we usually begin, by establishing mindfulness of the body.

- Find your posture—comfortable and upright. Let your eyes close.
- Listen to the sound of the bell with all of your attention, all the way to the end of the tone.
- Start feeling the relaxing effects of gravity. Let your body get heavy. Feel the points that are touching the ground and let them take the weight of your body.
- Take a few deep breaths, feeling any ease or relaxation that comes, as you exhale.
- You can even repeat "relax, relax" a few times silently to yourself. Let any excess tension present in your body drain down and out.
- As your body settles, feel the sensations of your whole body sitting.
- Now, direct your attention to the sensations of breathing.
- Each time you notice that your attention is drawn into thinking, silently say in your own mind "thinking." Once you've labeled the thought, direct your attention to awareness of your breath.
- If you like, you can use more specific labels, like "remembering" or "planning," or you can simply use "thinking." We'll do this for another couple of minutes.
- So, what we just did is a way of putting thinking aside. We're not trying to stop thinking; it's not our enemy. We're simply choosing to pay attention to the breath.
- Now, let's see if you can notice thoughts directly. You don't need to pay close attention to the breath anymore. Instead, pay attention to the words and pictures that you hear and see in your mind. Just notice those thoughts as they float through awareness.
- Sometimes, as soon as you notice thinking, it stops. As soon as you hear it, the sentence just ends; or as soon as you see the picture, it melts away or vanishes. That's fine. Just keep noticing the words and pictures without judgment.
- We'll go on like this for a few minutes.

*(Ring the bell.)*

- When you're ready, you can let your eyes open

slowly. Move your hands or feet and look around the room.

 **Discussion Questions**

– What was it like to label your thoughts and come back to mindfulness of breathing?

– What was it like to notice the thoughts directly, seeing the pictures and hearing the words in your mind?

– Who had more words than pictures? Who had more pictures?

– Which technique seemed better for you—labeling the thoughts and coming back to the body, or noticing the thoughts directly?

 **Take-Home Practice**

1. Pay attention to thinking this week. Notice how thoughts and feelings are connected.
2. If you're feeling down, see if you can notice the words and pictures that are going through your mind. Can you be aware of your thinking rather than believe it?

 **Journal Suggestions**

1. What surprised you about this lesson?
2. How does your inner narrator treat you? Is it kind or cruel?
3. How do you think you can use this lesson in your daily life?

 **Science Supplement**

**MIND-WANDERING AND THE BRAIN'S DEFAULT MODE NETWORK**

In an important study on brain function and mind wandering, Malia Mason of Columbia University (Mason et al., 2007) writes, "What does the mind do in the absence of external demands for thought? Is it essentially blank, springing into action only when some task requires attention? Everyday experience challenges this account of mental life. In the absence of a task that requires deliberative processing, the mind generally tends to wander, flitting from one thought to the next with fluidity and ease. Given the ubiquitous nature of this phenomenon, it has been suggested that mind-wandering constitutes a psychological baseline from which people depart when attention is required elsewhere and to which they return when tasks no longer require conscious supervision" (p. 393).

Because we've all practiced mindfulness meditation, we know that "the mind has a mind of its own." Even when we're intent on attending to the breath, for example, we are habitually pulled into the orbit of discursive thought. While there are likely some useful functions of mind wandering, it appears to have adverse effects on our happiness. Large studies have been conducted that randomly sample moments during people's day to determine the relationship between mind wandering and well-being. One notable study by Daniel Gilbert and colleagues (Killingsworth & Gilbert, 2010) found that approximately half (47 percent) of our waking life is spent with attention not on the task at hand, and that episodes of mind wandering were associated with lower levels of happiness.

So what happens to the brain when we are not dedicating our attention to a particular task? A network of brain regions known as the default mode network (DMN) becomes active. Importantly, there is substantial overlap between the DMN and self-referential thought. One region, the medial prefrontal cortex—a key node of the DMN—has consistently demonstrated increased activation during self-related tasks. Jennifer Beer (2007), a researcher at University of California, Davis, writes, "the increased resting metabolism of the medial prefrontal cortex is theorized to support a default psychological mode of self-evaluation that provides chronic, generalized

updates on the self" (p. 187–188). While it appears that various sensory, affective and motor processes are involved in self-experience, the DMN, including the medial prefrontal cortex, figures quite prominently in self-relevant thought.

We are probably quite familiar with these "chronic generalized updates on the self." This is the centerpiece of our running conversation with ourselves. We might be going about our day at school, but we're also narrating how we're doing. Often, we subtly assume that how we're doing means something important about who we are and our value. It is quite telling that the "default" position of attention is essentially self-referential thinking. When we're "lost in thought" we are taking the story of the self very seriously. We're embroiled in the drama of what's happened to us in the past, questions about what will unfold in the future, and there is typically a rigid notion of who we are. We lose touch with the arising of experience, with being here, now— and instead live in the cloistered world of thought.

## MINDFULNESS AND THE DEFAULT MODE NETWORK

In a study by Norm Farb and colleagues (2007), the research found that mindfulness shifted brain activation from narrative self-relevant thought, to brain regions associated with momentary experience of world and body. The authors conclude that mindfulness practice "allows for a distinct experiential mode in which thoughts, feelings and bodily sensations are viewed less as being good or bad or integral to the 'self' and treated more as transient mental events that can be simply observed. As such, the capacity to disengage temporally extended narrative and engage more momentary neural modes of self-focus has important implications for mood and anxiety disorders, with the narrative focus having been shown to increase illness vulnerability. Conversely, a growing body of evidence suggests approaching self-experience through a more basic present-centered focus may represent a critical aspect of human well-being" (p. 320).

Subsequent studies have echoed these findings. Judson Brewer suggests that "meditation practice may transform the resting-state experience into one that resembles a meditative state, and as such, is a more present-centered default mode" (p. 20255). The upshot of this research is that some of the beneficial effects of mindfulness practice on well-being may be explained by changes in the brain's DMN, and associated changes in self-focus.

## THINKING & RUMINATION

Not all forms of thought are equal. Some styles of thought appear to be detrimental. For example, obsessive ruminative thought—chewing on the same self-focused negative emotion in a passive, repetitive manner—is associated with poorer mental health. Rumination has links to negative automatic thoughts, self-focused attention, obsessive thought, worry and neuroticism. Although rumination is an attempt to resolve challenges and meet goals, the approach backfires and is linked with poorer well-being and a range of mental health disorders including depression and anxiety disorders.

Reviewing the subject, Smith and Alloy (2009) write:

"Over the past two decades, rumination has evolved as a critical construct in understanding the development and persistence of depressed mood. Hundreds of articles have addressed rumination related topics, and consistent evidence for the role of ruminative thought processes in depression has emerged . . . Rumination is best characterized as a stable, negative, broadly construed way of responding to discrepancies between current status and target status. Specifically, rumination may be triggered by both the realization that one is not where one desires, and the negative affect that is likely to accompany that realization. Further, the content of rumination is likely to center on

themes of discrepancies between actual and desired status" (p. 116).

Mindfulness may be a viable treatment for addressing rumination. Reviewing the treatments for rumination, Querstret and Cropley (2013) write:

"Perseverative cognitions such as rumination and worry are key components of mental illnesses such as depression and anxiety. Given the frequent comorbidity of conditions in which rumination and worry are present, it is possible that they are underpinned by the same cognitive process. Furthermore, rumination and worry appear to be part of a causal chain that can lead to long-term health consequences, including cardiovascular disease and other chronic conditions . . . Nineteen studies were included in the review and were assessed for methodological quality and treatment integrity. Results suggested that mindfulness-based and cognitive behavioral interventions may be effective in the reduction of both rumination and worry; with both internet-delivered and face-to-face delivered formats useful. More broadly, it appears that treatments in which participants are encouraged to change their thinking style, or to disengage from emotional response to rumination and/or worry (e.g., through mindful techniques), could be helpful" (p. 996).

## WHAT HAPPENS IN THE BRAIN BEFORE WE BECOME AWARE OF THOUGHT?

One fascinating study by Kalina Christoff and her colleagues examined brain activity before spontaneous thought arose (Ellamil et al., 2016). They used a neurophenomenological approach: They combined reports of subjective experience with neuroimaging techniques. Specifically, they used advanced meditators because they believed that these individuals could more accurately report when a spontaneous thought arose. Their findings were quite interesting.

A couple of seconds before a thought arose, certain brain regions were activated, including the medial temporal lobe. Previous studies have found that electrical stimulation of medial temporal lobe evokes thought-like or dream-like experiences far more frequently than stimulation of other regions. Christoff writes:

"The antecedent medial temporal lobe activation that we observed may reflect spontaneously occurring reactivation and recombination of memory traces—a process originally described during sleep but also more recently identified during waking rest. The medial temporal lobe is commonly associated with episodic memory retrieval, but has also been found to support thinking about the future, imagining novel situations, and generating creative ideas . . . Medial temporal lobe-driven spontaneous reactivation and recombination of memory traces may influence cortical activation patterns, in the process giving rise to spontaneously retrieved old episodic memories or spontaneously generated novel mental simulations. Memories or novel simulations are often said to "come to us"—a phrase reflecting the common subjective experience of mental content arising in a bottom-up fashion and capturing our attention reflexively in the process. The neural antecedents identified in the present study are consistent with this subjective experience . . . While the specific neural systems underlying the restless nature of our minds remain a mystery, the present findings bring us one step closer to understanding the neural basis of our thoughts' universal meanderings"(p. 193–195).

## THINKING IS NOT THE ENEMY!

Importantly, all this talk about self-referential thought and the problems it can create might lead us to the impression that meditation is a war with our thoughts. No! Over time, our thinking does quiet down, but that's only because we're NOT getting into a war with our thoughts.

When we privilege the silence of the mind over discursive thought, it becomes harder to be with discursive thought when it's arising, which is often! Here is Jason Siff (2010), a meditation teacher who wrote a book titled, "Unlearning Meditation."

"It is quite natural for us to develop a hierarchy of meditative states. At the top are what we consider optimal states of mind, such as mental clarity, equanimity, mindfulness and deeply tranquil experiences that are wakeful. Near the bottom are those experiences that are considered mundane or uninteresting. Generally, at the very bottom are negative emotional or painful states of mind. This hierarchy of meditative states may not be explicitly stated in anything you have read or heard, but it has been reinforced by other meditators and teachers alike. It comes up as a word or phrase describing how you feel about an experience. Or it is seen right there in the meditation as part of the running commentary on your experiences. When I ask people to look at how their hierarchy operates in their sittings, they sometimes feel as though they are being asked to let go of the optimal states they experience. That is not the case. It is not about letting go of optimal states but about seeing how you assess your experiences using them as a standard for comparison. And by asking you to look at those experiences that have been devalued on account of such comparisons, I am not asking you to dwell on those experiences but to consider that by devaluing them it becomes hard for you to be with them and learn from them" (p. 194).

**REFERENCES & FURTHER READING**

Beer, J. S. (2007). The default self: Feeling good or being right? *Trends in Cognitive Sciences, 11,* 187–189.

Brewer, J. A., Worhunsky, P. D., Gray, J. R., Tang, Y. Y., Weber, J., & Kober, H. (2011). Meditation experience is associated with differences in default mode network activity and connectivity. *Proceedings of the National Academy of Sciences, 108,* 20254–20259.

Ellamil, M., Fox, K. C., Dixon, M. L., Pritchard, S., Todd, R. M., Thompson, E., & Christoff, K. (2016). Dynamics of neural recruitment surrounding the spontaneous arising of thoughts in experienced mindfulness practitioners. *NeuroImage, 136,* 186–196.

Farb, N. A., Segal, Z. V., Mayberg, H., Bean, J., McKeon, D., Fatima, Z., & Anderson, A. K. (2007). Attending to the present: Mindfulness meditation reveals distinct neural modes of self-reference. *Social Cognitive and Affective Neuroscience, 2,* 313–322.

Killingsworth, M. A. & Gilbert, D. T. (2010). A wandering mind is an unhappy mind. *Science, 330,* 932–932.

Leary, M. R. & Gohar, D. Self-awareness and self-relevant thought in the experience and regulation of emotion. In J. J. Gross (Ed.). (2014). *Handbook of emotion regulation, second edition.* (pp. 376–392). New York: The Guilford Press.

Mason, M. F., Norton, M. I., Van Horn, J. D., Wegner, D. M., Grafton, S. T., & Macrae, C. N. (2007). Wandering minds: The default network and stimulus-independent thought. *Science, 315,* 393–395.

Querstret, D. & Cropley, M. (2013). Assessing treatments used to reduce rumination and/or worry: A systematic review. *Clinical Psychology Review, 33,* 996–1009.

Siff, J. (2010). *Unlearning meditation: What to do when the instructions get in the way.* Boston: Shambhala Publications.

Smith, J. M., & Alloy, L. B. (2009). A roadmap to rumination: A review of the definition, assessment, and conceptualization of this multifaceted construct. *Clinical Psychology Review, 29,* 116–128.

9

# The Movie in Your Mind: Mindfulness of Thinking

**9**

## Key Points

+ Thinking is totally natural; it's not an "enemy" of mindfulness practice!

+ If we don't honor the power of thought, negative thoughts can turn into negative feelings and affect our well-being.

+ We are generally spellbound by our inner dialogue.

+ Mindfulness lets us clearly observe our thinking and helps us to develop a wise relationship to our thoughts.

## Practice Instructions

+ Sit in a posture that's comfortable yet upright, feet on the floor and hands in your lap.

+ Let your eyes close or gaze down at the ground in front of you.

+ Feel gravity and the weight of your body. Notice where your body touches the ground.

+ Take a few deep breaths, noticing any ease or relaxation on the exhalation.

+ Become aware of your whole body sitting.

+ Take a few more moments to feel the sensations of breathing in and breathing out.

+ First, practice labeling thoughts. Every time a thought arises (a word or picture), make a soft mental note, "thinking." Gently let go, and bring your attention back to your breathing.

+ Next, practice being mindful of thoughts themselves. Pay attention to any words or images that appear in your mind. Try not to get lost or entangled in their stories; just observe. Notice what happens to them.

+ When you're ready, let your eyes open and look around the room.

 ### Take-Home Practice

1. Pay attention to your thinking this week. Notice how thoughts and feelings are connected.

2. If you're feeling down, see if you can notice the words and pictures that are going through your mind. Can you be aware of your thinking rather than believing it?

 ### Journal Suggestions

1. What surprised you about this lesson?

2. How does your inner narrator treat you? Is it kind or cruel?

3. How do you think you can use this lesson in your daily life?

# GROOVES IN THE MIND: HEARTFULNESS FOR ONESELF

## The Basics

This lesson follows up on the first heartfulness lesson by using a metaphor of water flowing down a hill for the way that neuroplasticity works when we practice heartfulness and cultivate positive mind states. Review neuroplasticity to explore how we can use heartfulness to create new, healthy habits that bring more happiness and ease.

---

**LEARNING OBJECTIVES**

1. To define neuroplasticity.
2. To understand the link between repeated practice—heartfulness—and changes in the body and brain.
3. To learn a method of practicing heartfulness for oneself.

---

**LESSON 10 IN BRIEF: A SYNOPSIS**

## Grooves in the Mind: Heartfulness for Oneself

**1. Check in & review:**
Who practiced at home? What experiences or questions came up?

**2. The mind is built to learn.**
Discuss how our minds learn through patterns and repetition. How did you learn how to tie your shoes? To walk? What is muscle memory? **Neuroplasticity** is the brain's ability to change shape and reorganize neural connections, especially in response to experience or following injury.

**3. We're always learning something.**
Use the analogy of water carving a channel in a hillside to discuss "neurons that fire together wire together." If we think angry thoughts, or stressful thoughts all day, we are practicing anger or stress just like playing scales or doing athletic drills can carve grooves in our mind.

Mindfulness practice increases pathways for attention, concentration, and balance. Heartfulness carves new pathways for kindness and other positive mind states.

### Practice Instructions: Heartfulness for self

◆ Sit in a posture that's comfortable and upright, feet on the floor and hands in your lap.

◆ Let your eyes close, or gaze down at the ground in front of you.

- Feel gravity and the weight of your body. Notice where your body touches the ground.

- Become aware of your whole body sitting and breathing.

- Picture someone you like who you see regularly. Notice how you feel inside.

- Imagine this person sending kind wishes *to you*, repeating three or four simple phrases silently, "May you be happy . . . May you be healthy . . . May you be peaceful."

- Let go of their image and begin offering those kind wishes to yourself. Repeat the phrases silently and slowly, "May I be happy . . . May I be healthy . . . May I be peaceful . . . May I be kind and accept myself just as I am." Feel free to choose different phrases of your own.

- When you're ready, let your eyes open and look around the room.

 **Discussion Questions**

- Were you able to imagine a friend or relative sending you good wishes? How did that feel?

- Were you able to send some good wishes to yourself? How did it feel?

- Did anyone notice a voice inside saying, "This is stupid," or "I don't deserve this?"

- How many people used the phrases I suggested? How many people used their own? Anyone willing to share one or two of their phrases? What else did you notice?

 **Take-Home Practice**

1. Try sending good wishes to yourself once or twice this week, perhaps before you go to bed or some other time when you're not doing anything.

2. If you notice yourself feeling stressed out, try taking a few mindful breaths and then send kind wishes to yourself. Notice how this feels.

# Grooves in the Mind:
# Heartfulness for Oneself

## Lesson Outline

- Our minds are built to learn. They learn through patterns and repetition.

- Just as water will carve a channel in the hillside, our thoughts and attention will create "grooves" in our mind.

- This is called neuroplasticity. A repeated thought or action will strengthen those pathways in our brain.

- Mindfulness practice increases pathways for things like attention, concentration and balance.

- Heartfulness practice carves new pathways for things like kindness and other positive mind states.

## Lesson

*(Organize the room for mindfulness and engage the students in a transitional activity.)*

Who practiced mindfulness between the last time we did a lesson and today? How did it go? Did anyone remember to use mindfulness during a tense moment?

Today we're going to talk more about how we can strengthen our mind. We understand a lot more today about the human mind than we did even 10 years ago. One thing we know is that it's built to learn. Especially in the first years of life, we're learning all the time. For example, every one of us in this room learned to walk, to talk, to tie our shoes. So, how'd you do that?

*(Students answer.)*

That's right, we figured it out by trying over and over again. We learn through repetition. We fumble around until our muscles learn the right patterns to do all these things. It's called muscle memory. Well, our brain works kind of like a muscle too: The more it does something, the easier it remembers it.

As we've said in an earlier lesson, the word for this in brain science is neuroplasticity, which means that the shape and the way the brain works is malleable. Its neural networks can change shape and reorganize connections. This happens when we learn, and also when we heal from an injury. It's true for what we do with our bodies, like tying your shoes, or playing sports AND it's true for what we do with our brains and minds—like our thoughts, our moods and emotions. Those get etched in too! Every time we think in a certain way, it's like water running down a hill. What's water do to the ground when it flows downhill?

*(Students answer.)*

Yeah, it carves a channel or groove in the earth. The more the water runs down that track, the deeper that groove gets carved into the hillside. Then, whenever there's water—guess which way it's going to go? Down that same channel.

So, you know what that means? **Because the mind is malleable, because it's designed to learn, it's always learning something.** If you spend your time stressing, you're training your mind to get really good at stressing out. You carve a groove in your mind for stress. If we spend our day feeling angry: guess what, you're training your mind to be angry.

Do you know anybody who's stressed or irritated all the time? Sometimes for no reason? We can teach our

10

minds to do anything—even to be harsh with ourselves! Anybody really hard on yourself sometimes? Maybe you say things to yourself in your mind that if anyone else said to you, you'd get angry? We can put up a good front on the outside, but hate ourselves a lot on the inside.

A lot of us have learned to criticize ourselves as a way of trying to fit in, or to motivate ourselves. The good news here is that we can actually make new tracks, carve new grooves in our mind. Practicing heartfulness can help to shift this pattern and create a new pathway in our minds.

It's just like practicing anything else. If you want to get good at math, or art, or music, or a certain sport—you practice it. You do it a lot, over and over again, and your mind learns and remembers. It's why musicians practice playing scales. You etch those grooves in your mind and those neural networks get stronger. In mindfulness practice, what pathways do you think we're carving out? What skills or qualities are getting stronger?

(*Students answer.*)

That's right. Studies in adults show that over time mindfulness practice strengthens brain circuits associated with attention, emotional balance and stress management.

And in heartfulness practice, we're strengthening kindness. We're running down the same track of certain thoughts and intentions again and again to make them stronger. We're carving that neural groove deeper in the mind. So that, over time, instead of defaulting to stress, or being so hard on ourselves, our mind will naturally tend toward being kind.

## Practice

Let's do some practice. We'll begin the way we usually do with some relaxation and mindfulness. Then we'll try doing some heartfulness practice in a new way.

— Find your posture—comfortable and upright. When you're ready, gently close your eyes (or gaze down in front of you).

— Feel the weight and heaviness of your body—that grounding downward force of gravity. Feel where your body touches the chair or the ground, and let everything sink down through there.

— Just relaxing. Maybe even saying that word silently to yourself, "Relax, relax." Let the tension drain out of your body.

— Take a few deep breaths, feeling any ease or relaxation that comes, as you exhale.

— Take a few moments to just feel your whole body sitting, and breathing.

### HEARTFULNESS PRACTICE

✦ Now let's do some heartfulness. Picture someone in your life that you see regularly who makes you smile. It could be a grandparent or parent; an aunt or uncle; a teacher. You know, it could even be your baby brother or sister, or a pet.

✦ See their face in your mind. Imagine them looking at you, smiling. See the warmth, the kindness in their eyes. Now imagine them sending these wishes to you. Hear their voice, or just imagine they're thinking these thoughts and sending them to you: "May you be happy . . . May you be safe . . . May you be peaceful."

✦ Repeat the phrases (or your own) slowly, one at a time. Hearing them sending these wishes to you. See if you can let their friendship and caring in.

✦ "May you be happy . . . May you be safe . . . May you be peaceful."

✦ Notice how you feel inside, receiving these wishes.

✦ Now, let's offer some of these good wishes to ourselves. If this is hard for you, you can try picturing yourself when you were younger. See yourself as a smaller child, and send the wishes to that part of yourself; just being a good friend to yourself.

✦ "May I be happy... May I be safe... May I be peaceful... May I be kind to myself, and accept myself just as I am."

✦ Repeat the phrases silently, sending these good wishes to yourself.

✦ If your mind wanders, that's okay. When you notice, gently let go and bring your attention back to offering those good wishes again.

*(Ring the bell.)*

✦ When you're ready, you can let your eyes open slowly. Look around the room. Notice how you feel, and how it feels in the room right now.

 ## Discussion Questions

— How many people were able to imagine their friend or relative sending them good wishes? How did that feel?

— How many people were able to send some good wishes to themselves? How did it feel?

— Did anyone notice a voice inside that argued, or said something like "This is stupid." Or "I don't deserve this?"

— What else did you notice?

— How many people used the phrases I suggested? How many people used their own? Anyone willing to share one or two of their phrases?

 ## Take-Home Practice

1. Try sending good wishes to yourself once or twice this week, perhaps before you go to bed or some other time when you're not doing anything.

2. If you notice yourself feeling stressed out, try taking a few mindful breaths and then send kind wishes to yourself. Notice how this feels.

 ## Journal Suggestions

— How was it for you to practice heartfulness (sending kind wishes) for yourself?

— Knowing that the mind is always learning, always practicing something, are there any current habits of thought or emotion that you want to change? What habits and why?

— When is it easiest for you to practice heartfulness? When is it hardest?

**ALTERNATE ACTIVITIES**

You can also have students try offering heartfulness to themselves as follows:

1. What specific things would you wish for yourself in your life, that would make you happy?

2. Who in your life has or shows heartfulness toward you? Break up in pairs and talk about those people, and what it feels like to be around them.

3. Go back and forth between practicing heartfulness for someone else, and imagining them sending heartfulness to you.

Sometimes, we've proposed that the student becomes the teacher. Here's the assignment: Have the student(s) record a heartfulness practice as if they were leading a period of heartfulness practice. They guide the heartfulness in a way that is tailored to their own particular mind. For example, they might use particular phrases that speak directly to their situation or sensibility. They can then use the recording to practice with their own guided heartfulness instructions.

10

Essentially, they are listening to a recording of their own voice, being guided to do heartfulness for oneself. (This activity requires the capacity to record and listen to audio files.)

## Teacher Notes

Heartfulness for self can be challenging. Be prepared for some students to have a hard time with this. Some may feel surprised that it's hard for them. Others may feel disappointed or dejected or worried.

As with any experience a student has in mindfulness practice, the first response is to connect with empathy and normalize their experience. You might share a personal story to help them recognize that it's okay to be hard on oneself.

Then, try to relate their experience back to the lesson. Point out how those ingrained thoughts are just a pattern, just a habit. They're a groove in the mind that's been carved by thinking in a certain way many, many times (and internalizing the way others may speak to or treat us). Try to emphasize the sense of possibility that this practice offers: a way to dam the river and redirect the flow of its water.

If heartfulness for self brings up a lot of distress, it's also completely fine to simply practice heartfulness for someone else. In this way, we can build up some strength of kindness, eventually offering it back to ourselves.

Sometimes, the grief or sadness that arises is a necessary phase of practice. When this happens, they might turn to mindfulness practice and use the emotional awareness practices described in other lessons of this curriculum.

## Science Supplement

### UNPACKING SELF-CRITICISM

How does self-criticism function in our minds? Sometimes, when we're harsh with ourselves, we're trying to motivate ourselves to reach some goal or accomplish-ment. When we don't succeed, we become rough with ourselves. Maybe we don't like how a project went or we feel disappointed by how we handled a situation. The "tone of voice" of thinking changes—all of a sudden, our thinking is critical and harsh. It's almost as if we're running a little behavioral modification program with ourselves!

In behavioral modification programs, undesired behavior or performance is discouraged by the introduction of an aversive experience. In the case of self-harshness, we are essentially punishing ourselves as a way of training ourselves to produce the desired behavior or outcome. But how well does this work? Is it worth it? Are there ways of motivating ourselves that don't rely on withholding our care from ourselves? With mindfulness, we can pay attention to the levers and mechanisms of self-harshness. And with this experiential insight, we can explore different ways of being with the inevitable joys and sorrows of being human. We can cultivate sources of wholesome intrinsic motivation that serve as the basis for our efforts and aspirations. Accomplishing our goals, when fueled by care and kindness, feels much better than accomplishing goals through self-harshness and judgment.

Sometimes, self-criticism arises as a strategy to stay safe amid threatening people. Hypervigilant self-monitoring may be a strategy to minimize the threat that others may play. Some of these strategies may have developed in childhood, when we were entirely dependent on the adults who cared for us. As the developer of Compassion Focused Therapy, Paul Gilbert (2006) writes, ". . . research suggests that when people feel insecure, because others are seen as threatening and more powerful than the self, heightened self-monitoring, self-blaming, self-criticism and striving to meet other people's expectations of the self can emerge as safety behaviors/strategies, especially where blaming powerful others for their punitive/neglectful behavior would accentuate risk from them. Conceptualizing self-criticisms as forms of safety behaviors/strategies has important implications . . . Rather than see these in terms of maladaptive schema or cognitive distortion, they are linked to safety and self-protection. Paradoxically, however, they can also increase the sense of internal threat" (p. 356).

When we see our self-critical tendencies more clearly, we don't have to battle with our minds or seek to protect ourselves. Instead, we connect moment-by-moment with our basic worth as a human being. We connect with a kind of innocence that is beyond self-blame and self-affirmation.

## RESEARCH FINDING ON SELF-COMPASSION

Mark Leary and a group of researchers from Duke University (Leary et al., 2007) conducted a series of studies examining whether self-compassion helps buffer people against unpleasant "self-relevant" experiences. Self-relevant means experiences where you feel the self is under pressure, like receiving critical feedback, for example. Here are three of their key findings:

1. Self-compassion buffered people against negative self-feelings when imagining distressing social events.
2. Low-self-compassionate people undervalued their videotaped performances relative to objective observers who rated their performances.
3. Self-compassion leads people to acknowledge their role in negative events without feeling overwhelmed with negative emotions.

This is their conclusion: "In general, these studies suggest that self-compassion attenuates people's reactions to negative events in ways that are distinct from and, in some cases, more beneficial than self-esteem" (p. 356).

Kristen Neff (2003), created the Self-Compassion Scale (to the right), which is a validated measure for assessing the level of self-compassion. People are asked to rate how often they behave in the following ways.

This questionnaire might be an interesting practice to complete and discuss.

## SELF-COMPASSION QUESTIONNAIRE

*Please read each statement carefully before answering. To the left of each item, indicate how often you behave in the stated manner, using the following scale:*

| ALMOST NEVER | | | | ALMOST ALWAYS |
| --- | --- | --- | --- | --- |
| 1 | 2 | 3 | 4 | 5 |

____ 1. I'm disapproving and judgmental about my own flaws and inadequacies.

____ 2. When I'm feeling down I tend to obsess and fixate on everything that's wrong.

____ 3. When things are going badly for me, I see the difficulties as part of life that everyone goes through.

____ 4. When I think about my inadequacies, it tends to make me feel more separate and cut off from the rest of the world.

____ 5. I try to be loving toward myself when I'm feeling emotional pain.

____ 6. When I fail at something important to me I become consumed by feelings of inadequacy.

____ 7. When I'm down and out, I remind myself that there are lots of other people in the world feeling like I am.

____ 8. When times are really difficult, I tend to be tough on myself.

____ 9. When something upsets me I try to keep my emotions in balance.

____ 10. When I feel inadequate in some way, I try to remind myself that feelings of inadequacy are shared by most people.

____ 11. I'm intolerant and impatient toward those aspects of my personality I don't like.

____ 12. When I'm going through a very hard time, I give myself the caring and tenderness I need.

____ 13. When I'm feeling down, I tend to feel like most other people are probably happier than I am.

_____ 14. When something painful happens I try to take a balanced view of the situation.

_____ 15. I try to see my failings as part of the human condition.

_____ 16. When I see aspects of myself that I don't like, I get down on myself.

_____ 17. When I fail at something important to me I try to keep things in perspective.

_____ 18. When I'm really struggling, I tend to feel like other people must be having an easier time of it.

_____ 19. I'm kind to myself when I'm experiencing suffering.

_____ 20. When something upsets me I get carried away with my feelings.

_____ 21. I can be a bit cold-hearted toward myself when I'm experiencing suffering.

_____ 22. When I'm feeling down I try to approach my feelings with curiosity and openness.

_____ 23. I'm tolerant of my own flaws and inadequacies.

_____ 24. When something painful happens I tend to blow the incident out of proportion.

_____ 25. When I fail at something that's important to me, I tend to feel alone in my failure.

_____ 26. I try to be understanding and patient toward those aspects of my personality I don't like.

**REFERENCES & FURTHER READING**

Gilbert, P., & Procter, S. (2006). Compassionate mind training for people with high shame and self-criticism: Overview and pilot study of a group therapy approach. _Clinical Psychology & Psychotherapy: An International Journal of Theory & Practice, 13,_ 353–379.

Leary, M. R., Tate, E. B., Adams, C. E., Allen, A. B, & Hancock, J. (2007). Self-compassion and reactions to unpleasant self-relevant events: The implications of treating oneself kindly. _Journal of Personality and Social Psychology, 92,_ 887–904.

Neff, K. D. (2003). The development and validation of a scale to measure self-compassion. _Self and Identity, 2,_ 223–250.

Neff, K. D. & Vonk, R. (2009). Self-compassion versus global self-esteem: Two different ways of relating to oneself. _Journal of Personality, 77,_ 23–50.

# Grooves in the Mind: Heartfulness for Oneself

## Key Points

- Our minds are built to learn. They learn through patterns and repetition.

- Our thoughts and attention will create "grooves" in our mind, like water coursing down a hill.

- In neuroscience, this is called neuroplasticity: "Neurons that fire together wire together." A repeated thought or action will strengthen those pathways in our brain.

- Mindfulness practice increases pathways for attention, concentration, and balance.

- Heartfulness practice carves pathways for kindness and other positive mind states.

## Practice Instructions

- Find your posture, comfortable and upright; feet on the floor and hands in your lap.

- Let your eyes close, or gaze down at the ground in front of you.

- Feel gravity and the weight of your body. Notice where your body touches the ground.

> **DEFINITION:** *Neuroplasticity* **is the ability of the brain to change shape and reorganize neural connections, especially in response to learning, to experience, or following injury.**

- Take a few deep breaths, noticing any ease or relaxation on the exhalation.

- Become aware of your whole body sitting and breathing.

- Picture someone you like who you see regularly. Notice how you feel inside.

- Imagine this person sending kind wishes *to you*, repeating three or four simple phrases silently, "May you be happy . . . May you be healthy . . . May you be peaceful."

- Let go of their image and begin offering those kind wishes to yourself. Repeat the phrases silently and slowly, "May I be happy . . . May I be healthy . . . May I be peaceful . . . May I be kind and accept myself just as I am." Feel free to choose different phrases of your own.

- When you're ready, let your eyes open and look around the room.

## Take-Home Practice

1. Try sending good wishes to yourself once or twice this week, perhaps before you go to bed or some other time when you're not doing anything.

2. If you notice yourself feeling stressed out, try taking a few mindful breaths and then send kind wishes to yourself. Notice how this feels.

## Journal Suggestions

1. How was it for you to practice heartfulness (sending kind wishes) for yourself?

2. Knowing that the mind is always learning, always practicing something, are there any current habits of thought or emotion that you want to change? What habits and why?

3. When is it easiest for you to practice heartfulness? When is it hardest?

10

# ENDING THE WAR WITHIN: EQUANIMITY

## The Basics

This lesson describes the skill of equanimity. Equanimity is about not fighting with our inner experience. When we develop equanimity, dealing with the challenges of life become easier.

**11**

---

**LEARNING OBJECTIVES**

1. To define equanimity.
2. To explain the limitations of always trying to avoid pain.
3. To give an example of how mindfulness practice builds equanimity.
4. To describe two ways of focusing attention to handle a difficulty.

---

**LESSON 11 IN BRIEF: A SYNOPSIS**

## Ending the War Within: Equanimity

**1. Check in & review:**
Who practiced at home? What experiences or questions came up?

**2. Define equanimity.**
Mindfulness is paying attention in a *particular* way. What is "equanimity?" It's about not fighting with our experience, staying balanced. We can go to war inside with a thought or emotion. Anyone know the opposite experience, of not getting bent out of shape and maintaining perspective?

**3. Life includes pleasure and pain; trying to control things makes it more difficult.**
We can't always control the pleasure and pain in life. Like an athlete training, we may need to go through hard stuff to accomplish our goals. Fearing pain makes life harder and wastes our energy.

**4. Equanimity helps us to stay balanced.**
We can train our bodies and our minds. Discuss the analogy of protecting your feet by covering the earth in leather or making shoes; or staying steady in a storm. Discuss how mindfulness practice develops equanimity (e.g., observing an impulse to scratch an itch or move).

### Practice Instructions: Equanimity

◆ Sit in a posture that's comfortable and upright, feet on the floor and hands in your lap.

◆ Let your eyes close, or gaze down at the ground in front of you.

◆ Feel gravity and the weight of your body. Notice where your body touches the ground.

- Become aware of your whole body sitting and breathing.

- When a difficulty or an urge comes up, relax your body or take some soothing breaths.

- Try turning your attention *away* from the difficulty, focusing on a place in your body that feels good or relaxed. You can even open your eyes and look at something soothing.

- Try focusing on the difficult sensations *directly*, staying balanced inside as you feel it. Breathe. Say gently to yourself, "It's okay," or "Just let it be." Be careful not to push yourself—if you start tensing up and can't relax inside, turn your attention away again.

- When you're ready, let your eyes open and look around the room.

 **Discussion Questions**

- How did that go for you? What kind of difficulties came up?

- What was it like to turn your attention away from difficulty? To focus directly on the difficulty?

- Did the breathing help? What about saying words in your own mind? Is this relevant for life?

 **Take-Home Practice**

1. Notice when you naturally exhibit equanimity, remaining aware of what's happening and feeling balanced.

2. When something is difficult this week, see how you can use equanimity to stay balanced. Decide whether you want to focus on the difficulty or turn your attention away from it.

3. When something really good happens this week, notice how your body feels. We can have equanimity with pleasure too. Let the sensations of pleasure flow through your body.

**11**

# Ending the War Within: Equanimity

## Lesson Outline

— We can't always control the flow of pleasure and pain in life.

— Being afraid of unpleasantness makes life harder, scarier, and wastes energy.

— Developing equanimity can lead us to have more confidence in meeting the challenges of being human and the problems that we all face.

— Equanimity is an inner balance that can be developed through mindfulness practice.

— We can find balance by turning our attention away from our difficulties, or by focusing right on them in a calm, steady way.

## Lesson

*(Organize the room for mindfulness and engage the students in a transitional activity.)*

We've been talking about mindfulness a lot, but I want to emphasize that mindfulness isn't just any kind of attention. Does anyone remember how we defined mindfulness? How do we pay attention for it to be mindful attention?

*(Students answer.)*

That's right: in a curious and open way. Another way of saying this is that mindfulness is paying attention with **equanimity**. That's an unusual word. Anyone know what it means? What word does it sound like?

*(Students answer.)*

Equanimity is about not fighting with our inner experience. Do you know that experience of having a thought or some emotion, and then you kind of go to war with it? You start trying to make it go away, or you blame yourself for having that thought or feeling? Maybe someone lets you down and you feel sad, but then you pretend like you don't care, or you just get angry, or you try to distract yourself by pulling out your phone or something? Raise your hand if you know what I'm talking about when I say "we go to war with our experience?"

How many people also know the opposite experience? Someone does or says something that normally would really upset you, or something you were hoping for doesn't work out, and you're disappointed but you don't get all bent out of shape? You're able to maintain some kind of balance inside and keep things in perspective?

Life is intense. Sometimes it can feel so good, and other times it can be really hard. The thing is, we can't totally control when unpleasant or difficult stuff happens. Sure, we can influence things. If we get uncomfortable sitting in one position, we can change positions, right? Or if there's some injustice happening we can get involved and work to change it. But sometimes, pain is unavoidable. And even when we work for change, most of the time the results aren't up to us.

Anybody here play sports?

*(Students answer.)*

So, you know that training to be an athlete is hard. Sometimes it's even painful. At the end of a long run when you're breathing really hard, it's intense. There's some pain. But if we don't have the capacity to stay balanced and hang in there, we're not going to get very far as an athlete.

It's the same in life. If all we ever do is try to avoid pain, life gets complicated and narrow and we might not be able to achieve some of our goals.

Equanimity gives us the ability to keep going even when things are intense. We can train our bodies, and we can train our minds. We can encourage ourselves to keep studying even when we want to get up. We can even train ourselves to stay calm when someone says something mean to us.

If we don't make some peace with pain, we keep fighting a war inside. Either that, or we wind up fidgeting our way through our life. We can spend our whole life fidgeting, trying to avoid pain. That's kind of tiring! We waste a lot of energy trying to avoid unpleasant things we can't actually control.

Do you know the saying that if you want to protect your feet, you can cover the whole world in leather, or you can make some shoes? What do you think that means?

(Students answer.)

Developing equanimity is a little like making your own shoes. We can't always control when our experience is pleasant, but we can prepare our hearts and minds to be balanced even when life is unpleasant.

I want to give you another analogy. When we feel difficult emotions, or something hard happens, we can think of it like facing strong winds. Anyone ever been in or seen a video of a hurricane?

The wind blows so hard that whole trees get uprooted, things get tossed around and busted. With mindfulness practice, we're learning that even though the winds are blowing in our emotional world, nothing inside can be blown over. Intense emotions like anx-

iety or anger can feel like they're going to tear us up inside if we don't act on them, but they won't if we know how to handle them. They won't blow anything over. We learn to accept and feel the impact of emotion and trust that we can weather the storm. And then, if and when we do act, we're coming from a place that's clearer and stronger inside.

This is the skill of equanimity. When we sit still in mindfulness practice, we're literally practicing equanimity. A million different impulses arise, and we just sit there. We feel an itch; we think we must do something *right now*; or we have an intense emotion—and we just let all of it flow through, like you're surfing the waves in your own heart and mind. Instead of going to war, we can roll with things. It's like giving ourselves permission to be right where we're at, letting things be just exactly the way they are inside. Of course, when we're done we might need to take action or make a decision. But while we're practicing, we can just relax and let things be.

As we do this in our mindfulness practice, we build confidence. We get confidence that we can meet the ups and downs of life without being overwhelmed. Mindfulness and equanimity can become like solid, steady friends that we know will be there for us whatever happens. Then some of our worries melt away and we can approach life with more relaxation and confidence.

Anyone ever feel like that? Like you can handle stuff? Come what may, you're going to be all right?

Yeah, that's a kind of equanimity. So, let's practice this. We can focus on relaxing our body and mind—even when something is happening that we don't like. We'll take some soothing breaths, and silently remind ourselves to stay strong and balanced even when things are intense.

## Practice

♦ Find your posture—comfortable and upright. Let your eyes close.

♦ Give your full attention to hearing the sound of the bell, continuing all the way to the end of the tone.

♦ Start feeling the relaxing effects of gravity. Let your body get heavy. Feel the points that are touching the ground and let them take your weight of the body.

♦ Take a few deep breaths, feeling any ease or relaxation that comes, as you exhale.

♦ You can even repeat "relax, relax" a few times silently to yourself. Let any excess tension present in your body drain down and out.

♦ As your body settles, feel the sensations of your whole body sitting.

♦ Bring your attention to your anchor spot, and begin to feel the sensations of breathing in and breathing out. *(Let them sit for at least a minute.)*

♦ Now, as you're sitting, notice if there are any ways that you're trying to change your experience. Maybe you're trying to make a painful sensation go away, or you're bored and want the bell to ring. Maybe you're thinking about food and you want to eat something.

♦ Anything that's pushing you to want something else, or avoid what's happening right now—notice that in your body and mind, and see if you can relax.

♦ If you want, try taking some slow, deep breaths and really focus on the exhale.

♦ Don't underestimate your strength and resilience. We can handle a lot more than we usually think.

♦ Sometimes, to deal with difficulty we turn our attention away from the difficulty and focus elsewhere. Sometimes, we turn toward it and focus right on the difficulty.

♦ To turn away from the difficulty, put your attention on a place in your body that feels relaxed and good. Maybe your hands, or your lips touching, or some other part.

♦ See if you can focus your attention with those pleasant sensations. The difficulty may be persistent—

it may pull your attention—but keep coming back to the pleasantness. You can even open your eyes and find something to look at that's relaxing.

♦ You can also try focusing on the intensity itself. If there's a part of your body that's uncomfortable—some physical pain or difficult emotional sensations—put your awareness into those sensations. Imagine looking through a microscope at those feelings and seeing all their details. See if you can breathe and just observe those feelings.

♦ You might silently whisper a word or phrase to yourself as you do this. Sometimes, I'll say to myself, "It's okay," or "Let it be." See what's useful.

♦ We'll keep going like this for a few more minutes. See if you can stay really still and make peace with whatever is happening right now. You don't have to do this forever—just one moment at a time.

*(Ring the bell.)*

♦ When you're ready, let your eyes open slowly. Notice how you feel; take a look around the room.

 ## Discussion Questions

— How did that go for you? What kind of difficulties came up?

— What was it like to turn your attention away from difficulty?

— What was it like to focus directly on the difficulty?

— Did the breathing help or not? What about saying words in your own mind?

— How do you think this is relevant for your life?

 ## Take-Home Practice

1. Notice any moments when you naturally have equanimity, when you're connected to what's happening and able to stay balanced.

2. When something gets difficult this week, see how you can use equanimity to stay balanced. Decide whether you want to focus on the difficulty or turn your attention away from the difficulty.

3. When something really good happens this week, notice how your body feels. We can have equanimity with pleasure too. Let the sensations of pleasure flow through your body.

 **Journal Suggestions**

1. How do you see equanimity fitting into your life or helping you?

2. In what aspects of your life do you already have a lot of equanimity?

3. In what aspects of your life or your feelings do you have less equanimity?

 **Teacher Notes**

One of the key points in this lesson comes during the practice instructions: "Don't underestimate your strength and resilience. We can handle a lot more than we usually think." In teaching this lesson, try to help students identify the ways in which they already have some equanimity, some balance and resilience, in their lives. Mindfulness helps to strengthen that natural ability we have by slowly building up our equanimity and associated states like patience.

When doing the practice, it's also important to distinguish between observing a difficult or intense experience with equanimity, and pushing oneself and tightening up inside. If we get too tight, resisting or forcing ourselves to stay with something painful, we don't actually develop equanimity. Some resistance is natural; we can place our attention there and work to soften any contraction of mind or body around the edges. But too much, and we just start waging war again inside.

If you engage in a discussion about where we do and don't have equanimity, students may focus automatically on the most difficult thing(s) in their life, the areas where they have the *least* equanimity. Explain that equanimity grows slowly, like an athlete building their endurance or strengthening a muscle. In thinking about the places they want more equanimity, encourage them to work first on areas that aren't as difficult.

 **Science Supplement**

The term "mindfulness" has been used in many different ways—it is like a bag into which many things have been put. Clarity is in order. In scientific descriptions of mindfulness, typically two aspects have been emphasized. One is present-time awareness. Present-time awareness can be considered a combination of *stability*, *clarity* and *alertness*. But present-time awareness is only one half of the picture. Mindfulness is present-time awareness *plus* equanimity. Equanimity can be defined as a sense of cognitive-emotional balance where there is no compulsion to act out our preferences. It has a number of connotations: ease, non-reactivity, non-manipulation of experience, and the toleration of the arising, intensification, weakening and disappearance of subjective experiences.

Equanimity is often confused with indifference or passive acceptance of suffering in the world. This is a misunderstanding. Equanimity only entails openness to this moment—it does not imply that we must passively accept the circumstances or should not make efforts to create change. We can be equanimous with our present-time experience and be deeply committed to changing and improving the conditions in the world.

In an important article on the topic, Desbordes and her colleagues (2015) write that "Equanimity is a state and dispositional tendency that can be developed over time through specific contemplative practices. Equanimity transforms our sensory-perceptual and cognitive-emotional systems to widen our perspective on experience, more readily engage incoming sensory information, and more efficiently disengage cognitive-evaluative and emotional-reactive behaviors when appropriate. Generally, this transformation is more gradual than the development of enhanced meta-awareness."

Let's unpack that sentence. The authors imply that equanimity develops with practice. When we sit still and attend in a careful, open-hearted way, we're developing equanimity. Every time we have an itch as we're sitting, and don't scratch, we're developing equanimity. When we allow the petty annoyances in experience to be in the background and don't get spun out by them, we're practicing equanimity. When we experience some kind of intensity, and neither try to make it last nor vanish, we're practicing equanimity.

In doing this, we often "widen our perspective." When we're struggling, our perspective tends to narrow. This is natural—we focus most of our energy on resolving the problem and protecting ourselves. However, this narrow, almost claustrophobic focus is subjectively unpleasant. Rather than focusing narrowly on the issue, we broaden the perspective to other information and create a sense of "spaciousness." The authors go on to say that the practitioner "more readily engage[s] incoming sensory information." In equanimity, we practice allowing sensory information to flow into awareness. Often, when something is unpleasant, we brace against it. In equanimity, we're allowing sensory experience to arise, intensify, weaken and disappear—all according to its own rhythm, not our preferences. Of course, we may have preferences. Equanimity is not about liking things we don't like. But even if we don't like something, we can relax the compulsion to act based on our preferences. This is alluding to Desbordes' comment that equanimity helps us "more efficiently disengage cognitive-evaluative and emotional-reactive behaviors when appropriate."

Lastly, the authors acknowledge that the development of present-time awareness is likely faster than the development of equanimity.

Equanimity—and related constructs such as nonjudgement—are being studied more carefully now. One study found that present-time awareness in the absence of equanimity was associated with more anxiety and depressive symptoms than if the person had high levels of equanimity but low levels of present-time awareness. Even those low in present-time awareness and low in equanimity seemed to fare better than those high in present-time awareness and low in equanimity. Findings such as these highlight the importance of this skill and the need to emphasize it as a component of mindful awareness.

As the Desbordes (Desbordes et al, 2015) paper acknowledges, equanimity skills tend to develop more slowly than present-time awareness skills. When we experience unpleasantness, it signals threat. Our self-preservation instincts interpret negative stimuli as potential threats, and seek to respond adaptively. Sometimes, however, the threat is essentially a false alarm. But it can be difficult to disengage from a false alarm. Consider the following from Shepherd and colleagues:

"Healthy, adaptive responding to self-relevant, negative emotional information (e.g., threats) entails allocating attentional and cognitive resources to the source of the information to coordinate a contextually appropriate response. In a high-threat context, for example, an appropriate response can be reflexive and involve little or no higher cognitive intervention (e.g., avoiding a snake in one's path without stopping to consider whether it is poisonous). However, if the threat becomes irrelevant (e.g., recognizing the snake is innocuous), an adaptive response is to flexibly disengage attention and redirect focus to other aspects of current moment experience, such as the pursuit of goals or rewards. By contrast, *cognitive and attentional biases that are characteristic of many forms of psychopathology increase the likelihood that individuals will orient attention to negative, self-relevant emotional information, and have difficulties disengaging attention from that material once it has entered the field of awareness"(p. 841).*

These difficulties can prolong and intensify cognitive and physiological responses to negative events, and lead to perseverative, negative self-referential thinking processes such as brooding, rumination and worry, that are known to increase risk for the development of most mood and anxiety disorders. One way that mindfulness practices aim to counter biased processing is through promoting and training nonjudgmental observation of experiences. In mindfulness practices, individuals monitor conscious experiences as they arise in awareness and practice shifting to an observing, "decentered" perspective on them with an attitude of curiosity and nonjudgment. This metacognitive shift in perspective—frequently termed "decentering"—is thought to foster a broad contextual awareness of mental events as subjective, transient events, rather than accurate reflections of reality, or "me." For example, the thought, "I am a failure," might instead be viewed as, "I am having a thought that I am a failure; my thoughts aren't facts."

The "decentering" that is mentioned here reflects an aspect of equanimity—we are widening our perspective and learning to disengage from false-alarm threats.

## REFERENCES & FURTHER READING

Desbordes, G., Gard, T., Hoge, E. A., Hölzel, B. K., Kerr, C., Lazar, S. W., . . . & Vago, D. R. (2015). Moving beyond mindfulness: Defining equanimity as an outcome measure in meditation and contemplative research. *Mindfulness, 6,* 356–372.

Pearson, M. R., Lawless, A. K., Brown, D. B., & Bravo, A. J. (2015). Mindfulness and emotional outcomes: Identifying subgroups of college students using latent profile analysis. *Personality and Individual Differences, 76,* 33–38.

Shepherd, K. A., Coifman, K. G., Matt, L. M., & Fresco, D. M. (2016). Development of a self-distancing task and initial validation of responses. *Psychological Assessment, 28,* 841–855.

**11**

## Ending the War Within: Equanimity

### Key Points

+ We can't always control the flow of pleasure and pain in life.

+ Being afraid of unpleasantness makes life harder, scarier, and wastes our energy.

+ Developing equanimity can bring more confidence in meeting the challenges of life.

+ Equanimity is an inner balance that can be developed through mindfulness practice.

+ We can find balance by turning our attention away from our difficulties, or by focusing directly on them in a calm, steady way.

> **DEFINITION:** *Equanimity* is the ability to stay balanced, with both pleasure and pain, and in dealing with the ups and downs of life.

### Practice Instructions

+ Sit in a posture that's comfortable yet upright, feet on the floor and hands in your lap.

+ Let your eyes close, or gaze down at the ground in front of you.

+ Feel gravity and the weight of your body. Notice where your body touches the ground.

+ Take a few deep breaths, noticing any ease or relaxation on the exhalation.

+ Become aware of your whole body sitting and breathing.

+ When a difficulty or an urge comes up, relax your body or take some soothing breaths.

+ Try turning your attention *away* from the difficulty, focusing on a place in your body that feels good or relaxed. You can even open your eyes and look at something soothing.

+ Try focusing on the difficult sensations directly, staying balanced inside, as you feel it. Breathe. Say gently to yourself, "It's okay," or "Just let it be." Be careful not to push yourself—if you start tensing up and can't relax inside, turn your attention away again.

+ When you're ready, let your eyes open and look around the room.

###  Take-Home Practice

1. Notice any moments when you naturally have equanimity, when you're connected to what's happening and able to stay balanced.

2. When something gets difficult this week, see how you can use equanimity to stay balanced. Choose to focus on the difficulty, or turn your attention away from the difficulty.

3. When something good happens this week, notice how your body feels. We can have equanimity with pleasure too. Let the sensations of pleasure flow through your body.

###  Journal Suggestions

1. How do you see equanimity fitting into your life or helping you?

2. In what aspects of your life do you already have a lot of equanimity?

3. In what aspects of your life or your feelings do you have less equanimity?

**11**

# HANDLING OVERWHELM: THE "FREAK OUT FORMULA"

## The Basics

This lesson explores methods to handle feeling overwhelmed, or when we "freak out." Mindfulness and heartfulness can provide a helpful balance for our nervous system in these states. This lesson can be taught in the regular cycle of the curriculum, or after a particularly stressful event in the school, community, or students' lives.

---

**LEARNING OBJECTIVES**

1. To describe the physiological and emotional signs of feeling overwhelmed.
2. To name the nervous system's three responses to threat.
3. To identify three strategies to handle overwhelm.

---

**12**

---

**LESSON 12 IN BRIEF: A SYNOPSIS**

### Handling Overwhelm: The "Freak Out Formula"

**1. Check in & review:**
Who practiced at home? What experiences or questions came up?

**2. What happens when we feel overwhelmed?**
Who feels overwhelmed sometimes, when things feel like they're bigger than you can handle? If you pour water into a cup that's full what happens? What happens when our nervous system overflows like that cup, when it gets more input than we can handle? Discuss fight, flight, freeze, and how those defense mechanisms are adaptive.

**3. Mindfulness can help us to handle overwhelm.**
Why is it important to learn how to handle overwhelm in life? The first step in learning to handle overwhelm is *recognizing* that we're starting to feel "full" inside. What's that feel like? What are some things you've already learned to do to handle that feeling and dissipate the intense energy?

Ways to handle overwhelm include: talking to a friend, changing your environment (go outside, take a walk), taking a break, or doing something physical.

One thing that happens when we're overwhelmed is that our attention gets fixated and trapped on a particular thought, feeling, or memory. We can balance that by using mindfulness to orient to and connect with our physical environment. The "Freak Out Formula" is one way to do that. Go slowly and keep it real, connecting with the actual experience of your senses more than the idea or thought.

## Practice Instructions

◆ To use the Freak Out Formula:

  – *Name three things you see.*
  – *Then name three things you hear.*
  – *Then name three things you can touch and feel with your hands.*

◆ Go slow and keep it real, focusing on the actual sensory experiences. You can also include smells or tastes.

 **Discussion Questions**

◆ How did it feel? How many people felt kind of silly or funny doing it? How many people felt more relaxed or settled after doing it once or twice?

◆ Why do you think noticing things around you might help you feel more relaxed or at ease?

◆ When are some times when you might want to use the Freak Out Formula? Is there anyone in your life to whom you'd like to teach this?

 **Take-Home Practice**

◆ Pay attention to how you feel this week. See if you can catch the first signs of starting to feel "full" *before* you get overwhelmed. How can you take a break, pause, or shift things?

◆ Try the Freak Out Formula a couple of times—if you're feeling overwhelmed, or even just as a way of practicing mindfulness. Notice any changes in how you feel.

# Handling Overwhelm:
# The "Freak Out Formula"

## Lesson Outline

— Feeling overwhelmed, or "freaking out" is completely normal and natural.

— It happens when the amount of stimulation (the energy or activation in our nervous system) is larger than our capacity to handle or metabolize that energy.

— How do you know when you're freaking out? What's it feel like?

— When overwhelmed we can freeze, go numb, melt down, go into hyperdrive, and so on.

— What are some ways that you've learned to handle overwhelm?

— One thing that happens when we're overwhelmed is that our attention gets fixated and trapped on a particular thought, feeling, or memory.

— We can balance that by using mindfulness to orient to and connect with our physical environment. The "Freak Out Formula" is one way of doing that.

## Lesson

*(Organize the room for mindfulness and engage the students in a transitional activity.)*

Did anyone remember to use mindfulness since our last lesson? When?

We've been talking about how mindfulness can help us feel less stressed and get better at the things we enjoy in life. Today, I want to talk about how it can help if we feel overwhelmed. How many people ever get overwhelmed, where it feels like things are bigger than you can handle?

*(Students answer.)*

Yeah, me too. We all feel overwhelmed sometimes; it's totally natural. What happens if you pour water into a cup, and you keep pouring after it's full?

*(Students answer.)*

Right—it overflows. Well, that's what happens when we get overwhelmed. When the amount of input we're getting in our nervous system is greater than our capacity to handle it, we feel overwhelmed. It's a bit like eating too much and feeling sick!

Does anyone know what our nervous system does when it's overwhelmed, when there's more sensory stimulation or input than it can handle?

*(Students answer.)*

Some of the "old brain" programs take over. We might try getting angry and aggressive—the fight response—or feel scared and try to get away—the flight response. Those are defense mechanisms to try to manage all the energy in our body. But if that energy keeps increasing, or if we can't fight or flee, you know what we do?

*(Students answer.)*

That's right—we freeze. We go numb, shut down, or just collapse. Anyone know why our old brain makes us freeze when we feel overwhelmed?

*(Students answer.)*

Yes, it's adaptive. That part of our nervous system thinks we might die! And in the wild, if you can't run and you can't fight, freezing and going numb is your next best option. Predators usually don't bother hunting something that already looks dead.

Sometimes we might actually be in a situation where our physical survival is threatened. But a lot of the time, we're just overwhelmed by stuff that isn't actually threatening our life—like a test, or what someone said to us before school. And if we don't know how to handle feeling overwhelmed, we can end up freaking out and doing all kinds of crazy stuff. We might say or do something we regret, blow up at someone, freeze, or get depressed and miss an opportunity.

The more tools we have to handle overwhelm, the better equipped we are for our lives, our work, and our relationships. **We can use mindfulness to handle feeling overwhelmed.** The first step is being mindful enough to **recognize** when we're starting to get overwhelmed. How does it feel for you when you start to get overwhelmed?

*(Students answer.)*

Great. Yeah, it can feel different for each of us, but basically there are all kinds of signs in our bodies, our hearts, and our minds.

*(Summarize as appropriate: changes in breath, body temperature, sensations of constriction, tightness, or buzzing; feelings of fear, anxiety, irritation, agitation; thoughts racing, going blank, and so on.)*

When we recognize those changes, we can use it as a signal to address the overwhelm. It's like noticing that the cup is almost full of water, and if we don't change something soon it's going to overflow! So, what have *you* found that helps you handle feeling overwhelmed?

*(Students answer.)*

We each know something about how to deal with this stuff already or we probably wouldn't be where we are today. A lot of the things you mentioned—including mindfulness—are basically helping us take a break and *shifting our physiology* so that our nervous system can relax some of the overcharge it's experiencing.

Remember, that feeling of overwhelm is a sign that there's too much input. So, if we can hit pause—if we can stop adding water into the cup—that usually helps. That might look like a change of scenery, going outside; it could be putting things on hold and dealing with them later. One of the main ways to help our body and mind come back into balance is talking to someone you trust who's not stressed. Conversation and social engagement is often a reliable way to help calm down.

How many people find talking to a friend, a buddy, or a close relative helpful when you're stressed out?

It's also good to have some tools we can use on our own. This is where what we call the "Freak Out Formula" comes in. It's like a recipe to keep from losing your cool when stuff gets hard.

When we're overwhelmed, our attention gets stuck on a certain thought, memory, feeling, or sensation. It's like getting pulled into a whirlpool. To keep from getting totally sucked in and spiraling down, we use mindfulness to pull our attention out and anchor it in our external, physical environment.

So, instead of letting our mind run wild with overwhelm, we help it slow down and come back to reality by practicing mindfulness of three things: things we can see, hear, and touch—concrete, direct, sensory experiences.

The Freak Out Formula goes like this: first, name three things you can see; then, three things you can hear; and last, three things you can touch and feel. Then repeat. You keep cycling through each of those senses until you start to feel more settled. We're using mindfulness to notice our actual experience of this moment. You can do it aloud, or silently.

There are two tricks to getting the Freak Out Formula to work. First, go slowly, really noticing each thing you name. Second, notice the actual, *real* experience rather than the *idea* about it. So, for example, instead of saying "I see a tree" you would say, "I see brown and green." Instead of "I hear a car" you would say, "I hear a rumbling sound."

So, let's give this a try together as a group. We'll name three sights, then three sounds, and then three things you can touch and feel. Raise your hand and I'll call on you. Each person offer just one thing you notice.

*(As the students offer their answers of things they notice in each sensory domain, help them to distinguish between the idea/concept and the actual experience. After three visual experiences are offered, prompt them to switch to sounds, and so on).*

Great. Let's try this on our own, silently now. Hopefully no one's feeling overwhelmed right now, but we can still go through the steps to learn how it works. We'll just do this silently, but you can you do it out loud when you're alone. We'll start with eyes open, using the Freak Out Formula, and then go right into some basic mindfulness of body and breath.

Who can tell me how it goes? Three things . . . *(Students answer.)*

That's right. Three things you see, three things you hear, three things you touch, then repeat. And the two tricks?

*(Students answer.)*

Yup—go slowly and keep it real, using mindfulness to name and notice the actual quality of the experience rather than the word or the idea we use to label it.

## Practice

So, you can start sitting in any position.

◆ Begin to look around the room slowly, and silently name three things that you see. *(Allow some time.)*

◆ When you're ready, pay attention to hearing. Silently name three sounds.

◆ And then notice three things you can touch, naming the textures you feel.

◆ When you're done with one cycle, start again. Take your time, and keep it real. *(Let students experiment for a couple of minutes.)*

◆ Notice how you feel now, after a couple of minutes of practicing the Freak Out Formula. Let's transition from here into some formal mindfulness practice.

◆ Find your posture, comfortable and upright. If it feels all right, let your eyes close.

◆ Feel the relaxing effects of gravity, noticing its downward force and letting the body get heavy. Let any excess tension present in your body drain down and out.

◆ Take a few deep breaths, and when you exhale, feel any relaxation in your body.

◆ Let yourself become aware of your whole body sitting.

◆ Allow your attention to settle on your anchor. Feel the sensations of breathing in and breathing out. Notice each in-breath and out-breath as clearly as you can.

*(Ring the bell.)*

◆ When you're ready, you can let your eyes open slowly. Notice how you feel.

**Discussion Questions**

— How many people were able to go through the steps of the Freak Out Formula before we started practicing mindfulness formally?

— How did it feel? How many people felt kind of silly or funny doing it? How many people felt more relaxed or settled after doing it once or twice?

— Why do you think noticing things around you might help you feel more relaxed or at ease?

— What are some times when you might want to use the Freak Out Formula? Is there anyone in your life to whom you'd like to teach this?

**TAKE-HOME SUGGESTIONS**

1. Over the next few days, pay attention to how you feel. See if you can catch the first signs of starting to feel "full" *before* you get overwhelmed. How can you take a break, pause, or shift things?

2. Try the Freak Out Formula a couple of times—if you're feeling overwhelmed, or even just as a way of practicing mindfulness. Notice any changes in how you feel.

 **Journal Suggestions**

1. Have you ever used mindfulness practice to help you when you feel overwhelmed? What did you do and how did it help?

2. Is there anything about what you learned today that might be helpful in times of great stress or difficulty? What?

**ALTERNATE ACTIVITIES**

If students have trouble focusing or settling down, you can have them write down each of the things they notice while doing the Freak Out Formula. You can also include other physical senses in the practice like smell and taste. (Since there is not always something to smell or taste, these are not emphasized in the lesson).

Another useful way of helping the nervous system to settle and relax is by modulating the out-breath. Breathe in and then extend the exhalation long and slow. If helpful, have them count silently to five as they breathe out.

You can also have students practice the Freak Out Formula in pairs, taking turns sharing out loud with one another three things they see, hear, and touch.

 **Science Supplement**

The practices in this lesson are based upon the trauma therapy work of Peter Levine. Orienting to the environment and social engagement are two primary methods for regulating the nervous system in response to an overload of sympathetic arousal (fight-flight). This can have a calming and grounding effect on the body-mind.

Levine writes that "Orienting responses are the primary means through which the animal tunes in to its environment. When an animal senses a change in its environment, it responds by looking for the source of the disturbance . . . The animal orients itself toward a potential mate or source of food, and away from danger. These responses are constantly merging into one another and adapting to allow for a range of reactions and choices."

Our autonomic nervous system (ANS) is often described as having two parts: the sympathetic and parasympathetic nervous systems. The former is akin to the gas pedal in a car, activating the mind-body with a range of arousal, from mild interest to intense fight or flight. The latter applies the brakes, responsible for our systems of "rest and digest" along with the freeze response.

Stephen Porges suggests that it's more accurate to think of the ANS as having *three parts*, adding the social engagement system as a corollary yet distinct part of the parasympathetic nervous system. Engaging the eyes, head, and neck by looking around and orienting to our environment in a relaxed and natural way activates the Ventral Vagus nerve and—when the environment is free of threat—sends signals of safety directly to the ANS, calming any excess sympathetic activation. The Freak Out Formula is meant to mimic and induce this basic practice of looking around and orienting to one's environment. You can supplement your discussion with the students by playing a You-Tube video of prey like deer or antelope grazing in the wild, and discuss why they pick their heads up and look around every few minutes. In a similar fashion, using the eyes, ears, and vocal chords to engage socially with a safe and friendly human being can dampen sympathetic arousal.

## THE "ARC" OF EMOTIONS

When we're freaking out, we're talking about intense emotion. David Barlow, a psychology professor at Boston University, is a leading researcher of interventions to support emotional well-being.

In managing difficult emotions, he highlights the centrality of understanding emotions—and becoming more aware of emotions. Often, mindfulness students are hungry for techniques to modulate or change their emotions. Those can be helpful, but it is critically important to become more awake to our emotional life and understand our emotions in empowering ways.

In Barlow's treatment guide, he highlights the value of tracking the **ARC** of emotions. **ARC** stands for: **Antecedent, Response, and Consequences**

Antecedents are the events, situations, memories, or imaginations that trigger emotional experiences. The Antecedent/trigger might have just occurred, or it might be in your distant memory. The Response includes all the emotions/thoughts/behaviors that follow the Antecedent. Consequences can be short or longer term. Emotional and behavioral Responses have Consequences on your life. Sometimes the short-term Consequences of our Responses are positive, but long-term Consequences might be problematic.

To support the growing awareness of the ARC, another prominent emotion researcher, Paul Ekman, recommends keeping a "trigger journal." Here's what Ekman recommends: when someone has an emotional episode, they should write down in detail what unfolded. They might include the Antecedent (trigger), the Response and any Consequences that might have unfolded. Do this for a few weeks and then read the journal to identify the themes. This can help people see where one's emotional Responses are appropriate and where the Responses cause trouble.

## A NOTE ON ATTRIBUTION

The "Freak Out Formula" was named by Anthony Twig Wheeler, based on the work of both Dr. Peter Levine and Steve Hoskinson, who granted permission to share these ideas.

### REFERENCES & FURTHER READING

Barlow, D. H., Farchione, T. J., Fairholme, C. P., Ellard, K. K., Boisseau, C. L., Allen, L. B., & May, J. T. E. (2010). *Unified protocol for transdiagnostic treatment of emotional disorders: Therapist guide.* New York: Oxford University Press.

Beauchaine, T. P., Gatzke-Kopp, L., & Mead, H. K. (2007). Polyvagal theory and developmental psychopathology: Emotion dysregulation and conduct problems from preschool to adolescence. *Biological Psychology, 74*(2), 174–184.

Levine, P. & Frederick, A. (1997). *Waking the tiger: Healing trauma: The innate capacity to transform overwhelming experiences.* Berkeley, CA: North Atlantic Books.

Porges, S. W. (2009). The polyvagal theory: New insights into adaptive reactions of the autonomic nervous system. *Cleveland Clinic Journal of Medicine, 76*(Suppl. 2), S86.

Wagner, D. (June 2016). Polyvagal theory in practice. *Counseling Today.* ct.counseling.org/2016/06/polyvagal-theory-practice

**12**

## Handling Overwhelm: The "Freak Out Formula"

### Key Points

◆ Feeling overwhelmed—"freaking out"—is completely normal and natural.

◆ It happens when the amount of stimulation (the energy or activation in our nervous system) is larger than our capacity to handle or metabolize that energy.

◆ When overwhelmed, we can freeze, go numb, melt down, go into hyperdrive, and so on.

◆ Being able to handle overwhelm makes us better equipped for life, work, or relationships.

◆ What are some ways that you've learned to handle overwhelm?

◆ Mindfulness gives us a lot of tools to handle overwhelm.

◆ One thing that happens when we're overwhelmed is that our attention gets fixated and trapped on a particular thought, feeling, or memory.

◆ We can balance that by using mindfulness to orient to and connect with our physical environment. The "Freak Out Formula" is one way of doing that.

**12**

### Practice Instructions

◆ Ways to handle overwhelm include: talking to a friend, changing your environment (go outside, take a walk), taking a break, or doing something physical.

◆ To use the Freak Out Formula:

– *name three things you see,*
– *then three things you hear,*
– *then three things you can touch and feel with your hands.*

◆ Go slow and keep it real, focusing on the actual sensory experiences. You can also include smells or tastes.

 ### Take-Home Practice

1. Over the next few days, pay attention to how you feel. See if you can catch the first signs of starting to feel "full" *before* you get overwhelmed. How can you take a break, pause, or shift things?

2. Try the Freak Out Formula a couple of times—if you're feeling overwhelmed, or even just as a way of practicing mindfulness. Notice any changes in how you feel.

 ### Journal Suggestions

1. Have you ever used mindfulness practice to help you when you feel overwhelmed? What did you do and how did it help?

2. Is there anything about what you learned today that might be helpful in times of great stress or difficulty? What?

# DIFFICULT EMOTIONS: ANGER

## The Basics

This lesson addresses mindfulness of anger, providing strategies for working with anger internally as well as working interpersonally.

---

### LEARNING OBJECTIVES

1. To identify two reasons that anger is important in our lives.
2. To explain what makes the difference between anger that helps and anger that harms.
3. To name the two habitual "anger styles" and identify one's own style.
4. To demonstrate the ability to use slow, deep breaths to soothe anger.

---

### LESSON 13 IN BRIEF: A SYNOPSIS

## Difficult Emotions: Anger

**1. Check in & review:**
Who practiced at home? What experiences or questions came up?

**2. Anger can help or harm us.**
"Emotions aren't our fault but they are our responsibility." What's that mean? How many people here feel angry? What's that like? How can anger *help* us? It's a natural response to threat and is there to protect us. How can anger *harm* us? What's it like to be around angry people? Anger can give us bad advice. What are some personal or historical examples of anger causing harm?

A student once came to a teacher, complaining of feeling angry toward someone else. The teacher told them to try "hatred meditation," focusing all their energy on hating that person for one whole hour. How do you think that would feel?

**3. The difference is in how we *relate*. What's your anger style?**
We may respond to anger by blowing up or by suppressing it. What's your anger style? Mindfulness can help us by learning to recognize when we're angry, to handle it early on before it gets too intense. Even when anger is strong, like a force pushing us inside, mindfulness can help soothe it so we can make better choices.

13

## Practice Instructions

- Sit in a posture that's comfortable yet upright, feet on the floor and hands in your lap.

- Let your eyes close, or gaze down at the ground in front of you.

- Feel gravity and the weight of your body. Notice where your body touches the ground.

- Take a few deep breaths, noticing any ease or relaxation on the exhalation.

- Become aware of your whole body sitting and breathing.

- Practice deep soothing breaths. Place one hand on your belly and one hand on your chest.

  - *In the first half of your inhalation, fill your belly. In the second half, fill your chest.*
  - *Breathe out long and slow.*
  - *Notice any relaxation or ease as you breathe out.*
  - *Repeat this a few times.*

- When you're ready, let your eyes open.

 ## Discussion Questions

- Do you think you could do this when you get angry?

- Let's think about a situation making you angry. See how the body feels. Is there any tightness? Is your mind starting to get mad?

- How might mindfulness help?

 ## Take-Home Practice

When something gets you angry this week, see if you can do two minutes of mindfulness practice and tune in to the emotional sensations in the body. When something really good happens this week, notice how your body feels.

**13**

# Difficult Emotions: Anger

## Lesson Outline

— The emotion of anger is a self-protective response designed to help us get safe in response to a threat.

— Anger also can cause harm to ourselves and our relationships.

— The difference is how we relate to anger.

— We usually relate to anger by exploding or imploding.

— Getting familiar with our "anger style" can help us learn how to handle it.

— Mindfulness can help soothe the intensity of anger so we can make choices.

## Lesson

*(Organize the room for mindfulness and engage the students in a transitional activity.)*

One of the things we're learning about emotions is that **they're not our fault, but they are our responsibility.** They're not our fault because we don't choose to feel angry or sad or afraid. Emotions show up inside of us on their own—they never ask our permission! And, we're the only ones who can take care of our emotions. We're like the caretaker for a piece of land. Looking over the land, tending to it, helping the crops grow well.

Today, I want to talk about anger. How many people here get angry? What is it like to be angry?

*(Students answer.)*

Anger is a really important emotion. It's important because it can help us, and because it can harm us. Who can tell me some ways that anger can help us?

*(Students answer.)*

Right, anger is there *to protect us.* It's a natural emotion that we feel when we're threatened. Think back to our ancestors living in the wild—the ones who were able to get angry and mobilize in response to a threat are the ones who survived! So anger is important first of all because it can help us get safe!

Next question: How can anger *harm* us?

*(Students answer.)*

Right, absolutely. It can cause arguments or fights and really mess up relationships. What's it like for you when people around you are angry?

*(Students answer.)*

And how about for you? How many people regret words that you've spoken when you're really angry? When you're angry, do you make your best decisions?

Sometimes I think of anger as giving us bad advice! We need to learn how to recognize when anger is giving us bad advice or it can really cause harm. It can harm our personal relationships. It can even cause harm between communities or countries. Who can give me an example of an episode in history (or currently) where anger and hatred caused a whole lot of pain?

*(Students answer.)*

From the interpersonal to the international level, anger is something we need to learn to deal with. Sometimes it can feel good to be angry, but after-

13

wards there are usually more bad feelings. It's a little like eating food that tastes good but makes you sick afterwards!

One time, a student went to their mindfulness teacher and described how annoyed and angry he was with someone. The teacher gave a strange assignment. The teacher said: I want you to go practice *hatred* meditation. For a whole hour, I want you to focus all of your attention on hating that other person. If your attention wanders off and you think about anything else, or you start paying attention to your breath, immediately bring the attention back to hating that person. How do you think it would feel to do that?

*(Students answer.)*

Yeah, it would be really tiring. It's not so pleasant to be really angry! So, are we in agreement that anger can help us, and it can harm us? Great. What do you think makes the difference between anger helping us or harming us?

*(Students answer.)*

Yeah. **It's all about how we relate to anger, how we respond to it.** We need to learn how to recognize when we're getting angry, and know how to respond.

Mindfulness helps us get familiar with our style of anger. Some of us explode. We get triggered quickly and lash out at others with words or actions. Some of us "implode," meaning that we keep all the anger inside. We stuff it down and don't say anything—sometimes we even blame or get angry at ourselves. What's your style? How many people tend to explode? How many tend to implode? How many people do both?

Mindfulness teaches us how to find that balance point between suppressing our feelings and acting them out aggressively.

There are a few more ways mindfulness can help with anger. First, mindfulness helps us stay more relaxed so anger doesn't build up steam. We learn to recognize anger when it first begins, before it gets really strong. If we can notice anger when it's not too strong, we can calm ourselves down and make better choices before we get overwhelmed.

Even when anger gets intense, mindfulness can help us. We can learn to soothe ourselves with mindfulness. Anger gets our body very agitated and reactive. Do you know that feeling where it seems like there's some kind of force pushing inside you? That's the feeling of anger in the body. How could mindfulness help in moments like that?

*(Students answer.)*

We can learn to soothe anger by breathing slowly, filling up the belly, chest—even up to the shoulders with our breath, then breathing out long and slow. We'll practice that in a minute.

Mindfulness can also help us to be wiser during moments of anger. In the intensity of the moment, we can remember maybe just one thing. For me, if I'm angry, I sometimes tell myself, "This can't end well. If I act out this anger, it can't end well." What would be one thing for you to remember when you get real mad? What words could you tell yourself?

*(Students answer.)*

## Practice: Introduction

Great. Let's practice taking some deeper breaths. First, let's practice getting the breath into the belly. Place one hand on your belly and one hand on your chest. Try breathing in through your nose so that your belly moves a lot but the hand on your chest stays almost totally still. When you breathe out, let it be long and slow. *(Allow some time.)*

Were people able to do that? Okay, good. Now let's try filling the belly with the first half of the breath and then breathing into the chest with the second half of the breath. Breathe out long and slow. Let's try that for a few breaths. *(Allow some time.)*

How did that feel? All right, now let's do some formal practice incorporating this deep breathing.

### PRACTICE

✦ Find your posture—comfortable and upright. If it feels all right to you, let your eyes close.

✦ Listen to the sound of the bell with all of your attention, all the way to the end of the tone.

✦ Start to feel the relaxing effects of gravity. Let your body get heavy. Feel the points that are touching the ground and let them take the weight of your body.

✦ Take a few deep breaths, feeling any ease or relaxation that comes, as you exhale.

✦ You can even repeat "relax, relax" a few times silently to yourself. Let any excess tension present in your body drain down and out.

✦ As your body settles, feel the sensations of your whole body sitting.

✦ Now, let's practice taking some of those deep breaths with a long, slow exhalation. Place one hand on your belly and one hand on your chest.

✦ On the first half of your in-breath, fill your belly. On the second half of your inhalation, fill your chest. Then breathe out long and slow.

✦ On the exhale, see if you can feel any relaxation in your body.

*(Ring the bell.)*

✦ You can let your eyes open slowly. Notice how you feel, maybe look around the room.

 ### Discussion Questions

— Do you think you could do this when you get angry?

— Let's think about a situation making you angry. See how the body feels. Is there any tightness? Is your mind starting to get mad?

— How might mindfulness help?

 ### Take-Home Practice

1. When something gets you angry this week, see if you can do two minutes of mindfulness practice and tune in to the emotional sensations in the body.
2. When something really good happens this week, notice how your body feels.

 ### Journal Suggestions

1. What surprised you about this lesson?
2. What did you learn about how anger works inside of you? What is your style of anger?
3. Why do you want to learn to manage anger more effectively?
4. If you could only remember one thing when you feel angry, what would you want to remember? Why?

**13**

## Science Supplement

Mindfulness skills run counter to many aspects of anger and thus may be relevant in the treatment of anger and aggressive behavior. The non-judgmental, accepting attention that characterizes mindfulness is directly relevant as anger is judgmental and impulsive.

Researchers have broken down the process of handling anger into three phases: (1) prevention, (2) working with the intensity once anger is present, and (3) the resolution of anger. Mindfulness can have a role in each of the three phases of managing anger.

Prevention means that we're aware of the process of escalating emotion and we attend to it effectively. For example, mindfulness may help us notice what's happening early in the process of becoming angry or resentful, giving us the opportunity to intervene. We might reappraise the situation in a more empowering way. We might notice changes in our arousal level.

Another key factor is the role that rumination plays in anger. Rumination is associated with increased anger and aggressive behavior, while mindfulness is inversely correlated with rumination. Mindfulness attenuates rumination and in turn, this may attenuate anger.

Mindfulness may also be helpful in the acute intensity of anger. Anger is typically a state of hyperarousal. Mindfulness has a soothing capacity that may be especially relevant for de-escalating intense episodes of anger. Further, mindfulness helps us to make wiser choices, to connect with our values, including our wishes not to cause additional harm. When we can be mindful of the intensity of bodily sensations during anger, we can avoid acting impulsively. This is a practice of equanimity: tolerating the sensations of anger. If the sensations of anger could speak, they would say something like, "Lash out, and I'll leave you alone and stop punishing you." This is a false promise. Acting out our anger can bring relief in the short-term, but it always compounds the problem in the long-term.

Lastly, mindfulness often integrates forgiveness practices that relate to the resolution phase of anger. Sometimes, anger leaves a trace for days, weeks, months, or even years. The reduction of rumination through mindfulness may be relevant here. Mindfulness curricula (including this one) commonly include practices on forgiveness. (See Extra Lesson 22) For some people, this may be especially important in reestablishing a sense of goodwill. Anger that lasts an hour or a day is clearly preferable to anger that lasts a month or a year, hardening into ongoing resentment.

Dr. Borders of The College of New Jersey and her colleagues (Borders, Earleywine, & Jajodia, 2010) conducted two studies examining the relationship between mindfulness and anger. In the journal *Aggressive Behavior*, she writes:

> "With two different samples, we found that people who are mindful are less angry and hostile. Moreover, our results are consistent with the proposed model that the relationships between mindfulness and anger and hostility are partly mediated by lower levels of ruminative thinking . . . Several other proposed mechanisms for mindfulness may influence behavioral aggression. Relaxation is one common outcome of mindfulness practice. Studies have also found that relaxation can decrease aggression, presumably because relaxation decreases physiological arousal. Thus, mindfulness practice may decrease aggression partially through making individuals more relaxed. Another possible mechanism between mindfulness and behavioral aggression is emotion regulation, or the ability to influence the experience and expression of emotions. Common emotion regulation strategies include altering thoughts or behavior in order to better cope with negative emotions. Two studies have found that mindfulness correlates with the ability to regulate negative affect. Moreover, Coffey and Hartman (2008)

found that emotion regulation mediated the association between mindfulness and depressive and anxious symptoms. Likewise, research has found links between aggressive behavior and poor emotion regulation. Thus, mindfulness may decrease aggressive behavior in part because it promotes the ability to cope with and even change negative internal emotions. Mindfulness may also promote better cognitive functioning and flexibility. As discussed above, mindfulness is associated with increased cognitive flexibility. A recent study also showed that participating in mindfulness training led to increases in working memory and sustained attention. Some researchers in fact suggest that mindfulness is a form of 'mental training' that involves self-regulation of attention and cognitive inhibition. On the other hand, aggression is associated with decreased cognitive performance, especially on tests of planning, attentional control, and goal directed behavior. Thus, mindfulness may actually promote better executive functioning, which may prevent some of the cognitive errors that contribute to aggressive behavior. Relatedly, mindfulness may decrease aggression because it decreases behaving in automatic or impulsive ways. Mindfulness should help make people aware of feelings and thoughts when they arise, rather than after they are already acted upon" (p. 40).

**REFERENCES & FURTHER READING**

Borders, A., Earleywine, M., & Jajodia, A. (2010). Could mindfulness decrease anger, hostility, and aggression by decreasing rumination? *Aggressive Behavior, 36,* 28–44.

Chambers, R., Gullone, E., & Allen, N. B. (2009). Mindful emotion regulation: An integrative review. *Clinical Psychology Review, 29,* 560–572.

Coffey, K. A., & Hartman, M. (2008). Mechanisms of action in the inverse relationship between mindfulness and psychological distress. *Complementary Health Practice Review, 13,* 79–91.

Lumma, A. L., Kok, B. E., & Singer, T. (2015). Is meditation always relaxing? Investigating heart rate, heart rate variability, experienced effort and likeability during training of three types of meditation. *International Journal of Psychophysiology, 97,* 38–45.

**13**

# Difficult Emotions: Anger

## Key Points

- Anger is a self-protective response designed to help us get safe in response to a threat.
- Anger can also cause harm to ourselves and our relationships.
- The difference is how we relate to anger.
- We usually relate to anger by exploding or imploding.
- Getting familiar with our personal "anger style" can help us learn how to handle it.
- Mindfulness can help soothe the intensity of anger so we can make better choices.

## Practice Instructions

- Sit in a posture that's comfortable yet upright, feet on the floor and hands in your lap.
- Let your eyes close, or gaze down at the ground in front of you.
- Feel gravity and the weight of your body. Notice where your body touches the ground.
- Take a few deep breaths, noticing any ease or relaxation on the exhalation.
- Become aware of your whole body sitting and breathing.
- Practice deep, soothing breaths. Place one hand on your belly and one hand on your chest.
  - *In the first half of your inhalation, fill your belly. In the second half, fill your chest.*
  - *Breathe out long and slow.*
  - *Notice any relaxation or ease as you breathe out.*
  - *Repeat this a few times.*
- When you're ready, let your eyes open.

 ## Take-Home Practice

1. When something gets you angry this week, see if you can do two minutes of mindfulness practice and tune in to the emotional sensations in the body.
2. When something really good happens this week, notice how your body feels.

 ## Journal Suggestions

1. What surprised you about this lesson?
2. What did you learn about how anger works inside of you? What is your style of anger?
3. Why do you want to learn to manage anger more effectively?
4. If you could only remember one thing when you feel angry, what would you want to remember? Why?

13

# HAPPINESS: GRATITUDE AND GENEROSITY

## The Basics

This lesson explores the cultivation of two positive mind states, generosity and gratitude, as a way of increasing happiness and well-being. It includes references to some of the research that's been done on happiness, as well as a guided practice for enhancing the effects of gratitude and generosity.

**LEARNING OBJECTIVES**

1. To explain societal definitions of happiness.
2. To describe the subjective aspects of genuine happiness.
3. To define the concept of a happiness "set point."
4. To list two ways to feel happier.

### LESSON 14 IN BRIEF: A SYNOPSIS

## Happiness: Gratitude and Generosity

**1. Check in & review:**
Who practiced at home? What experiences or questions came up?

**2. Discuss happiness.**
We all want to be happy. How many people are truly happy? What does society say about happiness? What is genuine happiness? Scientists say that we have a happiness "**set point**," a default level of subjective happiness that stays constant through our life. Research shows we can actually shift our set point.

**3. Generosity and gratitude make us happier.**
One study showed that people felt happier when they spent money on someone else rather than on themselves. How does it feel when you help someone out, or give something freely? Everything in society tells us the opposite—to get as much as we can for ourselves—but that doesn't make us happy! How does it feel to focus on things that you appreciate in life? What's the relationship between gratitude and generosity? Mindfulness can strengthen these qualities and bring more happiness into our lives. When we're happy, we have more happiness to share with others.

14

## Practice Instructions

- Sit in a posture that's comfortable yet upright, feet on the floor and hands in your lap.

- Let your eyes close. Feel gravity and the weight of your body.

- Take a few deep breaths, noticing any ease or relaxation on the exhalation.

- Become aware of your whole body sitting and breathing.

- Think of something you did for someone to help them out, or something you gave to someone.

- Picture it; let it become clear in your mind.

- How did it feel then to do that? How does it feel now? Enjoy any pleasant emotions you feel.

- Think of something specific you're grateful for. Picture it; let it become clear in your mind.

- Notice how it feels to think of that. Let yourself really enjoy any good feelings.

- To end, come back to just feeling your body sitting, breathing.

- When you're ready, let your eyes open and look around the room.

 ## Discussion Questions

- Was it easier to think of something generous? Something that you appreciate? The same?

- How did that work for you? What did you like? What was difficult?

- What were some of the things you did that were generous? For which you felt grateful?

- What's it like to be around someone who's generous? Or who's grateful?

- What's the relationship between generosity and gratitude?

 ## Take-Home Practice

1. Do three acts of generosity before we next meet. Write them down so you don't forget.

2. Each day, take a few minutes to reflect on anything you did that was generous, where you gave somebody something or helped someone. Notice how that feels.

3. Each day, take a few minutes to reflect on three things for which you're grateful. Take time to really feel your appreciation for each of them. Notice how that feels.

**14**

# Happiness:
# Gratitude and Generosity

## Lesson Outline

- We all want to be happy, but how many people are truly happy?
- Studies show that both gratitude and generosity make us happier.
- How does it feel when you help someone out, or give something freely?
- How about when you focus on the things you appreciate in life?
- Giving and receiving are two sides of the same coin. If we know where to look, we can see them flowing in each of our lives.
- We can use the tools of mindfulness to strengthen these qualities of gratitude and generosity, and bring more happiness into our lives.
- And when we're happy, we have more happiness to share with others.

## Lesson

*(Organize the room for mindfulness and engage the students in a transitional activity.)*

How many people did some mindfulness practice since the last time we met? Anyone want to share anything about what they noticed? Did it help you? How?

*(Students answer.)*

Today, I want to talk about being happy. Is there anybody here who *doesn't* want to be happy? We all want to be happy, right?

- Raise your hand if you know anyone who's *not* happy.
- Raise your hand if you know anyone who's *kind of* happy (maybe even you).
- How about this: anyone know someone who is *genuinely* happy?

What does it mean to be genuinely happy? Actually—let me ask you a different question first. What's our society *tell us* about what it means to be happy—the media, TV, music?

*(Students answer.)*

Right: success, money, fame, being young, having nice things. That does bring some happiness. But what if I asked you, what does it mean to be *genuinely* happy? What would you say?

*(Students answer.)*

That's beautiful. I agree—things like family, good friends, our health, education, meaningful work and helping others, expressing our skills, living in peace—those give us a deeper kind of happiness, don't they? Some people even say that the point of life is to learn how to be happy.

Social scientists have done a lot of studies on happiness. There's a theory, based on some of this research, that we each have a "set point" for happiness, **a kind of default level of subjective happiness that stays relatively constant in our life.** It's determined by factors like our genes and personality traits ingrained early in life. This theory has been used to explain why people winning the lottery experience a temporary improvement in their overall state of well-being, and then return to a baseline closer to how they felt before winning.

**14**

A little depressing, huh? Like we can only ever get so happy!

Here's the good news: **The research shows that we can actually change our "set-point."** There are specific things we can do to *increase* that baseline of happiness! For example, they did a study where they gave people between $5 and $20. They told half of them they could spend that money on anything they wanted for themselves, and they told the other half to buy something for someone else. Then they used some questionnaires to measure how happy people felt.

Who do you think was happier? Raise your hand if you think the people who spent the money on themselves felt happier? And who thinks the people who spent the money on someone *else* felt happier?

Those who spent the money on *someone else* reported greater feelings of happiness than those who spent it on themselves. Even when it's a small amount of money, **we feel happy when we give to others.**

Check it out and see if this matches your experience. Think about a time when you gave someone a gift, or helped them out—not because you had to (an adult told you to) but just because you wanted to. How did that feel?

*(Students answer.)*

Yeah, it feels good to be generous. When we give to one another, it makes us happy. Kind of wild, huh? Everything in our society is saying the opposite: get as much as you can for yourself. But giving to others actually makes us happy!

Giving once brings us a temporary, short-term happiness. If we make a habit of being generous, giving to others when we can, over time it can affect our set-point for happiness. Over time, it raises our default state of happiness.

How about when someone does something nice for you, gives you a gift or helps you out. How's *that* feel? Feels good, right? Anyone know the word for that emotion, the good feeling you get when someone does something kind or generous?

*(Students answer.)*

Right, gratitude or appreciation. That's the other side of generosity: When someone gives to us, we feel grateful. And gratitude *also* shifts our set-point for happiness. In fact, having a regular practice of feeling gratitude is one of the most reliable and consistent ways to increase our overall sense of happiness and well-being. If you want to be happier, think of three things you really appreciate every day!

This is where mindfulness comes in. Remember the property of the brain called neuroplasticity: that we can carve new grooves in our mind? Well, we can use mindfulness practice to heighten the effects of generosity and gratitude by paying close attention to how they feel and savoring them. Just like sending kind wishes, when we make a point of dwelling and focusing on these qualities they get stronger. That can help us to feel happier in a genuine way.

## Practice

Let's practice. We'll begin the way we usually do with some relaxation and mindfulness, and then I'll take you through a guided practice noticing how it feels to give and receive.

— Find your posture—comfortable and upright. If it feels all right to you, let your eyes close.

— Listen to the sound of the bell with all your attention, all the way to the end of the tone.

- Start feeling the relaxing effects of gravity. Let your body get heavy. Feel the points that are touching the earth and let them take the weight of your body.

- Take a few deep breaths, feeling any ease or relaxation that comes, as you exhale.

- You can even repeat "relax, relax" a few times silently to yourself. Let any excess tension present in your body drain down and out.

- As your body settles, feel the sensations of your whole body sitting.

## Generosity and Gratitude Practice

◆ Now, let's shift our attention to strengthening generosity and gratitude. We're going to use the same tools we learned to soak in the good.

◆ First, think of one thing you did or said in the last week that was generous: it could be giving something to someone, helping someone, even something simple like holding the door, saying hi, or smiling.

◆ Let that specific event become really clear in your mind. Try to remember where you were, what you or the other person were wearing, what time of day it was.

◆ Notice how it felt to do that generous thing. Can you feel any pleasant feelings or sensations in your body?

◆ How does it feel now to be remembering and reflecting on it? See if you can let yourself focus on and enjoy any feelings of happiness, warmth, or other good sensations you experience. Really let that in.

◆ Next, let's shift gears from giving to receiving. Think of something in your life right now that you're grateful for. Again, make it as specific as possible.

◆ As you think about that, notice how you feel. Let yourself really receive this thing for which you're grateful. How does it feel to appreciate it? Where do you feel that in your body?

◆ When you're ready, think of another thing you're grateful for: a person, something that happened, something you have or enjoy doing. With each thing that comes to mind, take some time to notice how it feels to think of and appreciate it. Let it affect you.

◆ To finish, let's return to mindfulness of the body. Let all of those things go, and just feel the sensations of your body sitting here. You might feel one or two mindful breaths.

*(Ring the bell.)*

◆ Let your eyes open slowly. Notice how you feel, maybe look around the room.

 ## Discussion Questions

- Raise your hand if it was easier to think of something you did that was generous?

- Raise your hand if it was easier to think of something that you appreciate?

- Raise your hand if it was about the same?

- How did that work for you? What did you like? What was difficult?

- What else did you notice?

- What were some of the things you did that were generous?

- What were some of the things for which you felt grateful?

- What's it like to be around someone who's generous? Or who's grateful?

- What's the relationship between generosity and gratitude?

That's right, they're two sides of the same coin: giving and receiving. When we give, we also get something, don't we? We get the pleasure of contributing to someone else. When we receive, we also give something: We give someone else the opportunity to contribute to us and feel good about that. Do you see how they fit together?

**14**

If you start to think about this and look for it in life, it's pretty fascinating. Everything in nature is a cycle of giving and receiving: All life on the planet depends on other life. When we breathe, we give and receive air with the trees; the water that cycles through the land and the atmosphere is giving and receiving. What other things function in this way? How about in human society, are there cycles of giving and receiving there?

 ## Take-Home Practice

1. Do three acts of generosity between now and the next time we meet. Write them down somewhere (or make a note in your phone) so you don't forget.
2. Each day, take a few minutes to reflect on anything you did that was generous, when you gave somebody something or helped someone. Notice how that feels.
3. Each day, take a few minutes to reflect on three things for which you're grateful. Take time to really feel your appreciation for each of them. Notice how that feels.

 ## Journal Suggestions

1. What information in this lesson was most useful or interesting to you?
2. Are there any times when the practice of generosity or gratitude might help you? When?
3. What are some things you can do today that are generous? Name at least three specific things. Tomorrow, come back and write if you were able to do them, and if so, how it felt.

### ALTERNATE ACTIVITIES

– Make a list of as many things as you can for which you feel grateful. Be as specific as possible; instead of "food" write down what you actually ate at a certain meal.

– Make a list of as many generous things as you can that you've done or said in the last week.
– Can you think of things you did that were generous to yourself?
– What are some things you can do that are generous before the end of the day today? Again, be as specific as possible.

 ## Science Supplement

Part of mindfulness is about getting clear about what we value most—what we care about. The trouble is that we've been told what to value by our society, and that may not be what truly matters to us. For example, society definitely tells us to value wealth. But how much happiness does money buy? If you won a million dollars in the lottery, how happy would you be? For how long would you be happy?

Some of the research about money goes against what we might expect. While avoiding poverty makes people happier, having a ton of money doesn't seem to boost happiness very much at all. Here are some conclusions from an important study reviewing the data (Ryan and Deci, 2001):

a. People in richer nations are, in fact, happier than people in poorer nations.
b. Increases in national wealth have not been associated with increases in well-being.
c. Richer people in the United States are only slightly happier than poorer people.
d. Getting richer does not usually result in increased happiness.
e. People who strongly desire wealth are *less happy* than those who do not strongly desire wealth.

One of the reasons that more money doesn't make us much happier is that once we get more, we often start comparing ourselves to people who have even more than we do. So, once you're a millionaire, you feel inferior to those who have ten million dollars. And on it goes . . .

Much of the impact of wealth on happiness seems to be about our thinking and about how we judge ourselves against our peers. One of the leading researchers on well-being, Ed Diener (Diener, Ng, Harter, & Arora, 2010), found that material prosperity predicted a positive *evaluation* of one's life, while psychological prosperity predicted a positive *feeling*. In a survey of worldwide data on income and well-being, he found that:

— Across the globe, income was associated with subjective well-being, but there were "declining marginal effects of income on subjective well-being," meaning that as people got richer, the next thousand dollars of income was less meaningful in terms of yielding well-being.

— Income was a moderately strong predictor of life evaluation but a much weaker predictor of positive and negative feelings.

— Possessing luxury conveniences and being satisfied with one's standard of living were also strong predictors of life evaluation.

— Feelings were most associated with the fulfillment of psychological needs: learning, autonomy, using one's skills, respect, and the ability to count on others in an emergency.

— Two separate types of prosperity—economic and social psychological—best predict different types of well-being.

## GENEROSITY, GIVING, AND HAPPINESS

In a widely cited article from the journal *Science*, Elizabeth Dunn (Dunn, Aknin, & Norton, 2008) explored the relationship between generosity and happiness. She writes:

"Can money buy happiness? A large body of cross-sectional survey research has demonstrated that income has a reliable, but surprisingly weak, effect on happiness within nations, particularly once basic needs are met. Indeed, although real incomes have surged dramatically in recent decades, happiness levels have remained largely flat within developed countries across time. One of the most intriguing explanations for this counterintuitive finding is that people often pour their increased wealth into pursuits that provide little in the way of lasting happiness, such as purchasing costly consumer goods. An emerging challenge, then, is to identify whether and how disposable income might be used to increase happiness. Ironically, the potential for money to increase happiness may be subverted by the kinds of choices that thinking about money promotes; the mere thought of having money makes people less likely to help acquaintances, to donate to charity, or to choose to spend time with others, precisely the kinds of behaviors that are strongly associated with happiness. At the same time, although thinking about money may drive people away from prosocial behavior, money can also provide a powerful vehicle for accomplishing such prosocial goals. We suggest that using money in this fashion—investing income in others rather than oneself—may have measurable benefits for one's own happiness" (p. 1687).

The studies conducted to examine this question found ". . . that spending more of one's income on others predicted greater happiness both cross-sectionally (in a nationally representative survey study) and longitudinally (in a field study of windfall spending). Finally, participants who were randomly assigned to spend money on others experienced greater happiness than those assigned to spend money on themselves" (p. 1687).

**14**

## REFERENCES & FURTHER READING

Diener, E., Ng, W., Harter, J., & Arora, R. (2010). Wealth and happiness across the world: Material prosperity predicts life evaluation, whereas psychosocial prosperity predicts positive feeling. *Journal of Personality and Social Psychology, 99,* 52–61.

Dunn, E. W., Aknin, L. B., & Norton, M. I. (2008). Spending money on others promotes happiness. *Science, 319,* 1687–1688.

Frey, B. S. & Stutzer, A. (2002). What can economists learn from happiness research? *Journal of Economic Literature, 40,* 402–435.

Ryan, R. M. & Deci, E. L. (2001). On happiness and human potentials: A review of research on hedonic and eudaimonic well-being. *Annual Review of Psychology, 52,* 141–166.

14

# Happiness: Gratitude and Generosity

## Key Points

- We all want to be happy, but how many people are truly happy?
- Studies show that both gratitude and generosity make us happier.
- Giving and receiving are two sides of the same coin. If we know where to look, we can see them flowing in each of our lives.
- We can use the tools of mindfulness to strengthen these qualities of gratitude and generosity, and bring more happiness into our lives.
- And when we're happy, we have more happiness to share with others.

## Practice Instructions

- Sit in a posture that's comfortable yet upright, feet on the floor and hands in your lap.
- Let your eyes close, or gaze down at the ground in front of you.
- Feel gravity and the weight of your body. Notice where your body touches the ground.
- Take a few deep breaths, noticing any ease or relaxation on the exhalation.
- Become aware of your whole body sitting and breathing.
- Think of something you did for someone to help them out, or something you gave to someone.
- Picture this and let it become really clear in your mind.
- Enjoy any pleasant emotions you feel.
- Next, think of something you're grateful for in your life. Make it really specific.
- Picture this and let it become really clear in your mind.
- Notice how it feels to think of that event. Let yourself really enjoy any good feelings.
- To end, come back to just feeling your body sitting, breathing.

 ## Take-Home Practice

1. Do three acts of generosity between now and the next time we meet. Write them down somewhere (or make a note in your phone) so you don't forget.

2. Each day, take a few minutes to reflect on anything you did that was generous, where you gave somebody something or helped someone. Notice how that feels.

3. Each day, take a few minutes to reflect on three things for which you're grateful. Take time to really feel your appreciation for each of them. Notice how that feels.

 ## Journal Suggestions

1. What information in this lesson was most useful or interesting to you?

2. Are there any times when the practice of generosity or gratitude might help you? When?

3. What are some things you can do today that are generous? Name at least three specific things. Tomorrow, come back and write if you were able to do them, and if so, how it felt.

14

# MINDFUL COMMUNICATION AND EMPATHY

## The Basics

This lesson introduces the practice of being mindful while communicating, with a focus on developing empathy. Feel free to supplement the mindful communication activity with variations as appropriate.

---

### LEARNING OBJECTIVES

1. To define empathy and its use in life.
2. To practice mindful listening.
3. To demonstrate the ability to offer an empathic reflection of another's statement.

---

### LESSON 15 IN BRIEF: A SYNOPSIS

## Mindful Communication and Empathy

**1. Check in & review:**
Who practiced at home? What experiences or questions came up?

**2. Communication is a central part of life.**
How often do we communicate? There are many ways to be smart: Social and emotional intelligence helps us navigate relationships and be successful in life. How do those intelligences help us in life?

**3. What is empathy?**
Empathy is the capacity to "feel with" someone else. It's an innate capacity that is hardwired in our brain and is adaptive in different contexts. How does it feel to be around someone who is really stressed or angry? We can feel others' emotions. How was it adaptive to our survival to read another's emotions?

How can empathy help us today? **Mirror neurons** fire when we see someone do something, including the way an emotion shows on their face.

**4. We can improve our capacity for empathy.**
What about our society discourages empathy? How is a lack of empathy as a society dangerous? We can improve empathy by practicing it, by listening fully, with a genuine intention to understand.

### Practice Setup

*Get agreement about ground rules for mutual respect, being real and honest.*

*Have students pair up; assign partners or let them choose. Explain that one person is going to tell a short story about something that's happened to them recently and that they care about—positive or negative—while the other person just listens. Give them a little time to consider silently and decide what they're going to share. Demonstrate the activity briefly by having a student tell you a one-minute story, then guessing at how they might be feeling and/or what matters to them in the situation.*

## Practice Instructions

♦ Find your posture, comfortable and upright; feet on the floor and hands in your lap.

♦ Let your eyes close, or gaze down at the ground in front of you.

♦ Feel gravity and the weight of your body. Notice where your body touches the ground.

♦ Take a few deep breaths, noticing any ease or relaxation on the exhalation.

♦ Become aware of your whole body sitting and breathing.

♦ Open your eyes and notice how it feels to be sitting across from your partner. Are you anxious? Do you want to laugh? (*Give one person one to three minutes to share*).

♦ When you listen, give the other person your full and complete attention.

♦ Consider how they might be feeling, or what they might need. What matters to this person? Can you take a guess?

 ## Discussion Questions

♦ Did you lose mindfulness while speaking? While listening?

♦ What made you lose mindfulness? Were you thinking, wanting to speak or respond?

♦ Raise your hand if it was easy to listen like this. Raise your hand if it was hard.

♦ Did anyone notice any impulses other than to listen? Like what? (*Point out that we often like to ask questions, give advice, or tell our own story instead of just listening*).

♦ How many people guessed how their partner felt or what mattered to them?

♦ How did it feel to have your partner listen to you in this way?

♦ How did it feel to hear their guess about how you felt?

 ## Take-Home Practice

1. Practice being mindful while you are speaking. Can you stay aware while you speak?

2. Practice being mindful while you're listening. Can you give whomever is speaking your full and complete attention?

3. Experiment with finding empathy for others. As you listen, consider how they might be feeling, or what matters to them. Take a guess and see if you're understanding them.

**15**

# Mindful Communication and Empathy

## Lesson Outline

- Communicating with and relating to others is a big part of life.

- It feels good to be seen and understood, and that's something we can give to each other.

- Having social and emotional intelligence can help us to navigate relationships and be more successful in life.

- Empathy is an innate capacity. It is hard-wired in our brain and is adaptive in different contexts.

- We can enhance our social and emotional intelligence by strengthening empathy.

- Learning to listen mindfully is one way of developing empathy.

## Lesson

*(Organize the room for mindfulness and engage the students in a transitional activity.)*

We've been expanding the different ways we can be mindful, different parts of our lives we can use to sharpen our mind. Today, I want to talk about an essential area of our lives—something we all do every day. It can make or break our relationships, and help or hinder us in our career. Anyone want to take a guess what that might be?

*(Students answer. Feel free to give them hints: "I'll give you a clue, we're doing it right now.")*

That's right! Communicating. How much time do you spend every day talking, listening, texting, or on social media? Engaging with others makes up a huge part of our life.

Let me ask you another question: How many of you know what it feels like to be misunderstood, or to have someone look right through you? Feels pretty awful, right? What about the reverse, how's it feel when someone really gets you? When you really feel seen and heard and understood?

*(Students answer. If you have more time, the above questions can be expanded into a longer discussion with the entire class or in small groups to increase intimacy and safety.)*

Yeah, it feels great. Well, here's the thing—we can actually get better at that skill of really seeing and understanding each other. And when we're good at that, it can take us real far in life.

At school, we talk a lot about learning. But being smart academically or intellectually is only one kind of intelligence. Does anyone know what other kinds of intelligence there are? How else can we be smart?

*(Students answer; examples: street smart, social, emotional, mechanical, kinesthetic . . .)*

Yeah, there are all of these different ways that we can be smart. When it comes to making a difference in the world and having a happy, meaningful life, *social* and *emotional* intelligence are key. This kind of being smart with people is how we get along and understand others. When we can do that, we're more likely to succeed in the things we care about. What have we learned already with mindfulness that can help us in our relationships?

*(Students answer. Examples: mindfulness of emotions; mindfulness of impulses / response vs. reaction; heartfulness, gratitude, generosity . . .)*

Today I want to talk about empathy, and then practice using it in our communication. Anyone know what that word "empathy" means?

(Students answer.)

Exactly. Empathy is what allows us to see and really "get" other people. Empathy literally means "to feel into." **It's the capacity to feel what someone else is experiencing from the inside, from their point of view.** What's fascinating about empathy is that it's innate; we're wired for it. We're designed to pick up on one another's emotions.

Ever been around someone who's really stressed and anxious, and you start feeling anxious too? If someone came in this room totally freaked out, shouting "Fire!" we'd all feel that in our bodies, right? We'd get a quick shot of adrenaline and fear, and be ready to respond immediately. Or, how about if you're at a store and you find a really young child lost, crying. You'd feel some concern and want to help, right?

So, we've got this natural ability to pick up on the emotions of others and feel them. Why? How could this have helped us when we were evolving? If one person was better at reading emotions on someone else's face—say fear, disgust, or anger—how might that be helpful?

(Students answer.)

Right. It might protect us from eating something that had spoiled, or from getting ourselves in a dangerous situation. What about these days? How might having empathy help us in life?

(Students answer.)

Part of this innate capacity for empathy has been connected to something called "mirror neurons."

Basically, if you see me do something, some of your brain's neurons mimic or "mirror" that behavior as if *you* were doing it yourself. When you see me raise my arms (*raise arms*), your brain pretends you're doing it too. And the same goes for my facial expressions; if my face looks angry, your brain detects that and may mirror the anger. Sometimes it's obvious what we're feeling, other times (especially if we're trying to hide how we feel), emotions flash across our face so quickly they're called micro-expressions.

All of these parts of empathy are innate to a certain degree, but we can develop them if we train ourselves. Our culture often says to do otherwise, though. Anybody have any ideas about things in our lives or society that discourage us from using or feeling empathy?

(*Discuss various aspects of modern life and social institutions that discourage empathy. This could include video games, performance driven academics, competitive economic structures, lack of healthy bonding with a primary caregiver, and so on.*)

If we're not developing empathy as individuals or as a society, how might that be dangerous, in ourselves or our communities?

(Students answer.)

We can train ourselves in empathy and increase our emotional intelligence. If we want to learn how to be mindful with other people, we've got to practice it! So today we're going to do something new. We're going to do an exercise in mindful communication, where we learn how to enhance our capacity to listen and read what's going on with one another.

We'll be practicing mindfulness with a partner, learning how to be present while speaking and listening. In particular, we're going to practice seeing if we can listen with some empathy—trying to really hear

15

and understand how somebody feels or what matters to them.

Developing the skill of listening with empathy can improve our relationships, help us make friends, land a job, and more. To practice this in a meaningful way, I'm going to invite you to share something real, something personal from your life with one another.

Now I don't know about you, but I don't feel so comfortable talking about personal stuff with just anyone. To share something real, I've got to be able to trust them, to know that they're going to have some respect for me. You know what I mean?

Before we do this activity, I want us to make some agreements together, kind of lay down some ground rules. Who's got an idea for what kind of agreements we can make to help get the most out of this activity?

*(Engage them in a short discussion. Or, if you already have ground rules in your class or for mindfulness, review those. Examples include: say what's true in a caring way; respect different points of view; keep confidentiality; and so on.)*

For me, it's important that we can all get on board with these agreements. That we can be real with and trust each other. Does that work for you? Are you willing to give this a try with me? Is there anybody who's not willing to do this experiment with interpersonal mindfulness?

*(Let them respond. It's important to get some buy-in.)*

## Practice Setup

*The following activity requires a higher level of maturity and emotional safety among students. If you are not confident that your students can engage with the dyad practice*

*effectively, we encourage you to use one of the Alternate Activities suggested below.*

*Have students pair up. You may want to assign partners or let them choose. Explain that one person is going to tell a short story about something that's happened to them recently that they care about—good or bad, positive or negative—while the other person just listens. Give them a little time to consider silently and decide what they're going to share. Demonstrate the activity briefly by having a student tell you a one-minute story, and then guessing at how they might be feeling and/or what matters to them in the situation (their needs).*

## Practice

I want you to sit across from your partner, and we'll begin as we usually begin, by establishing mindfulness of the body and doing a little mindful breathing.

✦ Find your posture—comfortable and upright. If it feels all right to you, let your eyes close.

✦ Listen to the sound of the bell with all of your attention, all the way to the end of the tone.

✦ Feel the relaxing effects of gravity. Let your body get heavy. Feel the points that are touching the ground and let them take the weight of your body.

✦ Take a few deep breaths, feeling any ease or relaxation that comes, as you exhale.

✦ You can even repeat "relax, relax" a few times silently to yourself. Let any excess tension present in your body drain down and out.

✦ As your body settles, feel the sensations of your whole body sitting. *(Allow some time.)*

✦ When you're ready, let your eyes open. You don't have to look at each other, just notice how it feels to be sitting across from your partner. What emotions are present? Do you feel anxious or awkward? Do you feel like laughing?

✦ We're going to practice being mindful while

15

talking and while listening. We can still be aware of our bodies, and we can be aware of our minds. As we practice, notice as much as you can: notice what thoughts go through your mind. See if you can notice the urge to talk, or maybe that you're not in the mood to talk much. Notice if silence is awkward. Notice that you are seeing the other person and hearing their voice. See if you can maintain some mindful awareness as we do this exercise.

*(This activity can be expanded into two separate practices: first, explore being mindful while listening and speaking in general; second, explore the empathic listening activity that follows. Decide who will speak first. It can be helpful to give them a random criterion, such as "The person with the longest hair will be speaking first.")*

✦ When you hear the sound of the bell, I want the first speaker to go ahead and tell your partner about something that happened to you recently that matters—good or bad, positive or negative. You'll have about two minutes. Listeners, I want you to practice listening mindfully. Give the speaker your full and undivided attention. Don't interrupt or say anything. Just listen completely. When you hear the bell again, after two minutes, stop talking and wait for more instructions.

*(Ring the bell and let the speakers begin their story. Ring it again after about two minutes and let the room return to silence).*

✦ Listeners, I want you to consider silently what you just heard. How do you think your partner feels about what they shared? If you had to guess, what do you think matters to them? Underneath the story— why's this important? (Give them a few moments to think). When I ring the bell, take a guess about how you think they feel or what you think might matter to them. Ask to see if your guess is on point.

✦ When you hear the bell the second time, stop speaking and come back to silence.

*(Ring the bell once for them to start. Allow a minute or so, then ring the bell again.)*

✦ Let your eyes close. Notice how that felt. What did you like about it? What was challenging? What was easy? Did it feel awkward? How did it feel to have your partner listen to you? How did it feel to guess?

*(Allow some time for them to feel their bodies sitting and breathing. Have them trade roles and repeat the exercise).*

 **Discussion Questions**

The discussion for this activity is critical. Draw out any insights or experiences that illustrate how easy it is to lose mindfulness when relating to others; how helpful it can feel to be listened to; how other impulses get in the way of listening; and how little energy it actually takes to listen with empathy. Here are some suggested questions to guide your discussion:

— How many people lost mindfulness while speaking?

— How many people lost mindfulness while listening?

— What made you lose mindfulness? Were you thinking . . . wanting to speak or respond?

— Raise your hand if it was easy to listen like this. Raise your hand if it was hard.

— Did anyone notice any impulses other than to listen? Like what? *(Point out that we often like to ask questions, give advice, or tell our own story instead of just listening).*

— How many people were able to come up with a guess about how their partner felt or what mattered to them?

— How many people felt like their partner's guess was in the right ballpark—maybe they weren't 100 percent on point, but close? Raise your hand.

15

— Did anyone find their partner's guess was off? Was it still helpful in any way? *(Even if the guess is inaccurate, students may report it helping them to understand themselves better. The aim isn't to "get it right" but to learn how to listen mindfully with an intention to understand.)*

— How did it feel to have your partner listen to you in this way?

— How did it feel to hear their guess about how you felt?

*(Close the discussion by summarizing any key points, and pointing out how good it can feel to relate with other people in this kind of honest, real way.)*

We all have the capacity to listen and empathize, but we don't use it very often. Like a muscle, it grows when we use it. We can use mindfulness to practice listening with empathy and improve our social and emotional intelligence.

 ### Take-Home Practice

1. Practice being mindful while you are speaking. Can you stay aware while you speak?

2. Practice being mindful while you're listening. Can you give whomever is speaking your full and complete attention?

3. Experiment with finding empathy for others. As you listen, consider how they might be feeling, or what matters to them. Take a guess and see if you're understanding them.

 ### Journal Suggestions

1. Was it difficult to be mindful while talking? How about while listening?

2. How did it feel to have your partner listen with empathy?

3. Are there any times in your life when listening to someone else with empathy might be helpful to you? When? Where?

4. How else might being mindful in conversation help?

**ALTERNATE ACTIVITIES**

✦ For smaller groups, you could try sitting in a circle and having one person share while everyone else listens. Take turns guessing how the person feels or what they need.

✦ If there is an insufficient level of safety socially for paired partner exercises, you could try reading a few quotes, snippets of stories from a novel or magazine article, play a short scene from a movie or TV show or a cut from an emotional song. Invite the students to practice listening and guessing with empathy.

✦ Try playing a short scene of an argument from a TV show or movie. Watch the scene through once; then replay it, pausing after each character speaks. Every time you pause the video, invite students to take empathy guesses about what the character is feeling or needing, instead of reacting or responding to the content of what they've just said.

 ### Teacher Notes

Some authors and social scientists have distinguished three kinds of empathy: cognitive, affective and either somatic or compassionate empathy. Generally speaking, cognitive empathy is the ability to understand another's point of view intellectually, often referred to as "perspective taking." Affective empathy is the ability to sense another's emotional state, their feelings and concerns. There are different categorizations of a third kind of empathy. Some highlight somatic empathy as a physical component of empathy rooted in the function of mirror neurons. Others (Goleman, 1995, 2006; Ekman, n.d.) suggest that compassionate empathy (or, "empathic concern") be considered a third kind of empathy, defining this

15

as the movement to help in order to alleviate another's pain or suffering.

Carl Rogers, one of the founders of humanistic psychology, contributed early research identifying empathy, authenticity, unconditional positive regard, and caring as keys factors in effective psychotherapy. His work further indicated the importance of these qualities in teachers working with children and students.

Dr. Marshall B. Rosenberg (2003), founder of Nonviolent Communication, codified some of Rogers's work on empathy and provided a structured, linguistic form of tracking feelings and needs to access and enhance empathy. In this form, one identifies the felt emotions and deeper human needs or concerns beneath a subjective statement as a method of stimulating and strengthening the natural empathic response.

 **Science Supplement**

Humans are social beings and positive relationships are important for our happiness. Empathy is a capacity that allows us to understand the hearts and minds of others and to resonate emotionally with those states. You're probably familiar with the saying, "to stand in someone else's shoes." That is an aspect of empathy. However, before we stand in someone else's shoes, we first need to know what it's like to stand in our own shoes! With mindfulness, we learn to truly stand in our own shoes. From this perspective, mindfulness is a practice of self–empathy. This kind of self-awareness allows us to develop empathic connections to others. As we experience the landscape of our inner life with more detail and richness, our ability to understand the inner lives of others expands.

## STRESS AS BARRIER TO EMPATHY

Mindfulness and empathy are linked through their shared relationship with stress. While mindfulness decreases stress, stress weakens empathy. When our attention is pooled up in our own stress, it's as if there is less "mental real estate" for the concerns of others. For example, after a long stressful day, perhaps you've noticed that you're probably less receptive to a letter, asking for donations to a good cause. It should come as no surprise that mindfulness programs that reduce stress also enhance empathy.

## EMPATHY AND MINDFULNESS: NEUROBIOLOGY AND RECENT RESEARCH

There are some intriguing results from brain studies on empathy and meditation practice. Tania Singer (Singer & Klimecki, 2014)—one of the leading scientists exploring empathy in the brain—has highlighted the anterior insula and the cingulate cortex as key brain regions for empathic responses. An important study recently examined the impact of meditation practice on brain structure. The results highlighted several brain regions impacted by meditative practice: the anterior cingulate and the insula were among the impacted regions.

Recent research has examined the relationship between mindfulness and empathy directly. In one study, participants either spent five minutes doing mindfulness practice or five minutes being distracted. After those five minutes, participants took a test where they saw photographs of people's eyes and were asked to identify the emotion that person was feeling. They also completed a writing assignment that assessed their level of empathy. Remarkably, after only five minutes of mindfulness practice, the mindfulness group dramatically out-performed the distraction group at detecting the correct emotion in the photographs. The mindfulness group was also judged to be more empathic in their written responses.

These findings are really interesting, but they leave an important question unanswered. Does the empathy generated through mindfulness practice lead to prosocial behavior? After all, if empathy doesn't change how we behave in the world, its value is diminished. There is evidence that mindfulness makes people more kind.

To assess the link between mindfulness and pro-social behavior, one research team devised a very cool study (Lim, Condon, and DeSteno, 2015). Here is what they did:

There were two groups—one mindfulness group and one cognitive training group. The mindfulness group received three weeks of online mindfulness instruction. The cognitive training group received three weeks of online training too, but their training did not include mindfulness. At the end of the three weeks, the researchers asked the participants to come to the research office to complete the study. But that was actually a set-up! Prior to a participant's arrival, two unknown people from the research team (referred to in the study as "confederates") pretended to be waiting in the lobby. There were three chairs and the confederates were sitting in two of them. When the real research participant arrived, they sat in the remaining chair. So that meant there were no chairs left. A minute later, a third confederate arrived. The third confederate had crutches and a walking boot. (She didn't actually have a broken foot; that was part of the study). The person with the "broken" foot winced visibly while walking and stopped just as she arrived at the chairs. She audibly sighed in discomfort, and leaned back against a wall. To assess kindness, the research team measured whether the participant offered their seat to the person with the broken foot to relieve her pain.

So, guess what happened? Good news! The mindfulness group gave up their chair at more than twice the rate as the individuals who got the cognitive training. A previous study including face-to-face mindfulness instructions reached similar conclusions. Findings such as these testify to the fact that as we pay attention to our breath, our body, and our lives in this simple and gentle way, a natural consequence is the opening of the heart.

## MIRROR NEURONS

Marco Iacoboni at UCLA (2009) has focused his research on mirror neurons. In a comprehensive review of the research on mirror neurons and empathy, he cites six key points listed below:

1. Imitation is pervasive and automatic in humans.
2. Psychological models of imitation that assume an overlap or strong associative links between perception and action are supported by neural mirroring.
3. The core neural circuitry of imitation is composed of a higher-order visual area (the posterior part of the superior temporal sulcus) and by the fronto-parietal mirror neuron system.
4. Empathy is implemented by a simulation of the mental states of other people.
5. A large-scale network for empathy is composed of the mirror neuron system, the insula, and the limbic system.
6. Mirror neurons were selected because they provide the adaptive advantage of inter-subjectivity.

Iacoboni concludes the review with this: "A further implication of the recent work on the relationships between mirror neurons, imitation, and empathy is the consideration that the evolutionary process made us wired for empathy. This is a major revision of widely held beliefs. Traditionally, our biology is considered the basis of self-serving individualism, whereas our ideas and our social codes enable us to rise above our neurobiological makeup. The research on mirror neurons, imitation, and empathy, in contrast, tells us that our ability to empathize, a building block of our sociality and morality has been built "bottom up" from relatively simple mechanisms of action production and perception" (p. 666–667).

## FUTURE DIRECTIONS

The scientific investigation of mindfulness, empathy and kindness is just beginning. Important questions remain. For example, Singer and her colleagues (2014)

15

distinguish empathic distress from compassion. While empathic distress is associated with negative emotion and burnout, compassion actually feels good and is associated with health and prosocial behavior. Crucially, most of the data discussed are from adults. Understanding the role of mindfulness and empathy at different developmental stages is an important area for future study. Childhood and adolescence may be a critical time for the cultivation of mindfulness, empathy, and kindness.

**REFERENCES & FURTHER READING**

Fox, K. C., Nijeboer, S., Dixon, M. L., Floman, J. L., Ellamil, M., Rumak, S. P., . . . & Christoff, K. (2014). Is meditation associated with altered brain structure? A systematic review and meta-analysis of morphometric neuroimaging in meditation practitioners. *Neuroscience & Biobehavioral Reviews, 43*, 48–73.

Goleman, D. (1995). *Emotional intelligence: Why it can matter more than IQ.* New York: Bantam Books.

Goleman, D. (2006). *Social intelligence: The new science of human relationships.* New York: Bantam Books.

Iacoboni, M. (2009). Imitation, empathy, and mirror neurons. *Annual Review of Psychology, 60*, 653–670.

Krasner, M. S., Epstein, R. M., Beckman, H., Suchman, A. L., Chapman, B., Mooney, C. J., & Quill, T. E. (2009). Association of an educational program in mindful communication with burnout, empathy, and attitudes among primary care physicians. *JAMA, 302(12)*, 1284–1293.

Lim, D., Condon, P., & DeSteno, D. (2015). Mindfulness and compassion: An examination of mechanism and scalability. *PloS one, 10(2)*, e0118221.

Rosenberg, M. B. (2003). *Nonviolent communication: A language of life.* Encinitas, CA: Puddle-Dancer Press.

Singer, T. & Klimecki, O. M. (2014). Empathy and compassion. *Current Biology, 24(18)*, R875–R878.

Weng, H. Y., Fox, A. S., Shackman, A. J., Stodola, D. E., Caldwell, J. Z., Olson, M. C., . . . & Davidson, R. J. (2013). Compassion training alters altruism and neural responses to suffering. *Psychological Science, 24(7)*, 1171–1180.

For more on the discovery of mirror neurons, see the work of neurophysiologist Dr. Giacomo Rizzolatti. gocognitive.net/interviews/discovery-mirror-neurons-1

For more on emotions and microexpressions, see the work of Dr. Paul Ekman. www.paulekman.com/resources/micro-expressions

**15**

# Mindful Communication and Empathy

## Key Points

◆ Communicating with and relating to others is a big part of life.

◆ Having social and emotional intelligence can help us navigate relationships and be more successful in life.

◆ Empathy is an innate capacity. It is hardwired in our brain and is adaptive in different contexts.

◆ We can enhance our social and emotional intelligence by strengthening empathy.

◆ Learning to listen mindfully is one way of developing empathy.

> **DEFINITIONS:** *Empathy* is the capacity to feel what someone else is experiencing on the inside. *Mirror Neurons* are a part of the brain that mimic the physical behavior we see in others.

## Practice Instructions

◆ Find your posture, comfortable and upright; feet on the floor and hands in your lap.

◆ Let your eyes close, or gaze down at the ground in front of you.

◆ Feel gravity and the weight of your body. Notice where your body touches the ground.

◆ Take a few deep breaths, noticing any ease or relaxation on the exhalation.

◆ Become aware of your whole body sitting and breathing.

◆ When you listen, give the other person your full and complete attention.

◆ Consider how they might be feeling, or what they might need. What matters to this person? Can you take a guess?

 ## Take-Home Practice

1. Practice being mindful while you are speaking. Can you stay aware while you speak?

2. Practice being mindful while you're listening. Can you give whomever is speaking your full and complete attention?

3. Experiment with finding empathy for others. As you listen, consider how they might be feeling, or what matters to them. Take a guess and see if you're understanding them.

 ## Journal Suggestions

1. Was it difficult to be mindful while talking? How about while listening?

2. How did it feel to have your partner listen with empathy?

3. Are there any times in your life when listening to someone else with empathy might be helpful to you? When?

4. How else might being mindful in conversation help?

---

Printable PDF available for download at http://wwnorton.com/mindschls

# MINDFUL EATING

## The Basics

This lesson explores the integration of mindfulness in a very common activity: eating! *Note:* you'll need some raisins for this lesson.

---

**LEARNING OBJECTIVES**

1. To learn how to apply mindfulness in the context of eating.

2. To report the effect of attention on ordinary activities like eating.

3. To reflect on one's relationship to food.

---

**LESSON 16 IN BRIEF: A SYNOPSIS**

## Mindful Eating

**1. Check in & review:**
Who practiced at home? What experiences or questions came up?

**2. Surprise the students with a gift**
Today we're going to learn about using mindfulness in a new way. I am going to say three sentences. Be mindful of your reaction to each one; notice any thoughts, responses, or feelings that occur. 1) I brought you something today. 2) I brought something you can eat. 3) I brought raisins. What was your reaction to each sentence?

Give out two raisins to each participant; have them observe their reactions inside, while waiting for further instructions.

### Practice Instructions

◆ Today we're going to be mindful of eating, first with eyes open, then closed.

◆ It's important to stay silent and focus all of your attention on your raisins (and not on each other).

◆ Imagine your raisins' story: Where did they grow? How did they get to you?

◆ Look closely and investigate them. How do they look, smell, feel, sound?

Mindfulness can help us not tighten when we're uncomfortable, and it can help us enjoy pleasure. Being mindful of eating can show us how we think about food, e.g. eating when we're stressed.

◆ Put one raisin in your mouth but don't chew it yet. Close your eyes and chew slowly, feeling all the sensations and flavors. What did you notice?

**16**

◆ Let's eat the second raisin slowly, with eyes closed. Notice anything different?

### Discussion Questions

◆ How did that work for you? Did the raisin taste different than you anticipated?

◆ Did the raisin taste good? Did you chew on the right or left side of your mouth?

◆ How did it taste compared to how your food normally tastes? How do you eat at home?

### Take-Home Practice

1. This week, eat three bites of each meal with mindfulness. See if you can taste all the flavors in those three bites. See how mindfulness affects the taste of the food.

2. Notice when you're eating without mindfulness. You don't have to slow down or change the way you're eating. Just notice what it's like to eat in a rushed way.

**16**

# Mindful Eating

## Lesson Outline

— Surprise the students with a gift of raisins as a way to inspect feelings and preferences about food.

— We can reflect on and contemplate where our food comes from, the way it connects us to others in the world, and how it nourishes our bodies.

— Mindfulness can make eating more pleasurable, fully experiencing the pleasure of eating.

— A highly ordinary experience, eating an ordinary food, can be experienced in a new and different way when done with mindfulness.

## Lesson

*(Organize the room for mindfulness and engage the students in a transitional activity. Then, check for updates on using mindfulness at home, in particular as it relates to the previous lesson.)*

Today we're going to learn about using mindfulness in a new way. I am going to say three sentences. Please just be mindful of your inner reaction to each sentence. Notice any thoughts, responses, or feelings that occur.

1. I brought you something today. (*Pause*)
2. I brought something you can eat. (*Pause*)
3. I brought raisins. (*Pause*)

What was your reaction to each sentence?

*(Students answer.)*

I am going to come around to each person and hand out a couple raisins. When you get your raisins, just hold them in your hand *but don't eat them yet!* Just keep your raisins until I give them to everyone and then I'll tell you what to do next.

While I'm giving out the raisins, notice if you like raisins and you're getting hungry. Notice if you don't like raisins and how that makes you feel. Maybe you wish I was giving out chocolate!

## Practice

*(Typically, we begin by establishing mindfulness of the body, but for this lesson, we recommend moving right into mindful eating.)*

Today, of course, we're going to practice mindfulness of eating. For the first part, we'll have our eyes open, but it is very important that we are silent, not talking to each other, and not looking at each other during this time. Keep all of your attention focused on yourself and the raisins! First, take one raisin in your hand and look at it.

Let's use our imagination to guess the story of the raisin. How did this raisin get to you? Think about the farm where the grapes grew, the people who picked the fruit, the people who packaged and transported the food, and the workers at the grocery store where I bought them.

Now look more closely at your raisin. Investigate everything you can about the raisin with your eyes, your ears, your nose. How does it look? How does it feel? What's it smell like? What's it sound like?

Mindfulness of eating is about allowing pleasure. We've talked a lot about not tightening when there's discomfort, but the same principle applies to plea-

**16**

sure. Mindfulness can make eating more pleasurable. Sometimes, mindfulness can show us how we think about food. For example, a lot of us eat when we're stressed, even if we're not hungry. There are lots of things we can learn when we practice mindfulness of eating.

Okay, so now, slowly put one raisin in your mouth but don't chew it yet. Close your eyes and then chew it as slowly as you can, feeling and tasting all of the sensations and flavors fully before you swallow the raisin. When you're done, just relax and see if the taste stays in your mouth.

What did you notice?

(*Students answer. Examples: the movement of the tongue; changing shape or flavor; liking or disliking; wanting more; wanting candy; and so on.*)

Now let's take another minute to eat the other raisin with eyes closed, noticing any ways in which the experience is different than the first. I will ring the bell to end. Listen to the whole sound of the bell, and when you cannot hear the sound of the bell anymore, open your eyes.

 **Discussion Questions**

– How did that work for you?
– Did the raisin taste differently than you anticipated?
– Did the raisin taste good?
– Did you chew on the right or left side of your mouth?
– How did it taste compared to how your food normally tastes?
– How do you eat at home?

Mindfulness opens up a whole new world of experience when eating, doesn't it? It can really help us to enjoy our food more. It also can have other benefits with eating. Anyone have any ideas about how mindful eating might be helpful?

(*Students answer.*)

Yeah, those are good ideas! How many people have ever eaten too much and felt sick afterwards? Me too! It doesn't feel good, right? Overeating isn't good for our health. If we eat mindfully, really enjoying and tasting the food, we're more likely to notice when we're full, feel satisfied, and stop there. Being mindful when we're hungry can also help us make better choices about *what* we eat. For example, if we want a snack and we're mindful of that we might choose something healthy like a piece of fruit instead of candy.

 **Take-Home Practice**

1. This week, eat three bites of each meal with mindfulness. See if you can taste all the flavors in those three bites. See how mindfulness affects the taste of the food.
2. Notice when you're eating without mindfulness. You don't have to slow down or change the way you're eating. Just notice what it's like to eat in a rushed way.

 **Journal Suggestions**

1. What surprised you about this lesson?
2. What are your thoughts and feelings about food?
3. How can mindfulness be useful in how you eat?

16

## Teacher Notes

This lesson often elicits strong reactions from students—both positive and negative. The more clear and well-paced your instructions are, the easier it will be to navigate and manage the energy in the room. Be sure to take your time and lay out the instructions step by step.

## Science Supplement

Food and eating is a necessary physiological behavior, yet it is deeply entwined with psychology. Eating has many meanings for us. It involves emotion, thoughts, self-evaluation (positive and negative), questions about identity, image and cultural factors, and has familial and sociocultural aspects.

Eating does not merely have individual effects but has societal and ecological impacts. Despite the widespread availability of food in economically advanced countries, hunger has not been eradicated and impacts tens of millions of people each day. The ecological impacts of certain food production—particularly large-scale factory farm animals—is tremendous. Eating behaviors exert powerful effects on public health systems in the United States. About 35 percent of American adults are classified as obese as are 17 percent of children. Obesity is predictive of poorer physical health and lower levels of well-being. At the same time, anorexia affects 2 to 3 percent of the population. These facts highlight the complexity of food and eating behavior.

These are recalcitrant problems and they will not be solved by simple approaches, nevertheless, mindfulness may be a resource. Researchers have highlighted a number of ways in which mindfulness may be helpful for people struggling with eating disorders—or with problematic eating that does not meet clinical criteria typically called "disordered eating." The helpful features of mindfulness include: cultivating awareness of internal experiences such as hunger and fullness, improving self-acceptance and self-compassion, and enhancing cognitive flexibility and emotional regulation.

One of the leaders in the field, Jean Kristeller (2014), writes,

"Eating can be a largely automatic and mindless behavior. Mindful eating is eating while fully aware of the process, noticing both the pleasantness and the internal and external states influencing hunger and satiety, and desire for food. Humans can eat mindfully naturally, but tend not to under the influence of habitual patterns, if they are in emotional states or even slightly distracted. Thus, mindless eating is the more common mode, and in the contemporary food-abundant environment, mindless food choices and overeating can be argued to be contributing substantially to the current epidemic of obesity. Engaging in mindful eating, regardless of how this is cultivated, is a critical aspect of healthy balanced eating and, presumably, weight management." (p. 913).

Kristeller is highlighting how mindfulness can help forge new healthy habits around eating. When we have healthier habits, we don't need to rely so much on will-power to make wise decisions.

Jordan and colleagues (Jordan, Wang, Donatoni, & Meier, 2014) conducted a series of studies echoing Kristeller's suggestions. Jordan writes:

"Across four studies, we established that mindfulness predicts reduced calorie consumption. Dispositional mindfulness was associated with reports of less uncontrolled eating, reduced calorie consumption in a spontaneous eating task, and greater likelihood of choosing fruit than sweets as a snack. In addition, we found evidence that general mindfulness causally affects eating behavior: an experimental manipulation

16

of state mindfulness led participants to consume fewer calories. Notably, this mindfulness induction made no reference to food or eating behavior. Taken together, these results provide strong evidence that mindfulness encourages healthier eating, even in the absence of specific instruction in mindful eating. Mindfulness may thus be a pertinent factor in a theoretical understanding of eating behavior. These results, moreover, tentatively suggest that generic mindfulness-based strategies could have ancillary benefits for enhancing healthy eating" (p. 110 ).

A recent review of mindfulness as an intervention for disordered eating by Katterman and colleagues (Katterman, et al., 2014) concludes:

"The current review adds to the accumulating evidence that interventions that include mindfulness meditation training hold promise in improving maladaptive eating behaviors. The available evidence suggests that a standard mindfulness-based training program does not produce consistent weight loss. This was the first review to examine the impact of primarily mindfulness based interventions on eating behavior and weight in a non-eating disordered population. Our review suggests that mindfulness meditation is effective in reducing binge eating behavior across a variety of populations, and may also reduce emotional eating. Thus, mindfulness meditation as an intervention for problematic eating warrants further clinical and empirical attention" (p. 203).

Of course, mindfulness is not merely about attenuating symptoms, it is also about enjoyment. Mindfulness can enhance pleasure from eating. As we develop equanimity with pleasure—we let pleasure be just as it is—the pleasure can spread unimpeded through the body and lead to greater feelings of satisfaction.

## A NOTE ON ATTRIBUTION
This activity is based upon a lesson from an advisory board member of Mindful Schools, Jon Kabat-Zinn.

### REFERENCES & FURTHER READING
Jordan, C. H., Wang, W., Donatoni, L., & Meier, B. P. (2014). Mindful eating: Trait and state mindfulness predict healthier eating behavior. *Personality and Individual Differences, 68,* 107–111.

Katterman, S. N., Kleinman, B. M., Hood, M. M., Nackers, L. M., & Corsica, J. A. (2014). Mindfulness meditation as an intervention for binge eating, emotional eating, and weight loss: A systematic review. *Eating Behaviors, 15,* 197–204.

Kristeller, J. L. & Epel, E. (2014). Mindful eating and mindless eating: The science and the practice. *The Wiley Blackwell handbook of mindfulness,* 913–933. West Sussex, UK: Wiley-Blackwell.

Kristeller, J., Wolever, R. Q., & Sheets, V. (2014). Mindfulness-based eating awareness training (MB-EAT) for binge eating: A randomized clinical trial. *Mindfulness, 5,* 282–297.

Ogden, C. L., Carroll, M. D., Kit, B. K., & Flegal, K. M. (2014). Prevalence of childhood and adult obesity in the United States, 2011–2012. *JAMA, 311,* 806–814.

16

# Mindful Eating

## Key Points

◆ Mindfulness can make eating more pleasurable.

◆ We can learn to fully experience pleasure.

◆ We can reflect on and contemplate where our food comes from, the way it connects us to others in the world, and how it nourishes our bodies.

◆ A highly ordinary experience, eating an ordinary food, can be experienced in a new and different way when done with mindfulness.

## Practice Instructions

◆ Practice mindful eating slowly by closing your eyes and experiencing all of the smells, sensations, and flavors of the food. How does it feel in your mouth? How does it taste? How does it change?

◆ Can you pay attention to when you swallow and notice how that feels?

◆ Practice mindful eating at a regular pace by bringing your attention to the sensations and flavors of the food. Eat in a normal way, but give as much of your attention as possible to the direct sensory experience of eating: seeing the food, smelling it, tasting and chewing, swallowing.

 ## Take-Home Practice

1. This week, eat three bites of each meal with mindfulness. See if you can taste all the flavors in those three bites. See how mindfulness affects the taste of the food.

2. Notice when you're eating without mindfulness. You don't have to slow down or change the way you're eating, just notice what it's like to eat in a rushed way.

 ## Journal Suggestions

1. What surprised you about this lesson?

2. What are your thoughts and feelings about food?

3. How can mindfulness be useful in how you eat?

**LESSON 17**

# MINDFUL WALKING

## The Basics

This lesson introduces students to the practice of mindful walking, further expanding the repertoire of activities in which we can be mindful and offering it as a helpful method for settling the mind and calming the nervous system.

---

**LEARNING OBJECTIVES**

1. To explain the importance of being able to be mindful while moving.
2. To describe the benefits of mindful walking.
3. To practice mindfulness of walking, feeling the sensations in the feet or legs while observing other sensory input.

---

**LESSON 17 IN BRIEF: A SYNOPSIS**

## Mindful Walking

**1. Check in & review:**
Who practiced at home? What experiences or questions came up?

**2. Why is the breath a good anchor for mindfulness? How is walking similar?**
Why is the breath a good anchor? It's rhythmic, it's both voluntary and involuntary, and we do it all the time. Most of us walk a lot, every day, and we can use this to develop mindfulness.

**3. Walking is healthy and a complex activity.**
Walking has many health benefits: It's good exercise and improves digestion. Adults are supposed to take 10,000 steps a day (approximately five miles)! Walking can soothe our emotions and calm our thoughts. Seated mindfulness limits distractions and helps us to focus. But if that's the only time we can be mindful, it's very limited. Learning to walk mindfully is a foundation for being mindful during other activities in life. In mindful walking, we use the sensations in our feet and legs as an anchor.

### Practice Instructions

♦ Have students stand and shift weight between legs, exploring how the sensations in their feet change. Have them take one or two slow, mindful steps, feeling all the sensations that occur.

♦ Instead of "taking a walk" and letting our minds wander, we're going to walk mindfully outside.

- Feel your body moving, your legs walking, using the sensations to stay in the present.

- As you walk, notice and observe as much as you can about all of your senses.

- You might notice sounds, sights, smells— anything. We'll do this in silence, to help stay focused.

- Notice the temptation to interact with your friends. Focus on yourself, your own experience.

- If you notice your mind has wandered, bring your attention back to the sensations in your feet.

- You can walk at whatever pace helps you stay mindful and present.

- So: Anchor your attention in your feet, and observe all that you can through your senses.

- When you hear the bell, head back to class.

 **Discussion Questions**

- Did your mind wander? Were you able to bring it back to the sensations in your feet?

- What was mindful walking like compared to mindful breathing?

- What else did you notice in your experience?

- What parts of our body move when we walk? How do they move?

- Did you feel your feet better when you were walking faster or slower?

- How can you adapt this to walking out in the world? What would need to change?

 **Take-Home Practice**

1. Choose a specific activity or time that you walk and try to remember to walk mindfully.

2. Try being mindful of your walking when you're out and about. Instead of stressing or letting your mind wander, see if you can notice how your feet and legs feel.

# Mindful Walking

## Lesson Outline

— Just like breathing or eating, walking is something most of us do every day.

— Walking has a variety of health benefits, and can help us practice mindfulness.

— Learning to walk mindfully is a foundation for being mindful during other activities in life.

— The rhythm of mindful walking can soothe our emotions and calm our thoughts.

— In mindful walking, we use the sensations in our feet and legs as an anchor.

## Lesson

*(Organize the room for mindfulness and engage the students in a transitional activity.)*

How's your mindfulness practice been going? Has anyone used mindfulness since our last lesson? *(Show of hands.)* When? How? *(Students answer.)*

Today I want to teach you about one of the most important complements to mindfulness of breathing. Who remembers some of the reasons why the breath makes a good anchor for mindfulness practice?

*(Students answer.)*

That's right. It's rhythmic, which can be soothing. It's both voluntary and involuntary, so we can use it to balance our nervous system. It's usually emotionally neutral, so it won't stress us out. **And it's always happening, so we can practice with it wherever we go.**

There's another thing humans do that shares most of these characteristics. Can anyone guess what it is? *(Let students guess. Feel free to give them clues: You did it on your way here to class; and so on.)*

Yeah, unless we're injured, we walk! (If you have a student who is unable to walk, see Alternate Activities below.) In fact, we walk a lot. How many of you walked to school or to a bus stop today? Who can give me some examples of other times we walk?

*(Students answer.)*

So, next question: how is walking kind of like the breath?

*(Students answer.)*

Yes, great ideas! It's rhythmic; we can do it almost anywhere; it's not exactly involuntary, but we don't have to think hard to do it; it's neutral and it can help us calm down. Sounds like an ideal way to practice mindfulness, right?

How many of you have ever taken a walk to cool out when you felt really stressed or upset? Ever taken a walk with a friend, or a family member? Walking tends to smooth out the hard stuff and enhance the good stuff. It's even good for our health! Our bodies are meant to walk a lot. Adults are supposed to take roughly 10,000 steps a day. That's about five miles; and it's more if you're young! Being sedentary and not getting enough physical activity is correlated with all kinds of health problems, like heart disease, obesity, and diabetes.

Walking *mindfully* adds to all of these benefits. It can be a reliable way to settle our minds, calming our thoughts and soothing difficult emotions.

We start out learning mindfulness by *sitting* in a particular posture to cut down on distractions, quiet the mind, and help us focus. But if mindfulness is going to be a resource in our lives, we need to be able to use it when we're moving, too! We've talked some about how mindfulness has helped certain athletes like Stephen Curry and Michael Jordan be at the top of their game. They're not just doing it when they sit; they're using mindfulness when they play!

The foundation of learning to be mindful in the rest of our lives is mindful walking. Are you ready to give this a try? We'll start here together with a focused exercise, and then take some time to practice walking outside (*or the space to which you have access*).

## Practice: Introduction

(*If possible, arrange things so there is room for each person to walk two or three steps.*)

Please stand up, push in your chairs, and take a step back from your desk. Close your eyes and let your body get still and quiet. Bring your attention to your body. Notice your posture, your balance, how you are standing. Feel the weight of gravity. Can you let your posture be relaxed and upright, just like when we do seated mindfulness?

(*Allow some silence.*)

Is it possible to *not* move at all, not even the slightest bit?

No, of course not. Our bodies are always in motion. It's just that we usually don't notice it.

Gently shift your weight into your left foot, letting you knee bend slightly. Notice how it feels there, as your weight moves into the left foot. Then shift your weight very slowly into your right foot, letting your

right knee bend slightly. Notice how the sensations in your feet change. Remember, a "sensation" just means anything you can feel in your body. Now shift back and forth, in a way that doesn't make you lose your balance. See what you can notice as you shift your weight. (*Allow some time.*)

Okay. Shift back so your weight is balanced equally on both feet; notice what your feet feel like.

When we walk mindfully, we anchor our attention with these sensations in our feet. First, we're going to do this slowly, all together, to see what we can notice. It might feel a little silly at first. Try to think of it like an experiment; we're just exploring here.

I want you to slowly lift one foot, and take one step forward. Notice the sensations in your foot and leg. Place the foot on the floor, then slowly lift your other foot, and bring it forward to take another step, feeling any of the sensations in your foot, ankle, and leg.

(*You may need to adjust these instructions to fit restrictions of time and space.*)

What sensations did you feel in your feet, in your ankles, in your legs?

(*Students answer. Examples: heaviness, lightness, tension, movement, nothing, and so on.*)

Great. Those are the sensations we pay attention to with mindfulness of walking!

## Practice: Walking

I'm going to give you a few more instructions, and then you're going to try this out on your own. How many of you feel like you've gotten better at being mindful of your breath these last few weeks? (*Students raise hands.*) You already knew how to breathe, but you had to practice being mindful of it. We all know how to walk, but we have to practice being mindful at it. (If you don't have access to an open or outdoor space, see Alternate Activities.) Here's how we're going to do this:

✦ Instead of just "taking a walk" and letting our minds wander, we're going to use the sensations in our feet as an anchor.

✦ I want you to go outside and use the sensations of walking to keep your attention grounded in the present moment. Try to feel your body moving, your legs walking.

✦ As you walk, notice and observe as much as you can about all your senses.

✦ You might notice sounds, sights, smells—anything.

✦ We'll be doing this in silence to help stay focused.

✦ Watch out for the temptation to look at your friends or interact. Keep your attention focused on yourself and your own experience.

✦ Whenever you notice that your mind has wandered, bring your attention back to feeling the sensations in your feet.

✦ You can walk at whatever pace helps you stay mindful and present.

✦ So, anchor your attention in your feet, and observe all that you can through your senses.

✦ When you hear the bell, head back to class.

Any questions? Okay. See if you can start being mindful of your walking now, as you head out to find your spot. I'll see you back here in about 10 minutes.

 **Discussion Questions**

– How many people noticed your mind wander? Were you able to bring it back to the sensations in your feet?

– What was mindful walking like compared to mindful breathing?

– What else did you notice in your experience?

– What parts of our body move when we walk? How do they move?

– Did you feel your feet better when you were moving faster or slower?

– How can you adapt this to walking out in the world? What would need to change?

 **Take-Home Practice**

1. Choose one specific activity or time that you walk during your day (walking to school, to the bus). Do your best to remember to walk mindfully during that time.

2. Try being mindful of your walking when you're out and about. Instead of stressing or letting your mind wander, see if you can notice how your feet and legs feel.

3. Practice mindful walking before our next session.

**Journal Suggestions**

1. Did you learn anything new about walking today? What?

2. Was it harder or easier for you to stay mindful while walking (versus sitting and breathing)? Why do think that might be the case?

3. What kinds of thoughts did you notice while you were walking?

4. What activities or times of your day would be best for you to practice mindful walking?

**ALTERNATE ACTIVITIES**

**Differently-abled Students:** If you have a student(s) who can't walk, you can give them another simple, rhythmic movement activity to practice. This can share some of the same benefits as mindful walking.

Choose an activity that is easy, comfortable, and repetitive. Have them focus on the sensations they feel as they move. Do a practice run together, just like you did with the other students before walking, in which you perform the activity slowly and describe the felt sensations. Examples:

+ Sit with both hands on the lap, palms down. Lift one hand at a time, turning the palm up, then replacing it palm down on the thigh. Repeat.
+ Rub the palms together slowly.
+ Place both hands palms up on the lap. Touch the tip of the thumb to each forefinger of one hand, then the other. Give the student a simple pattern to follow.

**Formal Walking:** Walking meditation can also be practiced more formally by pacing to and fro along a set path. We suggest introducing walking practice in this more open, relaxed way to pique students' interest in the richness of sensory experience. If you like, you can build on this lesson and teach students to train their minds through more formal walking exercises.

**Walking in a Circle:** If you don't have access to the outdoors, a hallway, or open space (or if time doesn't permit that kind of activity), you can have the students practice by walking slowly in a circle around the perimeter of the room. Clear a pathway and have the students spread out equidistantly, leaving some space between the first student and the last student. Explain that they'll need to walk at a steady, even pace, keeping roughly the same distance between themselves and the person in front of them. If things get bunched up or slow down, invite them to keep noticing the sensations in their feet and legs, even if they're standing still.

 **Teacher Notes**

Pacing back and forth can feel awkward at first, even for adults. Be sure to explain the purpose of structured walking: to support focus, reduce mind wandering, and guide their mental training.

Mindful walking is an essential complement to seated mindfulness practice. Walking has the bene-

fits of balancing our body's energy and providing relief from physical pain that can occur with more prolonged periods of seated mindfulness.

Additional benefits of mindful walking, not mentioned in this lesson, include having a gross, tangible object of attention. For many people, the physical sensations of walking are much easier to detect than the sensations of breathing. For this reason, walking can be a very helpful practice to develop mindfulness and concentration. However, due to stimulation of the other senses (seeing and hearing), it presents other challenges of distraction. The instruction to keep the eyes downcast while practicing formal mindful walking can help in this regard.

Informal mindfulness of walking (while walking for pleasure or performing other activities) involves a looser focus of attention. The sensations in the feet and legs (or the overall movement of the entire body) are still considered the anchor for attention, but other experiences of sights, sounds, and thoughts permeate the awareness in a natural and effortless way. We can become mindful of these other moments of experience in a flow of change, using the sensations of walking to ground the attention and reduce mind wandering.

 **Science Supplement**

Exploring the evolution, biomechanics, and health benefits of walking can be a rich way to supplement this activity. Our ability to walk—bipedalism—is an intricate and complex feat of balance and momentum for the human body to engage in. Although most healthy adults can stand and walk on two legs without much thought, it demands a continual, subtle effort of coordination.

The health benefits of movement—for adults and young people—and the risks of a sedentary lifestyle are well documented in the scientific literature:

There is a large body of evidence from all study designs which suggests that decreasing any type of sedentary time is associated with lower health risk in young people aged 5 to 17 years. In particular, the evidence suggests that daily TV viewing in excess of 2 hours is associated with reduced physical and psychosocial health, and that lowering sedentary time leads to reductions in body mass index (p. 1)

In addition to the standard benefits of physical activity, walking after meals helps to lower blood sugar and improve digestion. Walking in nature, specifically, seems to have emotional and attentional benefits. The data do not speak to mindful walking, but instead the interaction with nature.

Berman and colleagues (Berman, Jonides, & Kaplan, 2008) write: *"Attention restoration theory (ART) is based on past research showing the separation of attention into two components: involuntary attention, where attention is captured by inherently intriguing or important stimuli, and voluntary or directed attention, where attention is directed by cognitive-control processes . . .* According to ART, interacting with environments rich with inherently fascinating stimuli (e.g., sunsets) invoke involuntary attention modestly, allowing directed-attention mechanisms a chance to replenish (Kaplan, 1995). That is, the requirement for directed attention in such environments is minimized, and attention is typically captured in a bottom-up fashion by features of the environment itself. So, the logic is that, after an interaction with natural environments, one is able to perform better on tasks that depend on directed-attention abilities. Unlike natural environments, urban environments contain bottom-up stimulation (e.g., car horns) that captures attention dramatically and additionally requires directed attention to overcome that stimulation (e.g., avoiding traffic, ignoring advertising, and so on.), making urban environments less restorative" (p. 1207).

Studies find benefits of walking with an open awareness in nature. Our attentional resources are restored. We imagine that there are important parallels between the bottom-up quality of attention in nature and the characteristics of mindful awareness.

**REFERENCES & FURTHER READING**

Berman, M. G., Jonides, J., & Kaplan, S. (2008). The cognitive benefits of interacting with nature. *Psychological Science, 19,* 1207–1212.

Gotink, R. A., Hermans, K. S., Geschwind, N., De Nooij, R., De Groot, W. T., & Speckens, A. E. (2016). Mindfulness and mood stimulate each other in an upward spiral: A mindful walking intervention using experience sampling. *Mindfulness, 7,* 1114–1122.

O'Connor A. (2013, June 24). Really? The claim: Taking a walk after a meal aids digestion. *The New York Times.* Well. well.blogs.nytimes.com /2013/06/24/really-the-claim-taking-a-walk-after-a-meal-aids-digestion

Sofer, O.J. (2016, November 8). The Practice of Walking. *Mindful Schools Blog.*

www.mindfulschools.org/personal-practice/ walking

Tremblay, M. S., LeBlanc, A. G., Kho, M. E., Saunders, T. J., Larouche, R., Colley, R. C., . . . & Gorber, S. C. (2011). Systematic review of sedentary behaviour and health indicators in school-aged children and youth. *International Journal of Behavioral Nutrition and Physical Activity, 8,* 98.

# Mindful Walking

## Key Points

◆ Just like breathing or eating, walking is something most of us do every day.

◆ Walking has a variety of health benefits, and can help us practice mindfulness.

◆ Learning to walk mindfully is an important foundation for being mindful during other activities in life.

◆ The rhythm of mindful walking can soothe our emotions and calm our thoughts.

◆ In mindful walking, we use the sensations in our feet and legs as an anchor.

## Practice Instructions

◆ Walk outside in an open area.

◆ Anchor your attention on the sensations in your feet and legs as you walk.

◆ Keep some attention with your feet, and allow yourself to notice and observe other sensory experience: sights, sounds, smells. Notice as much as you can about the full experience of walking.

◆ If your mind wanders, bring your attention back to feeling the sensations in your feet.

◆ Try walking at different paces, slow, medium, fast, and see how the experience changes.

◆ Walk at whatever pace helps you stay mindful.

 ## Take-Home Practice

1. Choose one specific activity or time that you walk during your day (walking to school, to the bus). Do your best to remember to walk mindfully during that time.

2. Try being mindful of your walking when you're out and about. Instead of stressing or letting your mind wander, see if you can notice how your feet and legs feel.

3. Practice mindful walking at least once before our next session.

 ## Journal Suggestions

1. Did you learn anything new about walking today? What?

2. Was it harder or easier for you to stay mindful while walking (versus sitting and breathing)? Why do think that might be the case?

3. What kinds of thoughts did you notice while you were walking?

4. What activities or times of your day would be best for you to practice mindful walking?

# SEEING WITH FRESH EYES: MINDFULNESS AND IMPLICIT BIAS

## The Basics

This lesson addresses social identity and prejudice, and highlights the ways that mindfulness and heartfulness can undercut bias and lead us into deeper connection with others.

---

**LEARNING OBJECTIVES**

1. To understand bias as a way of being misunderstood by others.
2. To learn the difference between explicit and implicit bias.
3. To identify the role of love in Dr. Martin Luther King Jr.'s "beloved community."
4. To be able to describe the role of mindfulness and heartfulness in reducing bias.

---

**LESSON 18 IN BRIEF: A SYNOPSIS**

## Seeing with Fresh Eyes: Mindfulness and Implicit Bias

**1. It feels good to be understood, and it hurts to be misunderstood.**

How does it feel when someone understands you? When someone misunderstands you? People can think they know who we are based on one attribute: our skin color, age, religion, body shape, gender, and so on. What are some examples of being misunderstood in that way—personally, and as a group?

**2. Define and discuss implicit bias.**

Discriminatory views and assumptions can be explicit or implicit. Explicit bias is conscious; implicit bias is not. Discuss examples of implicit bias on personal or societal levels. Explore their origins.

**3. Discuss Kingian nonviolence**

The antidotes to prejudice and bias are understanding and kindness. Dr. Martin Luther King Jr. had a vision of the beloved community based in love, respect, and understanding. Violence will only create more of the very thing we want to change.

Mindfulness and heartfulness can reduce bias. They help us see our assumptions more clearly, and be more open-minded and kind. Research shows mindfulness and heartfulness can reduce implicit bias.

## Practice Instructions

- Sit in a posture that's comfortable yet upright, feet on the floor and hands in your lap.

- Let your eyes close. Feel the weight of your body, noticing where it touches the ground.

- Take a few deep breaths, feeling any ease or relaxation on the exhalation.

- Become aware of your whole body sitting and breathing.

- Imagine yourself surrounded by people who love and care for you. Offer yourself kind wishes, repeating silently: "May I be happy . . . May I be healthy . . . May I be peaceful."

- Reflect on the harm that bias, prejudice, and racism cause in your own life and in society.

- Think of someone who has been discriminated against: someone you know or someone you don't know; someone from a group you belong to or from a different group. Send them heartfulness, offering phrases of kindness. End by offering heartfulness for yourself again.

- When you're ready, let your eyes open and look around the room.

 ## Discussion Questions

- How many people felt some sadness or pain thinking about the suffering humans inflict on one another through discrimination and bias? Did anyone feel angry?

- How many people were able to connect with heartfulness for yourself or others?

- Would anyone like to share how that experience was?

 ## Take-Home Practice

1. Pay attention to the assumptions you make about others. What implicit biases do you carry?

2. Dedicate some time to do formal heartfulness practice for someone who really needs it, perhaps someone who has struggled in the face of bias and discrimination.

## Seeing with Fresh Eyes:
## Mindfulness and Implicit Bias

**18**

### Lesson Outline

- This is the last of our core 18 lessons.

- It feels really good to be understood, and it hurts to be misunderstood.

- Bias is a kind of misunderstanding, with implications on individual and societal levels.

- The goal of Dr. Martin Luther King Jr.'s work was the creation of the beloved community based in love and understanding.

- Mindfulness and heartfulness can reduce bias and help us understand each other more fully.

- We can practice heartfulness for someone from another "group," who is different from ourselves.

### Lesson

*(Organize the room for mindfulness and engage the students in a transitional activity.)*

Anyone have any experiences using mindfulness since our last lesson that you want to share?

This is the last lesson in our mindfulness program. Of course, we can keep practicing this stuff for years and continue learning, but this is the last one in the series. Today I want to talk about something important—it's important for us as individuals and it's important in our society.

Do you know the experience of someone listening to you really well, say a friend or a relative? They're the person you go to if you're upset because they really "get" you, they understand you. Like that empathy exercise we did—they have a lot of empathy. Do you know what I'm talking about?

If feels really good to be seen and understood for who we are. I love that feeling; it helps me relax. But it's not always like that, right? Sometimes people misunderstand us. Sometimes people can't see us for who we are. And that feels bad—sometimes really bad. When someone is making assumptions about me and isn't understanding who I am, I either want to get in their face and tell them they're wrong, or I just want to go away and disappear.

Raise your hand if you've ever felt like that?

People can misunderstand us in lots of ways. Someone might look at you and see your skin color, your body shape, your gender and make all kinds of judgments without even knowing you. They think they've got you pegged, but they're misunderstanding you.

For example, maybe you go into a store and realize that you're being watched or followed like you're going to steal something. You're just doing your thing, but someone else is judging you based on your appearance; maybe because you're younger, because of the way you dress, or because of the color of your skin. It's been documented that assumptions about race or age can create this kind of bias.

Now that's just one incident. But what happens when the same kind of stuff happens to you over and over again every day? Or when whole groups of people are discriminated against in this way? These judgments have real effects in our world. Sometimes, those judgments harden into hatred and fear and create incredible amounts of suffering.

What are some other examples of this—either on the personal level or on the group level?

*(Students answer.)*

Right. It gets heavy. Now sometimes people's discrimination—their views and assumptions that judge others—are *explicit*. That means the person knows they're discriminating; they're aware of it. Sometimes, discriminatory views are *implicit*.

How many people have heard the term "implicit bias"? What do you think it means?

*(Students answer.)*

**Implicit biases are attitudes and stereotypes that we can have without even knowing it.** We inherit a lot of ideas and biases from our culture and our community and we may not be fully aware of them. But these biases still affect how we treat other people. They can affect how decisions are made in institutions or government. Starting to see our biases is important. The author James Baldwin wrote, "Not everything that is faced can be changed, but nothing can be changed until it is faced."

What can we do and how might mindfulness help? The antidotes to discrimination and bias are understanding and kindness. Dr. Martin Luther King Jr. had a vision of a beloved community that is all about understanding, love, and mutual respect. He believed that through a path of nonviolence, we could develop societies that treated everyone with greater care; to really start seeing people for who they are. Wouldn't that be a beautiful thing?

Guess what he thought was the secret ingredient in creating a beloved community?

Love. He spoke of a love born from understanding and goodwill for all. In a speech in 1957, he spoke about an "overflowing love which . . . is purely spontaneous, unmotivated, groundless, and creative."

King said that we can't stand idly by and do nothing in the face of prejudice—but that violence won't bring about the kind of change we want either, because it just recreates the very thing we're fighting. The only choice is nonviolence. Here are his words, from 1959: "The way of acquiescence leads to moral and spiritual suicide. The way of violence leads to bitterness in the survivors and brutality in the destroyers. But the way of nonviolence leads to redemption and the creation of the beloved community."(p.75)

What's all this got to do with mindfulness? Part of what we're doing in our mindfulness practice is learning to be more open-minded with ourselves and others, to become aware of our assumptions, and to be kind instead of acting from our biases.

Mindfulness is about paying attention to experience with an open heart. That experience might be our breath, or it might be seeing another person. Heartfulness develops some of the love that Dr. King was talking about, kindness that isn't just about family or friends or the people we know. It's a kindness that is so big that it reaches everyone. There's even research showing that mindfulness and heartfulness can reduce implicit bias. Just a few minutes of practice has reduced implicit bias against groups that often face discrimination.

As we develop our minds and hearts through practice, this can have effects on all the different people we meet.

## Practice

So, let's begin as usual by settling and establishing mindfulness of the body.

✦ Find your posture—comfortable and upright. If it feels all right to you, let your eyes close.

◆ Listen to the sound of the bell with all of your attention, all the way to the end of the tone.

◆ Start to feel the relaxing effects of gravity. Let your body get heavy. Feel the points that are touching the ground and let them take the weight of your body.

◆ Take a few deep breaths, feeling any ease or relaxation that comes, as you exhale.

◆ Take a few moments just to feel your whole body sitting there, and breathing.

◆ Let's begin by doing some heartfulness for ourselves. Imagine being surrounded by people who care about you. Imagine that they're looking at you and just by the way they're looking, you can feel their love for you.

◆ Silently, you might say some of the phrases you've learned. Phrases like, "May I be safe, may I be happy, may I be at peace."

◆ Now, reflect on the harm that's been done in this country on the basis of bias and discrimination. Maybe this is harm you've suffered personally, harm that you've witnessed others suffer, or harm connected to our country's history. This isn't about getting depressed; we're just being real.

◆ Now, imagine someone from a group that's been discriminated against. It could be a group you belong to, or a group you don't belong to. It could be a person from this school or from your neighborhood.

◆ Reflect on how deeply they wish to be happy, how much they long to be safe. Imagine what it would be like for them to be totally understood and valued by every person they met.

◆ Silently say in your mind, with a heart full of care, "May you be safe, may you be happy, may you be at peace."

◆ Let's just stay with this for a minute or two, repeating the phrases and wishing them well.

◆ This can be heavy, so let's come back to offering some kind wishes to ourselves. "May I be safe, may I be happy, may I be at peace."

◆ Now, take a few deep breaths, feel your body sitting.

*(Ring the bell.)*

◆ When you're ready, open your eyes. Notice how you feel.

### Discussion Questions

— This is a sensitive subject and the practice can be hard. I want to respect that.

— How many people felt some sadness or pain thinking about the suffering humans inflict on one another through discrimination and bias?

— Did anyone feel angry?

— How many people were able to connect with heartfulness for yourself or others?

— Would anyone like to share how that experience was?

We end with this lesson on purpose. Mindfulness isn't just about our own happiness. The qualities we're developing are meant to show up in our lives and in the world. When we're mindful, we can treat people with kindness and patience. This practice can help us understand others—to become more aware of our assumptions and make an effort to see others freshly, for who they are. And when others don't treat us the way we'd like, it gives us the power to respond with wisdom instead of reacting from hatred or anger.

### Take-Home Practice

1. Pay attention to the assumptions you make about others. What implicit biases do you carry?

2. Dedicate some time to do formal heartfulness practice for someone who really needs it, perhaps someone who has struggled in the face of bias and discrimination.

## Journal Suggestions

- What interested you about this lesson?
- Did you learn anything about your own biases?
- Are there any ways you can use this in your own life?
- What do you think about Dr. Martin Luther King Jr.'s idea of the beloved community?

**ADDITIONAL ACTIVITIES**

You may want to supplement this lesson with information about explicit or implicit bias from history or current events. The material from this lesson may dovetail with historical lessons or discussion of current sociopolitical realities.

Another possible activity is to have students take an Implicit Association Test and discuss the results. Note that this can reveal surprising and unsettling information; be prepared to discuss the impact of the test: implicit.harvard.edu/implicit/index.jsp

 ## Teacher Notes

This is an especially sensitive lesson. Its intensity can be amplified or dampened depending on the context. Please use your judgment to determine how to adapt this lesson. Take into account the level of maturity of the students, their familiarity with these themes, the salience of the issues within the classroom and school, and the level of trust and safety in the class. You may want to follow this activity with the extra lesson on forgiving others (Extras 22).

 ## Science Supplement

In influential research from Devine and her colleagues (Devine, Forscher, Austin, & Cox, 2012), an intervention to reduce implicit racial bias was developed. It included five core strategies, quoted below.

1. **Stereotype replacement**: This strategy involves replacing stereotypical responses for non-stereotypical responses. Using this strategy to address personal stereotyping involves recognizing that a response is based on stereotypes, labeling the response as stereotypical, and reflecting on why the response occurred. Next, one considers how the biased response could be avoided in the future and replaces it with an unbiased response.

2. **Counter-stereotypic imaging:** This strategy involves imagining in detail counter-stereotypic others. These others can be abstract, famous (e.g., Barack Obama), or non-famous (e.g., a personal friend). The strategy makes positive exemplars salient and accessible when challenging a stereotype's validity.

3. **Individuation**: This strategy relies on preventing stereotypic inferences by obtaining specific information about group members. Using this strategy helps people evaluate members of the target group based on personal, rather than group-based, attributes.

4. **Perspective taking**: This strategy involves taking the perspective in the first person of a member of a stereotyped group. Perspective taking increases psychological closeness to the stigmatized group, which ameliorates automatic group-based evaluations.

5. **Increasing opportunities for contact**: This strategy involves seeking opportunities to encounter and engage in positive interactions with out-group members. Increased contact can ameliorate implicit bias through a wide variety of mechanisms, including altering the cognitive representations of the group or by directly improving evaluations of the group.

This intervention was not mindfulness-based, but it is easy to imagine the relevance of mindfulness and heartfulness to the strategies Devine (2012) highlights, especially strategies #1, #2 and #4. The relevance of mindfulness and heartfulness for addressing out-group bias is quite new, but there are some encouraging data.

Leuke and Gibson (2015) provide a background and a framework for this research:

— Implicit attitudes are based on the automatic association between ideas in our memory.

— A common method for measuring these associations is the implicit-association test (IAT).

— Research has shown that white participants who take the IAT tend to have stronger associations between white and good than between black and good.

— Similarly, young people tend to have stronger associations between young and good than between old and good.

— Exploring whether mindfulness can reduce automatic out-group bias is important because such bias can lead to a number of negative outcomes.

  — *It is well established that encountering an out-group member or related stimuli activates automatic out-group attitudes.*

  — *Once activated, these automatic evaluations cause a number of negative behavioral effects.*

  — *Implicit out-group attitudes are particularly important to understand because they have been shown to be more predictive of certain types of negative out-group behavior than explicit attitudes.*

Their experiments suggested that mindfulness can, in fact, reduce implicit bias, even when de-biasing is not explicitly named. In their conclusion, Leuke and Gibson (2015) write: "Brief mindfulness meditation reduced implicit race and age bias. Specifically, listening to a 10-min audiotape that focused the individual and made them more aware of their sensations and thoughts in a nonjudgmental way caused them to show less implicit bias against African Americans and old people on the race and age IATs than individuals who listened to a 10-min

audiotape describing historical events and geographical landmarks . . . This meditation was not directed specifically toward the remediation of bias or for any purpose other than to be mindful. For this reason, mindfulness meditation may reduce reactance from people resistant to more direct prejudice reduction strategies" (p. 288).

Despite the encouraging data, they acknowledge that the observed reduction in *implicit bias* may or may not translate into a reduction of *prejudiced behavior* in the world.

Heartfulness, or lovingkindness meditation, is a logical candidate for encouraging goodwill and reducing bias. Lovingkindness practice has been assessed as a way to decrease implicit bias toward African Americans. The researchers also examined lovingkindness practice as a means for decreasing implicit bias toward homeless people. Interestingly, this study featured a six-week lovingkindness practice course, but also included a group that simply discussed lovingkindness over a period of six weeks. While practicing lovingkindness meditation significantly decreased implicit bias toward African Americans and homeless people, merely discussing lovingkindness did not. This suggests that the actual practice is important rather than merely discussing themes of kindness.

Stell and Farsides (2016) attempted to change implicit bias with a dramatically shorter lovingkindness intervention: seven minutes! Here is their conclusion:

"We found that just seven minutes of lovingkindness meditation directed to a member of a racial out-group was sufficient to reduce racial bias toward that out-group . . . Additionally, lovingkindness meditation's effects on bias were mediated by the presence of other-regarding . . . positive emotions. Furthermore, lovingkindness appears to gain efficacy both by increasing controlled processing and by decreasing automatic processing. The current study is the first to successfully find a short-term positive emotion induction that reduces racial prejudice as measured by the IAT . . . No previously published study has demonstrated that a short-term emotional induction has the power to reduce racial bias as measured by the IAT . . . The present study helps identify the effect of positive emotions on implicit bias in loving-kindness meditation, and isolates positive other-regarding emotions, alongside changes in cognitive processing, as putative mechanisms toward intergroup harmony" (p. 145).

Taken together, these findings suggest that mindfulness and heartfulness practice can be a resource in mitigating the effects of implicit bias.

**REFERENCES & FURTHER READING**

Carson, C. (2001). *The autobiography of Martin Luther King, Jr.* London: Hachette UK.

Devine, P. G., Forscher, P. S., Austin, A. J., & Cox, W. T. (2012). Long-term reduction in implicit race bias: A prejudice habit-breaking intervention. *Journal of Experimental Social Psychology, 48*, 1267–1278.

Kang, Y., Gray, J. R., & Dovidio, J. F. (2014). The nondiscriminating heart: Lovingkindness meditation training decreases implicit intergroup bias. *Journal of Experimental Psychology: General, 143*, 1306.

King, M. L. (2013). In a single garment of destiny: A global vision of justice. Beacon Press.

Lueke, A. & Gibson, B. (2015). Mindfulness meditation reduces implicit age and race bias: The role of reduced automaticity of responding. *Social Psychological and Personality Science, 6*, 284–291.

Stell, A. J. & Farsides, T. (2016). Brief loving-kindness meditation reduces racial bias, mediated by positive other-regarding emotions. *Motivation and Emotion, 40*, 140–147.

For a summary of Kingian Principles of Nonviolence, see: www.thekingcenter.org/king-philosophy

**18**

# Seeing with Fresh Eyes: Mindfulness and Implicit Bias

## Key Points

- It feels really good to be understood, and it hurts to be misunderstood.
- Bias is a kind of misunderstanding, with implications on an individual and societal levels.
- The goal of Dr. Martin Luther King Jr.'s work was the creation of a "beloved community" based in love and understanding.
- Mindfulness and heartfulness can reduce bias against others.

> **DEFINITION:** *Implicit bias* refers to attitudes or stereotypes that affect our understanding, actions, and decisions in an unconscious manner.

## Practice Instructions

- Sit in a posture that's comfortable yet upright, feet on the floor and hands in your lap.
- Let your eyes close, or gaze down at the ground in front of you.
- Feel gravity and the weight of your body. Notice where your body touches the ground.
- Take a few deep breaths, noticing any ease or relaxation on the exhalation.
- Become aware of your whole body sitting and breathing.
- Imagine yourself surrounded by people who love and care for you. Offer yourself kind wishes, repeating silently: "May I be happy . . . May I be healthy . . . May I be peaceful."
- Reflect on the harm that bias, prejudice, and racism cause in your own life and in society.
- Think of someone who has been discriminated against. It could be someone you know or someone you don't know. It could be someone from a group you belong to or from a different group. Send heartfulness to that person, offering phrases of kindness.
- End by offering some heartfulness for yourself again.
- When you're ready, let your eyes open and look around the room.

 ## Take-Home Practice

1. Pay attention to the assumptions you make of others. What implicit biases do you carry?
2. Dedicate some time to do formal heartfulness practice for someone who really needs it, perhaps someone who has struggled in the face of bias and discrimination.

 ## Journal Suggestions

1. What interested you about this lesson?
2. Did you learn anything about your own biases?
3. Are there any ways you can use this in your own life?
4. What do you think about Dr. Martin Luther King Jr.'s idea of a beloved community?

18

# OWNING YOUR ATTENTION: MINDFULNESS AND TECHNOLOGY

## The Basics

This lesson is primarily a didactic lesson, with the practice component figuring less prominently than other lessons. The lesson draws attention to the ways that technology disrupts attention, highlights the potential role of mindfulness in mitigating this, and offers some concrete steps to take control of one's attention.

---

**LEARNING OBJECTIVES**

1. To understand the connection between mindfulness, attention, and how technology disrupts attention.
2. To learn concrete technological tips for managing our relationship with technology.
3. To develop mindfulness in relation to technologically associated sounds.

---

### EXTRA LESSON 19 IN BRIEF: A SYNOPSIS

## Owning Your Attention: Mindfulness and Technology

**1. Discuss the benefits of technology.**
What does technology do that helps us? We used to carry around a road atlas, now we just use GPS.

**2. Discuss the drawbacks of technology.**
Ever feel like your phone makes you unhappy sometimes? Why? Raise your hand if you ever:

* Stayed up so late online you were exhausted the next day?

* Had trouble falling asleep because of something you saw or read on your phone?

* Feel distracted by your phone in class or doing your schoolwork?

* Had someone say something about you online that was mean or hurtful?

* Said something about someone else online that you might not have said in person?

* Feel hurt or annoyed because someone paid more attention to their phone than to you?

**3. Attention is one of our most precious resources.**
Why is our ability to pay attention important? If you want to listen to a friend, read a book, or do anything, you need to be able to pay attention. Where we put our attention impacts our lives.

Technology (especially phones) is altering the quality of our attention. Phones and apps are engineered to keep us focused on the screen for as long as possible; this is how companies make money. Technology grabs our attention and can make us less happy. The average person checks their phone

150 times a day. Discuss the ways that phones are designed to be addictive:

- Creating special sounds and icons for notifications

- YouTube autoplays more videos to keep us from leaving

- Instagram shows new likes one at a time, to keep us checking for more

- Facebook wants to show whatever keeps us scrolling

- Snapchat turns conversations into streaks we don't want to lose

- Our media turns events into breaking news to keep us watching

Mindfulness is about using our attention wisely, and can help us take control of this precious resource.

## Practice Instructions:

- Sit in a posture that's comfortable and upright, feet on the floor and hands in your lap.

- Let your eyes close, or gaze down at the ground in front of you.

- Feel gravity and the weight of your body. Notice where your body touches the ground.

- Take a few deep breaths, noticing any ease or relaxation on the exhale.

- Be aware of your whole body sitting, feeling the sensations of breathing in and breathing out.

*(Turn on your phone and play various notification sounds from the sound preferences.)*

- Notice how the sounds impact your body. What thoughts come up?

- Take some deep mindful breaths and feel the weight of your body resting in the chair.

- Picture in your mind your phone or device

you use at home (a tablet or laptop). It's closed or in sleep mode. Just see it in your mind and notice how you feel.

- Imagine opening it or picking it up. Notice how you feel. Notice any reaction or impulse.

- Imagine seeing some notifications, but not checking them. Can you feel the pull, the urge to click or tap the notification and check? Where do you feel it? What's it feel like?

- Imagine checking a notification. How do you feel inside? Notice any emotions or feelings.

- Imagine putting the device down. See it closed, the screen dark. Notice how you feel.

*(Ring the bell.)*

- When you're ready, open your eyes. Notice how you feel.

 ## Discussion Questions

— How did that work for you? Did anything surprise you?

— How many people spend more time on screens than you want to? Anyone spend less?

— How does it feel when the attention is being pulled in different directions?

— How can you take more control of your screen time?

 ## Take-Home Practice

1. Make it a practice this week to notice the impulse to look at your phone, and consciously decide if you need to look or can leave it alone.

2. Experiment with leaving a device at home when you're going out with friends; see how it impacts the connection with them.

# Owning Your Attention: Mindfulness and Technology

## Lesson Outline

- Technology has incredible benefits, but it is problematic too.

- Our attention is a precious resource; where we give attention impacts our lives.

- Technology (especially smartphones) is altering our attention in unprecedented ways.

- Phones and applications are engineered to keep us on the screen for as long as possible; this is how companies make money.

- Technology is negatively impacting where we put our attention and how long it stays there—and in some ways, may make us less happy.

- Mindfulness is about using our attention wisely, which can help us take control of this precious resource.

## Lesson

*(Organize the room for mindfulness and engage the students in a transitional activity.)*

Technology has done some pretty amazing things. In our pocket, you can carry a computer that is more advanced than even huge supercomputers from years ago. Do you know what you used to have to do if you were driving somewhere new?

Yeah, you would carry a road map. Some of them were so big they had hundreds of pages with maps of the entire country! It was called a "road atlas," and you'd keep one in your car wherever you went.

Now what do you do? Yes, our GPS even tells us the traffic, how long it will take, the best route or where to change buses or trains. Kind of amazing.

If you wanted to meet someone at an event or a concert, you'd have to plan a specific time and place to meet: "I'll meet you across the street from the entrance at 7 p.m." Now we just text one another!

Technology lets us connect with each other and share our lives; it adds a lot of good things. What do you like about technology, smartphones, and apps?

*(Students answer.)*

Right—it gives us all of those benefits (fun, exploration, learning, and so on). How many of you ever feel like your phone makes you unhappy? *(Students raise hands.)*

Okay, how about this:

- Raise your hand if you ever stayed up so late online you were exhausted the next day.

- How many of you ever had trouble falling asleep because of something you saw or read on your phone?

- How many people ever feel distracted by your phone in class or doing your schoolwork?

- Did you ever have someone say something about you online that was mean or hurtful?

- How many people ever said something about someone else online that you might not have said to them in person?

- Anyone ever feel hurt or annoyed because a friend was paying more attention to their phone than to you?

19

Yeah, so technology has its problems too, huh? It doesn't always make us happier. **Our ability to pay attention to what we want is so important.** We need our attention to be able to listen to a friend who's telling you something important, to read a book, even to watch a show or movie! To play a sport, we need to pay attention to our teammates. Or, when we do mindfulness practice, we pay attention to our breathing. All of this is important; our attention helps us to live life!

But here's the thing: The companies that design phones and apps want our attention. They *need* our attention. Facebook, Twitter, Whatsapp—all these companies—are competing for our attention. You know why? Who can take a guess why?

(*Students answer.*)

It's how they make money. The way they make more money isn't necessarily to make you happy—it's to keep you glued to the screen for as long as possible. The longer we look at something, the more revenue companies can generate through advertisements.

How many people sometimes spend more time on a screen than you want? Guess how many times people check their phone each day on average?

*They check them 150 times per day.* There's a former tech developer, Tristan Harris, who's trying to bring more awareness to this issue. Sometimes, he holds up a phone and says, "This thing is a slot machine." Do you all know what a slot machine is?

When you play a slot machine, sometimes you win a prize. But it's unpredictable, and that makes them addictive. You might win, but you never know when. So what do you think he means by that, stating this phone is a slot machine?

Yeah, they're addictive! Each time we look at our phone, we might win a little prize. We don't know what the prize will be, or when it will come, but the *chance* is there. Maybe you get a bunch of likes on Facebook, or someone tags you in a photo, or there's some event, and you're afraid you'll miss out. So, you compulsively check your phone. Here are some examples of how tech companies keep us glued to our screens:

- Creating special sounds and icons for notifications.
- YouTube autoplays more videos to keep us from leaving.
- Instagram shows new likes one at a time, to keep us checking for more.
- Facebook wants to show whatever keeps us scrolling.
- Snapchat turns conversations into streaks we don't want to lose.
- Our media turns events into breaking news to keep us watching.

Is this all making sense? Can you feel what I'm talking about? The pull to check your phone even when there's nothing specific going on? Who wants to check their phone right now?

We turn our phone from a tool into something like a best friend. It's there when we're bored or sad. But our technology doesn't always connect us, sometimes it leaves us distracted and lonely. So how do you think mindfulness relates to all of this?

Mindfulness and technology are both about attention. Technology is trying to keep you thinking about your phone all the time, and mindfulness is about being right where you are, in the moment. So, do you think mindfulness could help us deal with the ways that we can get hooked on technology?

We can be more mindful of when we pick up our device. We could be aware of the impulse to pick up the phone. We can pause and try to feel what we really need in the moment. Maybe sometimes we don't need our phone, we need to go spend time with someone we care about.

Mindfulness can help, but there are also other simple things we can do to reclaim our attention, to own our attention, instead of selling it to tech companies for free!

That same guy, Tristan Harris recommends these steps:

1. Turn off notifications; only use notifications for people trying to reach you.
2. Limit the home screen to tools, things you use for tasks like Maps, Camera, or Calendar. Move the rest of your apps off the first page and into folders. That way you only look at them when you want, rather than opening them just because you see them.
3. Charge your device outside your bedroom, or use an alarm clock to wake up.
4. Track the time you spend on your device with apps like Moment or Rescue Time.

## Practice

(*Teacher Note: If you know that every single student in the class has a smartphone, have them place their phones face down on their desks and use this activity to guide them through mindful use of their phones—seeing the phone, picking it up, putting it down, looking at an app, and so on. Otherwise, use the visualized practice below, so as not to exclude anyone.*)

So, let's begin as usual, by establishing mindfulness of the body.

◆ Find your posture—comfortable and upright. If it feels all right to you, let your eyes close.

◆ Listen to the sound of the bell with all of your attention, all the way to the end of the tone.

◆ Start feeling the relaxing effects of gravity. Let your body get heavy. Feel the points that are touching the ground and let them take the weight of your body.

◆ Take a few deep breaths, feeling any ease or relaxation that comes, as you exhale.

◆ Take a few moments just to feel your whole body sitting there.

◆ Bring your attention to your anchor spot, and feel your breathing.

◆ Now you're going to hear some familiar sounds. When you hear them, keep breathing, and see what reactions you have.

(*Turn on your own phone and play various notification sounds from the sound preferences.*)

◆ What do the sounds make you think about? How do they impact your body? Your mind?

◆ Take some deep, mindful breaths and feel the weight of your body resting in the chair.

◆ I want you to picture in your mind your phone or a device that you use at home (a tablet or laptop, for example). It's closed or in sleep mode. Just see it in your mind, and notice how you feel.

◆ Next, imagine opening it or picking it up. Notice how you feel. Notice any reaction or impulse inside.

◆ Imagine seeing a few notifications, but not checking them. Can you feel the pull, the urge to click or tap the notification, and check it? Where do you feel it? What does it feel like?

◆ Now imagine checking the notification. How do you feel inside? Notice any emotions or feelings that come up.

◆ Imagine putting the device down. See it closed, the screen dark. Notice how you feel.

(*Ring the bell.*)

◆ When you're ready, open your eyes. Notice how you feel.

### Discussion Questions

— How did that work for you? Did anything surprise you?

— How many of you spend more time on screens than you want to? Does anyone spend less?

— How does it feel when your attention is being pulled in different directions?

— How can you take more control of your screen time?

### Take-Home Practice

1. Make it a practice this week to notice the impulse to look at your phone, and consciously decide if you need to look or can leave it alone.
2. Experiment with leaving a device at home when you're going out with friends; see how it impacts the connection with them.

### Journal Suggestions

— If you have a phone, how does it function in your life?

— Do you use it more than you want to? Why?

— What effect does your phone have on your emotions? In what ways is it positive? In what ways is it negative?

### Science Supplement

A study conducted by the Moment Application (inthemoment.io) and the Center for Humane Technology (humanetech.com) on 200,000 iPhone and iPad users to determine how much time they spent on certain applications and how happy or unhappy that activity made them.

Some applications are considered valuable by users, while others are not. For example, users of Google Calendar, Podcasts, and Spotify were almost universally appreciated and on average, people spent between three and eight minutes on these apps. The fact that the most *disliked* applications actually compel *enormous* amounts of time is itself suggestive of a perverse incentive structure. Facebook, Instagram, and WeChat made a clear majority of users unhappy with their usage. These users spent between 43 minutes and 92 minutes on these apps each day.

Research on the effects of high technological use is just emerging, but there are some preliminary warning signs. For example, Kross (2013) found that Facebook usage was associated with declines in well-being. He concludes: "The human need for social connection is well established, as are the benefits that people derive from such connections. On the surface, Facebook provides an invaluable resource for fulfilling such needs by allowing people to instantly connect. Rather than enhancing well-being, as frequent interactions with supportive 'offline' social networks powerfully do, the current findings demonstrate that interacting with Facebook may predict the opposite result for young adults—it may undermine it" (p. 5 ).

Subsequent research has examined these findings. Fox and Moreland (2015) write that, ". . . although Facebook users often experience negative emotions, they feel pressured to access the site frequently due to the fear of missing out and to keep up with relationship maintenance demands . . . Facebook's visibility, connectivity, and persistence . . . afforded constant social comparison to other network members, which triggered jealousy, anxiety, and other negative emotions. Relational turbulence occurred due to the public nature of conflict on Facebook. Many participants' responses revealed overarching contradictions: initially they claimed Facebook was inconsequential, yet

19

later recounted significant stressful or hurtful events associated with Facebook" (p. 168).

Researchers have highlighted a difference between active and passive use. While active usage refers to direct exchanges with others (e.g., posting status updates, commenting on posts), passive usage is the consumption of information without any direct commenting or exchanges. It appears that passive Facebook usage may be more closely associated with compromised well-being than active usage. Verduyn and colleagues (2015) found that passive Facebook use led to a decline in well-being and this decline was a function of increased envy.

Of course, much more is to be learned. Clearly, not all effects of technology or social media are negative; many are positive. Further, it is not clear what role mindfulness will have in mitigating the problems. As Harris says, there are thousands of gifted engineers working all the time to design ways to keep us glued to our screens. Some of the solutions will require new technological designs that meet our needs, rather than increase time spent on-screen. Mindfulness may not be sufficiently developed to meet the intense appeal of devices for adolescents. Nevertheless, the stability and clarity of mindfulness is a powerful contrast with the compulsive and automatic process that typifies much of our engagement with technology.

**REFERENCES & FURTHER READING**

Fox, J. & Moreland, J. J. (2015). The dark side of social networking sites: An exploration of the relational and psychological stressors associated with Facebook use and affordances. *Computers in Human Behavior*, 45, 168–176.

Kross, E., Verduyn, P., Demiralp, E., Park, J., Lee, D. S., Lin, N., . . . & Ybarra, O. (2013). Facebook use predicts declines in subjective well-being in young adults. *PloS One*, 8(8), e69841.

Verduyn, P., Lee, D. S., Park, J., Shablack, H., Orvell, A., Bayer, J., . . . & Kross, E. (2015). Passive Facebook usage undermines affective well-being: Experimental and longitudinal evidence. *Journal of Experimental Psychology: General*, 144(2), 480–488.

Tristan Harris and attention hijacking: humantech.com. We need to talk about kids and smartphones. (2017, October 10). *Time Magazine*. time.com/4974863/kids-smartphones-depression

**19**

# TAKING OFF THE MASK: MINDFULNESS AND AUTHENTICITY

## The Basics

This lesson explores the masks that we wear and the ways in which we can reclaim our authenticity. It is meant to generate discussion, and can be integrated into your classroom as you see fit. It is not meant to introduce a new practice but instead considers how mindfulness and authenticity are connected.

**20**

---

### LEARNING OBJECTIVES

1. **To explain the concept of wearing a mask.**
2. **To define authenticity.**
3. **To name at least one mask that students wear in life.**

---

### EXTRA LESSON 20 IN BRIEF: A SYNOPSIS

## Taking Off the Mask: Mindfulness and Authenticity

**1. Discuss masks. What kinds of masks do we wear?**

What is a mask? What does it do? Masks conceal; they make us look like something we're not. Why might we put on a mask or "front?" It may protect us. Wearing a mask always hurts a little, because they force us to hide the truth and pretend to be something we're not.

What masks do we wear here at school? No one can wear a mask all the time. Follow anyone around 24/7, and you'll start to see more of who they are.

**2. Authenticity brings connection.**

Authenticity helps us to make deeper connections with others and to feel more at home with our-

selves. Mindfulness can help us connect with our authentic experience.

### Practice Instructions

◆ Sit in a posture that's comfortable and upright, feet on the floor and hands in your lap.

◆ Let your eyes close, or gaze down at the ground in front of you.

◆ Feel gravity and the weight of your body. Notice where your body touches the ground.

◆ Take a few deep breaths, noticing any ease or relaxation on the exhale.

- Be aware of your whole body sitting, feeling the sensations of breathing in and breathing out.

- Notice how you feel inside. What would it be like if you didn't have to pretend anything, if you didn't have to feel or look any particular way?

- As we sit quietly, see if you can take off the mask that you wear here at school. Just be yourself inside. However you feel is completely okay.

- How would it be to be yourself completely, no need to pretend or be anything for anyone?

- Bring your attention to your face. Relax your jaw. Relax the muscles around your eyes. Let your forehead be soft. Relax all the muscles in your face, letting your whole face be relaxed.

- Let's sit like this for a few more moments, feeling your breathing, letting yourself feel exactly the way you feel right now.

 **Discussion Questions**

*(These questions can be used in small groups, dyads, or for journaling.)*

- What masks do you wear?

- When do you feel most authentic? What's it like to not wear a mask?

- How does mindfulness relate to authenticity?

**20**

# Taking Off the Mask:
# Mindfulness and Authenticity

## Lesson Outline

- We wear masks to hide things about ourselves.

- Sometimes, we have very good reasons to wear masks.

- However, our authenticity is also important, as it helps us to make deeper connections with others and to feel more at home with ourselves.

- Mindfulness can help us connect with our authentic experience.

## Lesson

*(Organize the room for mindfulness and engage the students in a transitional activity.)*

What is a mask, what does it do?

*(Students answer.)*

It conceals—it makes us look like something we're not. Maybe sometimes it protects us.

We all wear masks. In some situations, there may be good reasons to wear a mask. But wearing a mask when we don't want to always hurts at least a little bit. **Masks force us to hide the truth, to pretend to be something we're not.**

Who knows what I'm talking about, the way we front sometimes?

Any time we try to conceal a truth about ourselves, it gets tiring. Do you know that experience when you tell a lie, and you've got to keep your story straight and remember who you told the lie to and who knows the truth . . . and the whole thing is just *stressful?*

Nobody can be just like their mask. There's always the risk of being found out, right? Lots of people try to look cool; that's one mask we wear. Here's the thing, though: Nobody is cool all the time! Follow someone around 24/7, and nobody—not even the coolest cat— is going to always seem cool. So, what kind of masks do people wear here at school? Who can give me an example?

*(Students answer.)*

Right. What's the opposite of wearing a mask?

*(Students answer.)*

Yeah, being real, being ourselves. That's called authenticity. What are some examples of authentic people from our culture?

*(Students answer.)*

With famous people, we might celebrate authenticity! But do we give ourselves permission to be fully authentic? I mean sometimes, we wear a mask so much that we forget to take it off. We can feel so much pressure from the outside to look a certain way that we get confused about who we are under the mask.

Mindfulness is a way of being authentic. It's a way of taking off the mask *to yourself*. You can sit there just as you are—however cool or awkward or brave or scared you are in that moment, it's all okay. Mindfulness is a training in authenticity.

What would it be like if you didn't have to prove anything to anyone? What would it be like if we all dropped our mask?

## Practice

✦ Find your posture—comfortable and upright. If it feels all right to you, let your eyes close.

✦ Listen to the sound of the bell with all of your attention, all the way to the end of the tone.

✦ Start feeling the relaxing effects of gravity. Let your body get heavy. Feel the points that are touching the ground, and let them take the weight of your body.

✦ Take a few deep breaths, feeling any ease or relaxation that comes, as you exhale.

✦ Take a few moments just to feel your whole body sitting there.

✦ Bring your attention to your breathing, and see if you can let it be completely natural—long or short, deep or shallow.

✦ Next, notice how you feel inside. What would it be like if you didn't have to pretend anything, if you didn't have to feel or look any particular way?

✦ As we sit quietly, with our eyes closed, see if you can take off the mask that you wear here at school. Just be yourself inside. However you feel is completely okay.

✦ What would it be like to be yourself completely, to not have to pretend or be anything for anyone?

✦ Bring your attention to your face. Relax your jaw. Relax the muscles around your eyes. Let your forehead be soft. See if you can relax all the muscles in your face, letting your whole face be relaxed.

✦ Let's sit like this for a few more moments, feeling your breathing, letting yourself feel exactly the way you feel right now.

*(Ring the bell.)*

✦ When you're ready, open your eyes. Notice how you feel.

 ## Journal Suggestions

1. What masks do you wear?
2. When do you feel most authentic? What's it like to not wear a mask?
3. How does mindfulness relate to authenticity?

### DYAD OR SMALL GROUP DISCUSSION

The questions listed for the journal suggestions can be used in dyads or small groups. Students can take turns sharing in a structured way, or they might have a free-form conversation about one or more of the questions. After the small groups, it can be useful to reconvene as a whole class to discuss themes and insights.

# A DAY OF HEARTFULNESS

## The Basics

This lesson guides students through visualizing an entire day using heartfulness.

---

**LEARNING OBJECTIVES**

1. To describe ways to practice heartfulness throughout the day.

---

**21**

---

**EXTRA LESSON 21 IN BRIEF: A SYNOPSIS**

## A Day of Heartfulness

**1. We can use heartfulness to change our disposition.**

We can imagine using heartfulness throughout the day. The more time we spend cultivating states like kindness, the more we strengthen those neural pathways in our mind.

**2. A moment of heartfulness doesn't take much energy.**

How much energy does it really take to smile or say hello or be kind, right? The hard part is *remembering*. We can always change the channel to heartfulness. If we can picture some of the different moments and ways that we can be kind, we're more likely to remember during the day.

**Practice Instructions**

◆ Sit in a posture that's comfortable and upright, feet on the floor and hands in your lap.

◆ Let your eyes close, or gaze down at the ground in front of you.

◆ Feel gravity and the weight of your body. Notice where your body touches the ground.

◆ Take a few deep breaths, noticing any ease or relaxation on the exhale.

◆ Be aware of your whole body sitting, feeling the sensations of breathing in and breathing out.

◆ We're going to imagine going through one complete day with heartfulness—using as many moments as we can to strengthen that quality and carve that groove into our mind.

◆ Imagine waking up in the morning. See yourself and imagine taking a moment to send heartfulness to yourself. Maintain that feeling as you get out of bed and get ready for school.

◆ Imagine the first person you see at home. Send them a silent wish, "May you be happy, may you be well." Try to maintain that kind intention as you interact with them.

◆ Imagine the first person you see at school. Take a moment to send them a little kindness: say hello, or wave. Carve that groove into your mind, just wishing them well.

◆ Imagine walking into class and seeing your teacher. Send them heartfulness: "May you be happy and well. May you be peaceful." Keep that intention as you participate in class.

◆ *(Do a few more instructions. You can include after-school activities, meals, and going to bed.)*

◆ Let's send heartfulness to everyone here in class, wishing everyone well in your own words.

## Discussion Questions

◆ Were you able to do some of that visualization, seeing those people and places in your mind?

◆ How did it feel to send kind wishes to them? How many people felt calmer? Happy? Joyful?

◆ Did anyone notice any other feelings or experiences?

## Take-Home Practice

1. Do some heartfulness silently during the rest of the day today, sending a few kind wishes to anyone you meet, as often as you remember.
2. Try having an attitude of kindness toward yourself as you go about your daily activities.
3. Practice heartfulness at home for 10 minutes during the day or before bed.

**21**

## A Day of Heartfulness

### Lesson

Let's do some heartfulness practice today. Instead of doing it for ourselves, or a few specific people, I want to see if you can imagine using heartfulness throughout the day. The more time we spend cultivating states like kindness, the more we strengthen those neural pathways in our mind.

It's not that hard to have heartfulness and send some good wishes. How much energy does it really take to smile or say hello or be kind, right? The hard part is *remembering*. We can always change the channel to heartfulness. One way to help ourselves remember that is by imagining ourselves going through a single day with heartfulness. If we can picture some of the different moments and ways that we can be kind, we're more likely to remember during the day!

### Practice

*(Organize the room for mindfulness and engage the students in a transitional activity.)*

Let's do some practice with this. We'll begin the way we usually do, with some relaxation and mindfulness, and then I'll take you through a guided heartfulness practice where we imagine what it would be like to strengthen kindness throughout an entire day.

◆ Find your posture—comfortable and upright. If it's all right to you, let your eyes close.

◆ Listen to the sound of the bell with all of your attention, all the way to the end of the tone.

◆ Start feeling the relaxing effects of gravity. Let your body get heavy. Feel the points that are touching the ground and let them take the weight of your body.

◆ Take a few deep breaths, feeling any ease or relaxation that comes, as you exhale. Just relaxing. You can even say silently to yourself, "Relax, relax."

◆ Take a few moments to feel your whole body sitting.

◆ Bring your attention to your anchor, and feel your breathing there.

### HEARTFULNESS

◆ Now we're going to imagine going through one complete day with heartfulness—using as many moments as we can to strengthen that quality and carve that groove into our mind.

◆ Imagine waking up in the morning. See yourself and imagine taking a moment to send heartfulness to yourself. If you like, put one hand on the center of your chest. Take that feeling with you as you get out of bed and get ready for school.

◆ Imagine the first person you see at home. Take a moment to send them heartfulness. Just sending them a silent wish, "May you be happy, may you be well." Try to maintain that kind intention as you interact with them.

◆ Now imagine the first person you see at school. Take a moment to send them a little kindness. Maybe you say hello, or wave. Carve that groove into your mind by maintaining that intention as you interact with them—just wishing them well.

◆ Imagine walking into class and seeing your morning teacher. Send them heartfulness: "May you be happy and well. May you be peaceful." Carve that groove in your mind, keeping that intention as you participate in class.

*(Do a few more instructions. You can include after-school activities, meals, and going to bed.)*

◆ To finish, let's send some heartfulness to everyone here in the class today. In your own words, in your own way, wishing everyone well.

*(Ring the bell.)*

21

◆ You can let your eyes open slowly. Notice how you feel, and how it feels in the room.

## Discussion Questions

— How many people were able to do some of that visualization, see those various people and places in your mind's eye?

— How did it feel to send kind wishes to them?

— How many people felt calmer? Anyone feel happy, or joyful, or good inside?

— Did anyone notice any other feelings or experiences?

## Take-Home Practice

1. Do some heartfulness silently during the rest of the day today, sending a few kind wishes to anyone you meet, as often as you remember.
2. Try having an attitude of kindness toward yourself. Send good wishes to yourself as you go about your daily activities.
3. Practice heartfulness at home for 10 minutes during the day or before bed.

## Journal Suggestions

1. How did it feel to imagine going through one day with heartfulness?
2. What do you enjoy most about heartfulness practice? What do you enjoy least?
3. Are there any times in particular in your life that you've found heartfulness helpful? When? How?

### ALTERNATE ACTIVITIES

If students have difficulty staying focused during this activity, you can also invite them to do any of the following:

1. Write a list of six different people or situations during your day for which you could practice heartfulness.
2. Break up into pairs and share about each of the people or situations during your day that you want to practice heartfulness toward. What phrases would you use?
3. Draw a picture of how you and/or the person you're sending heartfulness to might feel when doing this practice.
4. Practice saying the phrases silently, but moving your lips while you say them.

**21**

# FORGIVING OTHERS

## The Basics

This lesson teaches the practice of forgiveness. Specifically, it explores what it means to forgive others, and what forgiveness is not. This lesson is emotionally evocative. Gauge the maturity of the class to determine if this lesson is appropriate.

---

**LEARNING OBJECTIVES**

1. To define forgiveness.
2. To identify one benefit of forgiveness.
3. To explain the difference between forgiveness and reconciliation.

---

**EXTRA LESSON 22 IN BRIEF: A SYNOPSIS**

## Forgiving Others

**1. We all make mistakes.**

Part of being human is making mistakes. Life is complicated and none of us gets it right all of the time. I've made a lot of mistakes, even some big ones. How about you? Mistakes are part of how we learn.

**2. What is forgiveness (and what it isn't)?**

Forgiveness doesn't mean we condone harm that's been done to us, and it doesn't mean we accept situations that cause us harm. To practice forgiveness, we first need to make sure we're safe.

How does it feel to hold a grudge? Forgiveness is motivated by not wanting to live with the pain of resentment. It means we stop drinking poison hoping the other person will get sick. We can try to understand what was behind someone's actions. What do you think "hurt people hurt people" means?

Forgiveness takes time. Sometimes, all we can do is have the intention to forgive. Forgiveness is something we do to free ourselves; we don't need to reconcile with the other person to forgive.

### Practice Instructions

- Sit in a posture that's comfortable and upright, feet on the floor and hands in your lap.

- Let your eyes close, or gaze down at the ground in front of you.

- Feel gravity and the weight of your body. Notice where your body touches the ground.

- Take a few deep breaths, noticing any ease or relaxation on the exhale.

- Be aware of your whole body sitting, feeling

the sensations of breathing in and breathing out.

◆ Now bring to mind someone you want to forgive. Don't choose the person you have the most resentment toward! Pick someone you genuinely feel ready to forgive.

◆ First, whatever happened, whatever hurt you, offer yourself some kindness.

◆ If you're angry, take time to pause and breathe, calming the anger like we've practiced.

◆ Let yourself notice the pain you've felt. If you're feeling steady and strong, let yourself feel some of that pain. Forgiveness helps us get out from under that pain.

◆ Bring the person to your mind who hurt you in some way. Take some deep breaths.

◆ If resentment or anger comes up again in your mind, that's all right.

◆ Silently say to yourself "Just as I've hurt others, I too have been hurt. To the extent that I'm ready, I offer my forgiveness."

◆ Try saying, in your own mind, "I forgive you."

◆ Notice any resentment that comes up. Soften your body, soften your mind.

◆ Feel the feelings and continue saying those words in your own mind. "Just as I've hurt others, I too have been hurt. To the extent that I'm ready, I offer my forgiveness. I forgive you."

◆ If you get stuck or it feels like too much, come back to your breath; be mindful of your body.

◆ As we finish, come back to the relaxation of the body.

 ## Discussion Questions

◆ How did that go for you?

◆ What did you do when you felt resentful or angry?

◆ Did anyone have feelings of genuine forgiveness?

◆ What about self-kindness? Could you feel some kindness for yourself?

◆ Did anyone get stuck in the resentment, and it just seemed to get worse?

 ## Take-Home Practice

1. Practice forgiveness this week once or twice, for 5 to 10 minutes each time.

2. Focus on how it feels to say, "Just as I've hurt others, I too have been hurt. To the extent that I'm ready, I offer my forgiveness." What sensations and feelings arise when you say this?

3. If this is challenging, try doing heartfulness for yourself.

4. Notice resentment or grudges. How does your body feel? What happens in your mind?

**22**

# Forgiving Others

## Lesson Outline

— Part of being happy is learning to forgive.

— Mistakes are an important way to learn from life.

— Forgiveness doesn't mean we condone harm that's been done to us and it doesn't mean we accept situations that cause us harm.

— Forgiveness is motivated by not wanting to live with the pain of resentment.

— Forgiveness means we stop drinking poison hoping the other person will get sick.

## Lesson

*(Organize the room for mindfulness and engage the students in a transitional activity.)*

Human beings make mistakes all the time. We get things right a lot of the time—but being human is so complicated that we often mess up. Maybe we just didn't know better. Maybe we acted impulsively and did something we now regret. I know I've made many mistakes in my life. I've made decisions that didn't work out, that didn't make me happy. Some of my words have caused others emotional pain.

Raise your hand if you've ever made a big mistake in your life.

So there you go. It's not just you; all of us do this. We can't expect to get everything right. **Mistakes are a key way that we learn and grow**! Part of mindfulness practice is to learn and heal from mistakes, mistakes that we make and mistakes that others make. In other words, we learn to forgive ourselves and to forgive others. Just as we make mistakes, so do others.

Today, I want to talk about forgiving others. When you hear the word "forgiveness," what does it make you think?

*(Students answer.)*

Yes, those are really common associations. Let's start by talking about what forgiveness is *not*.

Forgiveness is not about pretending that someone didn't cause harm. It's also not about condoning the hurt that they caused. It's not saying that it's okay. Maybe someone treated you really badly—harmed you emotionally or physically. That's *not* okay. I'm not going to stand up here and say that it's okay in any way. I want all people to be safe, to be treated with dignity and respect, and to have enough of what they need to live.

To practice forgiveness, we first need to make sure that things are safe now, that whatever happened, we're out of danger and not being harmed anymore. That's the first part.

Even though someone may have harmed us, we still may want to forgive. We don't do this for the other person, but for ourselves. We do it when we feel ready, when we feel like we're tired of holding resentments and grudges. How does it feel to hold onto a grudge?

*(Students answer.)*

There's a saying that holding onto resentments and grudges is like drinking poison and expecting the other person to get sick. We're the one that gets sick! We want to make the other person suffer with our resentment, but we're the one who's actually suffering.

You can think about it this way: Imagine you're on a long journey, and along the way you meet someone. While you're with them, they put a big, heavy stone in your bag, so that when you leave—even when they're gone—there's something weighing you down. Wherever you go, that stone is there in the bottom of your bag, and you're carrying it around everywhere. Until one day someone asks you, "Hey, why don't you just take that rock out of your bag and leave it here on the ground?" Grudges can be like that stone.

Do you know what I mean?

You don't "have to" forgive anyone—it's not an obligation. It is something you may want to do, something you can choose to do, to take a weight off your own heart. Here's what Martin Luther King, Jr. had to say about forgiveness. I find these words so powerful. Listen to this and see what you think:

> Forgiveness does not mean ignoring what has been done or putting a false label on a [harmful] . . . act. It means, rather, that the . . . [harmful] act no longer remains as a barrier to relationship. Forgiveness is a catalyst creating the atmosphere necessary for a fresh start and a new beginning. It is the lifting of a burden or the cancelling of a debt.

So to forgive, we must first become mindful that we were hurt. Our anger or fear is totally understandable. We don't blame ourselves for our reactions. But we also don't want to live with a closed heart forever—we don't want to carry around that stone.

Instead, we can try to understand the behavior of the person who hurt us. Sometimes we think, "They're evil." But it's never that simple. Maybe they behave the way they do because they're also in pain. Maybe they can't control themselves. Maybe they're confused or angry or greedy or just plain old hurt.

Someone once said, "hurt people hurt people." What do you think that means? What are some reasons why people might behave in a mean or hurtful way?

*(Students answer.)*

If we really knew what was going on inside someone else, we might see their actions differently. The more we understand their inner life, the easier it becomes to forgive a person.

Forgiveness doesn't happen all at once. It usually takes time. *We* have to decide when we're ready to forgive. Still, we might find that on one day we feel very forgiving; it's as if we've let it go. Then the following week, the resentment might be back. That still counts! Some relief is better than no relief. And then, someday, we may find that we've really let go. The anger is gone and we can truly move on with our lives. We might even feel like we've gained some wisdom in the process.

Forgiveness is different than reconciliation. What does it mean to "reconcile" with someone?

*(Students answer.)*

That's right. It means that we work things out, or come to some kind of understanding together. Both people need to be involved to reconcile. But forgiveness is something we can do on our own, regardless of our desire to reconcile, or the other person's capacity to apologize or reconcile. If reconciliation is a possibility, then practicing forgiveness is often the first step toward that goal, but it's not necessary in order to forgive in our hearts.

**22**

Let's do some practice. We'll begin in the usual way, and then try using mindfulness to explore what it's like to forgive—or the *possibility* of forgiving someone in the future.

## Practice: Forgiving Others

✦ Find your posture—comfortable and upright. If it feels all right to you, let your eyes close.

✦ Listen to the sound of the bell with all of your attention, all the way to the end of the tone.

✦ Start feeling the relaxing effects of gravity. Let your body get heavy. Feel the points that are touching the ground and let them take the weight of your body.

✦ Take a few deep breaths, feeling any ease or relaxation that comes, as you exhale.

✦ Take a few moments just to feel your whole body sitting.

✦ Bring your attention to your anchor and feel your breathing there. We'll stay with this for a minute or two.

✦ Now bring to mind someone you want to forgive. Don't choose the person you have the *most* resentment toward! Pick someone you genuinely feel ready to forgive.

✦ First, bring some kindness to your own experience. Whatever happened, whatever hurt you, offer yourself some kindness.

✦ If you notice yourself feeling angry, take a few moments to pause and breathe, calming the anger like we've practiced.

✦ See if you can let yourself notice the pain you've felt. If you're feeling steady and strong, let yourself feel some of that pain. Forgiveness helps us get out from under that pain.

✦ Bring the person to your mind who hurt you in some way. Take some deep breaths to settle your body and mind.

✦ If resentment or anger comes up again in your mind, that's all right.

✦ Silently whisper to yourself "Just as I've hurt others, I too have been hurt. To the extent that I'm ready, I offer my forgiveness."

✦ Try saying, in your own mind, "I forgive you."

✦ Notice any resentment that comes up, and soften this. Soften your body, soften your mind.

✦ Feel the feelings and continue whispering those words in your own mind. "Just as I've hurt others, I too have been hurt. To the extent that I'm ready, I offer my forgiveness. I forgive you."

✦ If you get stuck or it feels like too much, come back to your breath and be mindful of your body.

✦ As we finish, come back to the relaxation of the body.

*(Ring the bell.)*

✦ When you're ready, open your eyes. Notice how you feel; look around the room.

 **Discussion Questions**

— How did that go for you?

— What did you do when you felt resentful or angry?

— Did anyone have feelings of genuine forgiveness?

— What about self-kindness? Could you feel some kindness for yourself?

— Did anyone get stuck in resentment and it just seemed to get worse?

 **Take-Home Practice**

1. Practice forgiveness at least twice this week for 5 to 10 minutes each time.

2. Focus on how it feels to say, "Just as I've hurt others, I too have been hurt. To the extent that I'm ready, I offer my forgiveness." What sensations and feelings arise when you say this? Do they change as you practice this, and if so how?

3. If this activity is challenging, try doing heartfulness for yourself.
4. When you feel resentment or grudges, notice what effect it has on you. How does your body feel? What happens in your mind?

 **Journal Suggestions**

1. What surprised you about this lesson?
2. How might forgiveness benefit you?
3. What are the obstacles to forgiving others?

 **Teacher Notes**

To teach this lesson effectively, it's essential to have some experience with forgiveness practice yourself. If you have not done forgiveness practice before, we encourage you to use the instructions in this lesson for a few weeks first, exploring the practice and developing your own understanding of its nuances. Notice when the mind conflates forgiveness with condoning action, or when it confuses forgiveness with reconciliation. Observe how it feels to hold on to anger or resentment, and—to whatever degree possible—the relief that comes when putting it down. The more you understand the process of forgiveness in your own heart, the more you will be able to support your students to explore this practice in an authentic and balanced way.

As we note above, this is an advanced lesson and may not be appropriate for all students or classes. Be sure to make clear the distinctions between what forgiveness is and what it is not. Take care that students begin this practice from a grounded, well-resourced place. It may be useful to do heartfulness for self before or after this activity. Some students may feel compelled to begin with the person who has caused the most harm in their lives. Explain how this isn't helpful, how it makes it harder to learn the practice and can stimulate strong, disturbing emotions rather than healing and strengthening the heart.

 **Science Supplement**

Although our culture has long placed value in forgiveness, scientific attention to the concept has been recent and relatively minimal compared to other prosocial emotions. Nevertheless, there has been more interest in recent decades. In their 2016 review, Akhtar and Barlow (2016) describe the evolution of the field and their meta-analytic findings synthesizing all available data:

"Over the last 20 years or so, clinicians and researchers have also become increasingly interested in the health benefits of forgiveness, largely because of its potential for reducing negative thoughts and emotions stemming from interpersonal hurts. In addition, improving general population well-being, such as reducing common mental health problems, as well as increasing positive emotions and relationships, is a key policy goal in many countries. This is largely because well-being is linked to reduced health risk behaviors such as smoking and excessive drinking, improved learning and educational attainment, greater work productivity as well as improved physical health. Understanding what promotes mental well-being is therefore vitally important, and it is argued that interventions that facilitate positive actions and attitudes have a key role to play in enhancing psychological health . . . This review provides moderate quality evidence indicating that process-based forgiveness interventions are effective in improving mental well-being following a range of significant hurts among diverse population groups. These findings suggest that forgiveness interventions could have an important role to play in promoting the general psychological well-being of individuals and populations who experience a range of problems resulting from having been traumatized" (p. 108).

22

The practice of forgiveness, however, is not only for individuals who might have suffered greatly because of another's actions. Even relatively modest interpersonal hurts can be effectively addressed by forgiveness practices.

Worthington and Scherer argue that the opposite of forgiveness—resentment—is stressful. Further, they suggest that forgiveness reduces this stress and is a coping strategy that may promote health.

We know that hostility is not good for our well-being, and forgiveness interventions can reduce hostility. Studies have suggested that developing *empathy* for the person who caused harm is the key element of forgiveness practices. This is an intriguing point and we suggest emphasizing this element in your presentation of forgiveness. Mindfulness is known to promote empathy and it is conceivable that the practice of mindfulness enhances our ability to forgive. However, research has highlighted that true forgiveness often takes time; small "doses" of forgiveness interventions are typically inadequate to resolve interpersonal hurt. Students may be supported by practicing forgiveness in an ongoing way. Forgiveness practice can often be a preparatory practice for heartfulness practice.

## REFERENCES & FURTHER READING

Akhtar, S. & Barlow, J. (2016). Forgiveness therapy for the promotion of mental well-being: A systematic review and meta-analysis. *Trauma, Violence, & Abuse, 9,* 107–122.

Lim, D., Condon, P., & DeSteno, D. (2015). Mindfulness and compassion: An examination of mechanism and scalability. *PloS One, 10*(2), e0118221.

Washington, J. (Ed.) (1986). *A testament of hope: The essential writings and speeches of Martin Luther King, Jr.* New York: Harper & Row.

Worthington, E. L., Witvliet, C. V. O., Pietrini, P., & Miller, A. J. (2007). Forgiveness, health, and well-being: A review of evidence for emotional versus decisional forgiveness, dispositional forgivingness, and reduced unforgiveness. *Journal of Behavioral Medicine, 30,* 291–302.

Worthington, E. L., & Scherer, M. (2004). Forgiveness is an emotion-focused coping strategy that can reduce health risks and promote health resilience: Theory, review, and hypotheses. *Psychology & Health, 19,* 385–405.

**22**

# ACTING OUT THE MIND

## The Basics

This lesson is a role play of various aspects of our internal life. Using different class members to represent different aspects of internal experience, this lesson is an attempt to clarify the practice of mindfulness in a playful way. It is most appropriate where the classroom environment is supportive and there is a sufficient level of emotional safety.

---

**LEARNING OBJECTIVES**

1. To develop greater clarity regarding the attentional and cognitive processes involved in mindfulness of breathing.
2. To have a playful experience of mindfulness.

---

**EXTRA LESSON 23 IN BRIEF: A SYNOPSIS**

## Acting Out the Mind

**1. Begin with mindfulness of breathing.**

**2. Introduce the activity and choose volunteers.**
*Explain that you're going to act out mindfulness of breathing. Recruit two volunteers. One will play the role of the breath, the other will play the role of attention. Position them face-to-face in front of the classroom.*

**3. Narrate mindfulness of breathing.**
So, here we are. The attention is looking at the breathing, being mindful of breathing. What happens to the attention after a few seconds when we place it on the breath?

We get distracted!

*(Recruit another student to come up and play the role of the distraction. Pick a specific distraction—thoughts about lunch, having a crush. Invite that student to the front of the room; narrate what happens. Distraction grabs the attention and drags them away from the breath to the other side of the room.)*

So, now the distraction has the attention. Sometimes we like our distractions, right?

*(Recruit another volunteer to play the role of "liking." Liking joins the distraction and the attention and they're hanging out together—attention, the distracting thought, and liking. Narrate how much they're enjoying being together.)*

**23**

Eventually, we remember we're paying attention to our breath, right? That's mindfulness!

(*Mindfulness enters the picture. Recruit another student for this role. Have mindfulness gently address the distraction and the liking:*) "Hello distraction, hello liking. I don't want to fight with you, but right now, we're attending to the breath."

(*Invite mindfulness to gently tug the attention back toward the breath. As the mindfulness and attention become more closely linked with the breathing, the three characters can get closer and closer, perhaps hugging.*)

Mindfulness and attention are really intimate with the breathing now, it's the only thing they're noticing, the only thing they're doing.

(*Lastly, you can recruit another student to play the role of peace, or calm, or a similar factor. Have them come up to the front of the room and explain their presence.*)

**23**

## Acting Out the Mind

### Lesson Outline

— Begin with mindfulness of breathing.

— Choose a few student volunteers to personify different aspects of the mind: e.g., one person is the breath, a second is attention, and so on.

— Add more characters to the drama one at a time, so students get a clearer sense of different aspects of the mind. Keep the story light and humorous.

*(Organize the room for mindfulness and engage the students in a transitional activity.)*

### Practice

✦ Let your body be comfortable and upright, feeling your spine. Feet on the ground, hands on your lap. Let your eyes close (or gaze down at the ground).

✦ When you hear the bell, listen with all of your attention all the way to the end of the tone.

✦ Start feeling the relaxing effects of gravity. Let your body get heavy. Feel the points that are touching the ground and let them take the weight of your body.

✦ Take a few deep breaths, feeling any ease or relaxation that comes, as you exhale. Just relaxing. You can even say silently to yourself, "Relax, relax."

✦ Take a few moments to just feel your whole body sitting.

✦ Bring your attention to your anchor spot and feel the sensations of breathing in and breathing out. Let's do a couple of minutes of mindful breathing.

*(Ring the bell.)*

✦ When you're ready, let your eyes open slowly.

### Lesson

*(Begin by recruiting two volunteers. One will play the role of the breath, the other will play the role of attention. Position them face-to-face in front of the classroom. Narrate this so that the students understand that they are essentially acting out mindfulness of breathing practice.)*

So, here we are. The attention is looking at the breathing, being mindful of breathing. Okay, what happens to the attention after a few seconds, when we place it on the breath?

*(Students answer.)*

Yeah, we get distracted! Okay, we're going to need another volunteer to play "distraction."

*(Recruit another student to come up and play the role of distraction. Pick a specific distraction—thoughts about lunch or a crush on someone, for example. Invite that student to the front of the room and narrate what happens. Distraction grabs hold of attention, and drags them away from the breath to the other side of the room.)*

So now the distraction has hold of the attention. Sometimes we like our distractions, right?

*(Recruit another volunteer to play the role of "liking." Liking joins the distraction and the attention and they're hanging out together—attention, the distracting thought, and liking. Narrate how much they're enjoying being together.)*

Eventually, we remember we're paying attention to our breath, right? That's mindfulness!

*(Mindfulness enters the picture. Recruit another student for this role. Have mindfulness gently addresses the distraction and the liking:)* "Hello distraction, hello lik-

23

ing. I don't want to fight with you, but right now, we're attending to the breath."

*(Invite mindfulness to gently tug the attention back toward the breath. As the mindfulness and attention become more closely linked with the breathing, the three characters can get closer and closer, perhaps hugging.)*

Mindfulness and attention are really intimate with the breathing now, it's the only thing they're noticing, the only thing they're doing.

*(Lastly, you can recruit another student to play the role of peace, or calm, or a similar factor. Have them come up to the front of the room and explain their presence.)*

 **Teacher Notes**

This activity can be repeated to dramatize real-life situations and clarify the mechanisms of mindfulness. For example, the students might create a play or skit for when the individual is experiencing a specific struggle: test anxiety, an argument with a parent or fellow student. Feel free to modify this lesson to demonstrate heartfulness practice.

### A NOTE OF ATTRIBUTION

This lesson has been adapted, with permission, from Dr. Marvin Belzer.

**23**

# GETTING BUY-IN

## The Basics

This lesson can be used if you're having trouble establishing relevance and getting buy-in from the class. This is not meant to introduce a new practice. Instead, it can help build a relationship with the students and establish an informal "contract" or agreement around mindfulness lessons.

---

**LEARNING OBJECTIVES**

1. Model the shared decision-making and nuanced ways of holding authority that is key to mindfulness programming.

2. Develop mutual respect and shared ownership regarding the success of the lessons.

---

**EXTRA LESSON 24 IN BRIEF: A SYNOPSIS**

## Getting Buy-In

**1. What's the most valuable thing you have?**
Invite answers. We can work to get more money, make new friends, grow more food. But once time is gone, you can never get it back. Time is our most precious resource in life. None of us knows how much time we really have, and we can't get more of it.

**2. How does it feel to have someone waste your time?**
Wasting someone else's time can be like an insult; it's not respectful. How much time will you be spending here doing mindfulness? (Add up all the time.) That's significant.

If I stood here for that many hours, and you

didn't learn one thing that was useful, that would be pretty wasteful, right? That would be insulting, even disrespectful.

**3. Make an agreement.**
Let's agree not to waste each other's time. I will agree to do my best *not* to waste your time.

I'm going to show up, listen, and do my best to teach you something useful. And I ask you to do the same: to show up, listen, and share what you know with me. And in that way, we won't be wasting each other's time.

Is this something we can agree to? If not, let's discuss it. What do you need to know so we don't waste each other's time?

**24**

# Getting Buy-In

## Lesson Outline

— Time is our most precious resource in life. None of us knows how much time we really have, and we can't get more of it.

— Wasting someone else's time can be like an insult; it's not respectful.

— Add up all the time we will spend doing mindfulness lessons: It's significant.

— Let's agree not to waste each other's time:

  – *Instructor agrees to do their best to provide something of value.*
  – *Students agree to have an open mind and give their full attention.*

## Lesson

I want to ask you a question: What's the most valuable thing you have? What's the most precious resource in your life?

*(Students answer.)*

Yes, I'd agree all of those things are pretty important. I'll tell you what I think is the most valuable out of all of them: time. I say that for two simple reasons: one, none of us knows how much time we really have; and two, we can't get more.

You can work and get more money. You can plant a garden and grow more food. You can get new clothes. You can make new friends. But once time is gone, it's gone forever. You can't get it back.

We're going to be doing mindfulness for about half an hour, twice a week, for eight weeks. Who can do the math and tell me how many hours that is in total? It's eight hours; that's an entire day of school!

So, let me ask you a question. If I stood up here for eight hours over the next two months, and you didn't learn one thing that was useful—wouldn't you say that was a waste of time?

I certainly would. And that'd be kind of insulting, to you. I mean, that'd be disrespectful to take the most precious thing you have and just waste it. Are you with me here?

So, I want to make an agreement with you. Here's my part of the agreement: I'll do my best *not* to waste your time. That means that with these lessons, every day I'm going to try to teach you at least one thing that's useful to you in your life. How's that sound?

Okay, now here's your part. If I came here for all this time, and you didn't listen—you never gave me a fair chance to share something with you—you'd be wasting *my* time.

But if you show up, and have an open mind, tell me about who you are honestly, what you know and how you see things: Then, we're having a real conversation, right? Not only am I more likely to teach you something important, but I might also learn something important from you. Because we've each got gifts. Each one of us is unique, and has something important to share with others.

So that's the agreement I want to make with you: I'm going to show up, listen, and do my best to teach you something useful. And I ask you to do the same: to show up, listen, and share what you know with me.

24

And in that way, we won't be wasting each other's time.

So, what do you say? Anyone not down with this? Because if you're not, I want to know what you need, to get on board—we don't want to waste each other's time.

*(Give students a chance to respond; discuss any genuine reservations they might have.)*

Cool. So, let's talk about mindfulness.

**24**

# MINDFULNESS FOR TESTS

## The Basics

This lesson offers two brief practices to help students prepare for taking a test. The first practice uses creative imagination to practice taking a test; the second practice offers an activity to help students calm their bodies and settle their minds before an actual test.

---

**LEARNING OBJECTIVES**

1. To practice using mindful breathing during a test when anxiety arises.
2. To practice using mindfulness of the body and mindful breathing before a test.

---

**EXTRA LESSON 25 IN BRIEF: A SYNOPSIS**

## Mindfulness for Tests

**1. Important events (like tests) can bring up anxiety and mindfulness can help.**

When there's a lot at stake, we get nervous. This is totally normal. While a small amount of nervousness might serve us, when we get really nervous, our performance suffers. This is where mindfulness can help. Doing a little mindfulness before or during a test can calm you down, and help shift what's happening inside. If we've trained our minds, we can stay cool under pressure, just like a basketball player shooting free-throws in the last quarter of a game. So today, we're going to learn how to use mindfulness to prepare for taking a test.

**Pretest Practice:**

*You can use this brief practice to help students settle their body and clear their minds before a test.*

◆ Find your posture and place your hands in your lap. If it feels all right, let your eyes close.

◆ Listen to the sound of the bell with all of your attention, all the way to the end of the tone.

◆ Start feeling the relaxing effects of gravity. Let your body get heavy.

◆ Take three slow, deep, breaths and pay particular attention to any ease or relaxation that you feel as you breathe out. You can even say to yourself silently, "Relax, relax."

**25**

- Notice how your body feels. If you feel anxious, nervous, or tense, notice where you feel that in your body. If you feel anxious, breathe in one deep breath, and as you breathe out, breathe out the anxiety.

- If you feel nervous, breathe in one deep breath, and as you breathe out, breathe out the nervousness.

- If you feel tension in your body, breathe in one deep breath. As you breathe out, breathe out the tension.

- Take your next breath, imagining ease coming into your body.

- Breathe calm into your body.

- Imagine yourself taking your test with ease. Imagine ease in your body and in your mind, through the entire test.

- Imagine putting your pencil down at the end of your test, feeling relieved and confident.

*(Ring the bell.)*

- When you're ready, let your eyes open and please begin your test.

**25**

# Mindfulness for Tests

## Lesson Outline

— Important events (like tests) can bring up stress and anxiety, which makes it harder to think and to do our best.

— Mindfulness can help us to manage those feelings and focus our attention.

## Lesson

Today I want to talk about how mindfulness can help us when we're under pressure: a job interview, a big game, a test. How many people feel stressed before something really important? How about when you're taking a test? (*Students raise hands.*)

What are some of the feelings you have during a test, or even *before* the test, while studying or thinking about a test that's coming up?

(*Students answer. They may identify feeling nervous, being afraid, wanting to do well, and so on.*)

And when you're stressed like that, it's harder to think and focus, right? When we're nervous or anxious, our body releases certain stress hormones, and our brain function can change in a way that actually prevents us from thinking clearly.

This is where mindfulness can help us. Doing a little mindfulness before or during a test can calm you down, and help shift what's happening inside. If we've trained our minds, we can stay cool under pressure, just like a basketball player throwing free-throws in the last quarter of a game in the finals. So today, we're going to learn how to use mindfulness to prepare for taking a test.

## Practice

Let's begin as usual, by establishing mindfulness of the body.

✦ Find your posture—comfortable and upright. If it feels all right to you, let your eyes close.

✦ Listen to the sound of the bell with all of your attention, all the way to the end of the tone.

✦ Start feeling the relaxing effects of gravity. Let your body get heavy.

✦ Take a few deep breaths, feeling any ease or relaxation that comes, as you exhale.

✦ Take a few moments just to feel your whole body sitting.

✦ Bring your attention to your anchor spot, and feel your breathing.

✦ Now imagine that you're taking a test. See the test in front of you, your pencil in hand. So far so good; you're answering questions easily.

✦ Then you come to a question that's really hard. You know you learned it, but you can't remember this now. Notice how you start to feel. It's a tough question; you're unsure that you'll be able to answer it.

✦ Without mindfulness, you might get psyched out and feel discouraged for the rest of the test. Imagine that when you reach that hard problem, instead of getting discouraged or frustrated, you remember to be mindful.

✦ Imagine putting down your pencil and closing your eyes. You take a few deep breaths. (Actually take those breaths right now.)

✦ Feel the weight of your body on the chair. Begin to feel your breathing, staying with the sensations of breathing in and out until you feel a bit calmer.

✦ Now imagine that you open your eyes, you look at the problem and your mind feels clear again. You con-

25

tinue your test and finish. Imagine putting your pencil down and feeling calm and satisfied.

*(Ring the bell.)*

✦ When you're ready, open your eyes. Notice how you feel; look around the room.

**PRETEST PRACTICE:**
*You can use this brief practice to help students settle their body and clear their minds before any tests or quizzes.*

✦ Find your posture and place your hands in your lap. If it feels all right, let your eyes close.

✦ Listen to the sound of the bell with all of your attention, all the way to the end of the tone.

✦ Start feeling the relaxing effects of gravity. Let your body get heavy.

✦ Take three slow, deep, breaths and pay particular attention to any ease or relaxation that you feel as you breathe out. You can even say to yourself silently, "Relax, relax."

✦ Notice how your body feels. If you feel anxious, nervous, or tense, notice where you feel that in your body. If you feel anxious, breathe in one deep breath, and as you breathe out, breathe out the anxiety.

✦ If you feel nervous, breathe in one deep breath, and as you breathe out, breathe out the nervousness.

✦ If you feel tension in your body, breathe in one deep breath. As you breathe out, breathe out the tension.

✦ Take your next breath, imagining ease coming into your body.

✦ Breathe calm into your body.

✦ Imagine yourself taking your test with ease. Imagine ease in your body and in your mind, through the entire test.

✦ Imagine putting your pencil down at the end of your test, feeling relieved and confident.

*(Ring the bell.)*

✦ When you're ready, let your eyes open and please begin your test.

25

## Gratitude

We would like to express our heartfelt gratitude for all of your work with young people. We hope this curriculum supports you well in serving adolescents.

Cropley, M., 99
Csikszentmihalyi, M., 65
culture(s)
    body-related ideas of, 88
Curry, S., 24, 167

day of heartfulness, 192–95. *see also* heartfulness
"decentering"
    equanimity and, 119
default mode network (DMN)
    mindfulness and, 98–99
    mind-wandering and, 97–98
delayed gratification
    defined, 53
depression
    kindness-based practice for, 83
Desbordes, G., 117, 118
Descartes, 95
development
    body image effects on, 90
Devine, P.G., 177
Diener, E., 143
differently-abled students
    movements for, 168–69
Dijkstra, P., 91
directed attention, 170
discrimination
    defined, 175
    described, 175
discursive thought
    silence of the mind over, 100
DMN. *see* default mode network (DMN)
Duke University, 56, 109
Dunn, E.W., 143

eating
    meanings of, 161
    mindful, 157–63 *see also* mindful eating
    societal and ecological impacts of, 161
eating behaviors, 161
    mindfulness in understanding, 162
eating disorders
    body dissatisfaction associated with, 90

emotion(s)
    ARC of, 127
    basics, 68–69
    defined, 73
    described, 68–69
    difficult, 129–36 *see also specific types and* anger
    feelings and, 70
    mindfulness of, 68–76 *see also* mindfulness of emotions
    myths about, 68, 70–71
    types of, 68, 70
    well-being linked to, 18
emotional changes
    neurobiological changes associated with, 40
emotional habits
    function of, 73
emotional sensations
    physical sensations *vs.*, 69
emotion regulation
    attentional deployment in, 74
    cognitive appraisal in, 74–75
    mindful, 74
    mindfulness and, 18
    response modulation in, 75
    situation modification in, 74
    situation selection in, 74
    types of, 74–75
empathic concern, 152–53
empathy, 146–56
    affective, 152
    compassionate, 152–53
    defined, 146, 149, 156
    described, 174
    developing, 146–56
    forgiveness and, 202
    future directions in, 154–55
    improving capacity for, 146
    mindful communication and, 146–56 *see also* mindful communication
    mirror neurons and, 146, 149, 152, 154
    neurobiology of, 153–54
    research on, 153–54
    sample script, 148–55
    science supplement, 153–55

DMN and, 98–99

eating-related, 157–63 *see also* mindful eating

of emotions, 18, 68–76 *see also* mindfulness of emotions

empathy and, 146–56 *see also* empathy

enjoyment related to, 162

equanimity and, 5, 5*f*, 6, 112–20 *see also* equanimity

in feeling less stressed, 123

feeling overwhelmed and, 121–28 *see also* "freak out formula"; overwhelm; overwhelmed

focus strengthened by, 35

forgiveness and, 196–202 *see also* forgiveness; forgiving others

formal practice of, 5

"freak out formula," 121–28 *see also* "freak out formula"

function of, 157

getting buy-in and, 207–9 *see also* getting buy-in

habitual tendency of, 5

in handling feeling overwhelmed, 124

happiness and, 137–45 *see also* generosity; gratitude; happiness

heartfulness and, 192–95

heartfulness for oneself, 103–11 *see also* heartfulness for oneself

higher trait-level, 5

implicit bias and, 172–80 *see also* implicit bias

introduction, 13–34

key skills of, 2–3

kindness in, 176

mechanisms of, 1

as mental training, 24, 38

mindful communication in, 146–56 *see also* mindful communication

mind power in, 13–20 *see also* mind power

moment of, 5

non-judgment and, 91

in noticing impulses and patience, 51–58, 176 *see also* impulses and patience

patience in, 51–58, 176 *see also* impulses and patience

as paying attention to experience with open heart, 175

present-time awareness in, 5, 5*f*, 6, 117

for PTSD, 83

in reducing bias, 172

role of disseminating, 1

in savoring the good, 59–67, 61*f*

secularity of, 4

secular teaching guidelines for, 4

self-awareness skills related to, 18

in self-control, 53

in self-regulation, 74

soaking in the good, 59–67, 61*f see also* soaking in the good

of sound, 35–42 *see also* mindfulness of sound

in strengthening positive experiences, 59–67, 61*f*

stress and well-being, 28–34

technology impact on, 181–87 *see also* attention; technology

for tests, 210–13 *see also* mindfulness for tests

of thinking, 93–102 *see also* mindfulness of thinking

transitional activities, 11–12

in understanding eating behavior, 162

user manual for the mind in, 21–27 *see also* user manual for the mind

uses for, 157, 159

walking-related, 164–71 *see also* mindful walking

working with adolescents, 7–10 *see also* adolescent(s)

mindfulness-based curricula

SEL curricula *vs.*, 2

mindfulness for tests, 210–13

basics, 210–11

pretest practice, 213

sample script, 212–13

synopsis, 210–11

mindfulness of body, 89–90

in mind power, 14, 16–18

in stress and well-being, 29, 32–33

in user manual for the mind, 22, 25–26

mindfulness of breathing, 43–50, 203

basics, 43–44

as resetting router, 43

sample script, 45–49

science supplement, 48

student takeaways, 50

synopsis, 43–44

mindfulness of emotions, 68–76. *see also* emotion(s)

basics, 68–69

sample script, 70–75

science supplement, 73

student takeaways, 76

synopsis, 68–69

thinking (continued)
    mindfulness of, 93–102 see also mindfulness of thinking
    as not an enemy, 100
    rumination and, 99
    "tone of voice" of, 108
    as totally natural, 95
    ways of, 96
    in words and pictures, 93
thought(s)
    awareness of, 48
    brain activity before we become aware of, 99–100
    discursive, 100
    impact on mood, 96
    importance of, 96
    negative, 96
    obsessive ruminative, 99
    power of, 95
time
    in mindfulness, 5, 5f, 6
    as most precious resource in life, 207–9
    wasting someone else's, 207
"tone of voice"
    of thinking, 108
transitional activities
    mindfulness-related, 11–12
Twitter
    compulsiveness of checking, 184

understood
    what it feels like to be, 172, 174
University of California, Davis, 98
University of California, Los Angeles, 154
Unlearning Meditation, 100
user manual for the mind, 21–27
    basics, 21–22
    mindfulness in, 21–27
    mindfulness of body in, 22, 25–26
    sample script, 23–26
    science supplement, 26
    student takeaways, 27
    synopsis, 21–22

Verduyn, P., 187
violence
    nonviolence vs., 175
visual orienting, 12
voluntary attention, 170

walking
    benefits of, 169, 170
    in a circle, 169
    formal, 169
    health benefits of, 164
    informal mindfulness of, 169
    mindful, 164–71 see also mindful walking
    in nature, 170
    practice for, 167–68
wandering minds, 36
want(s)
    resisting, 56
wanting
    liking vs., 56–57
war within
    ending, 112–20 see also equanimity
wasting someone else's time, 207
WeChat, 186
well-being
    emotions and, 18
    gratitude and generosity in achieving, 137–45 see also
        generosity; gratitude
    mindfulness in, 28–34 see also stress and well-being
    mind-wandering and, 98
    stress and, 28–34 see also stress and well-being
Whatsapp
    compulsiveness of checking, 184
Wheeler, A.T., 127
"widen our perspective"
    through equanimity, 118
Williams, L.M., 66
Woollett, K., 41
word(s)
    thinking in, 96
Worthington, E.L., 202